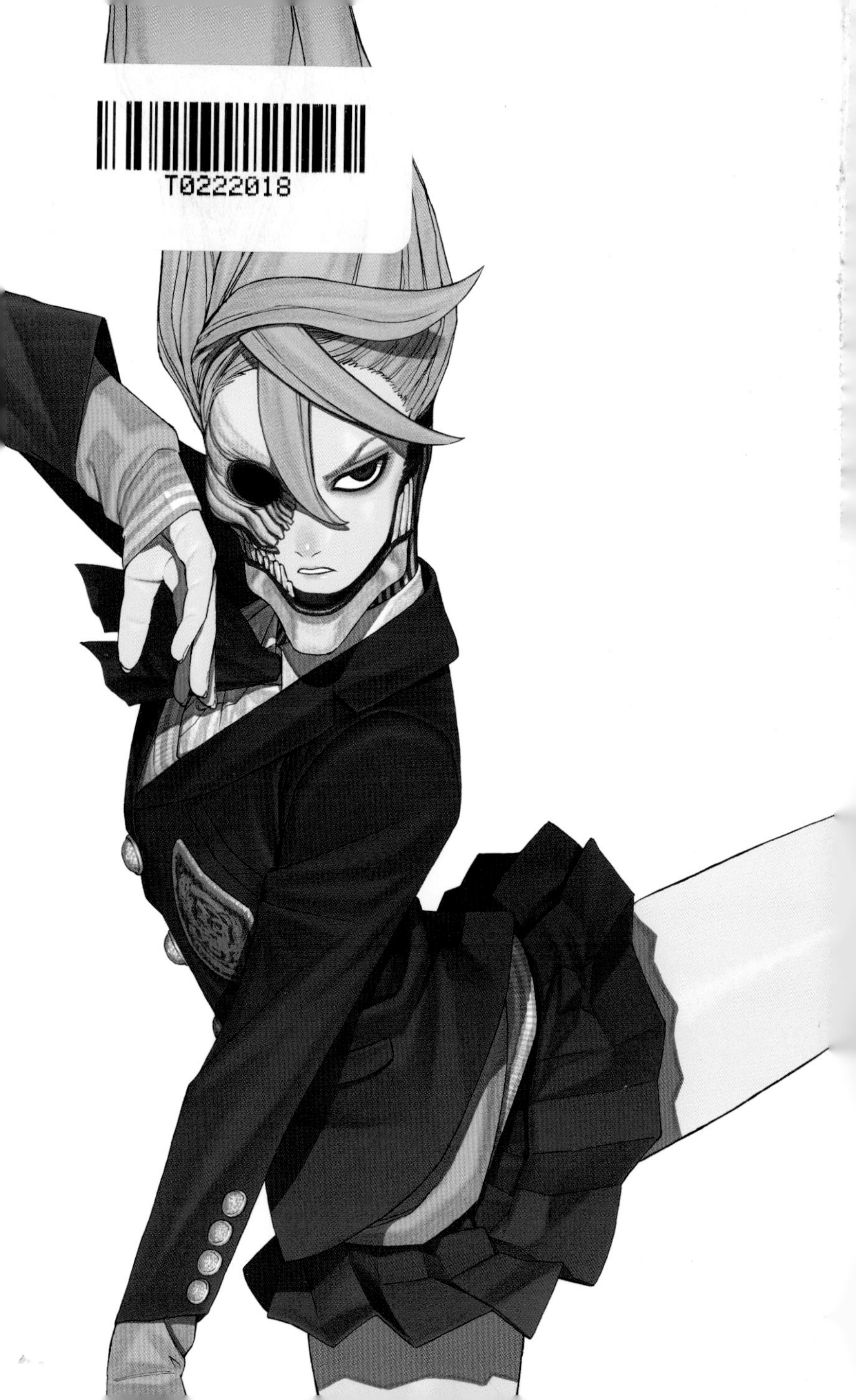

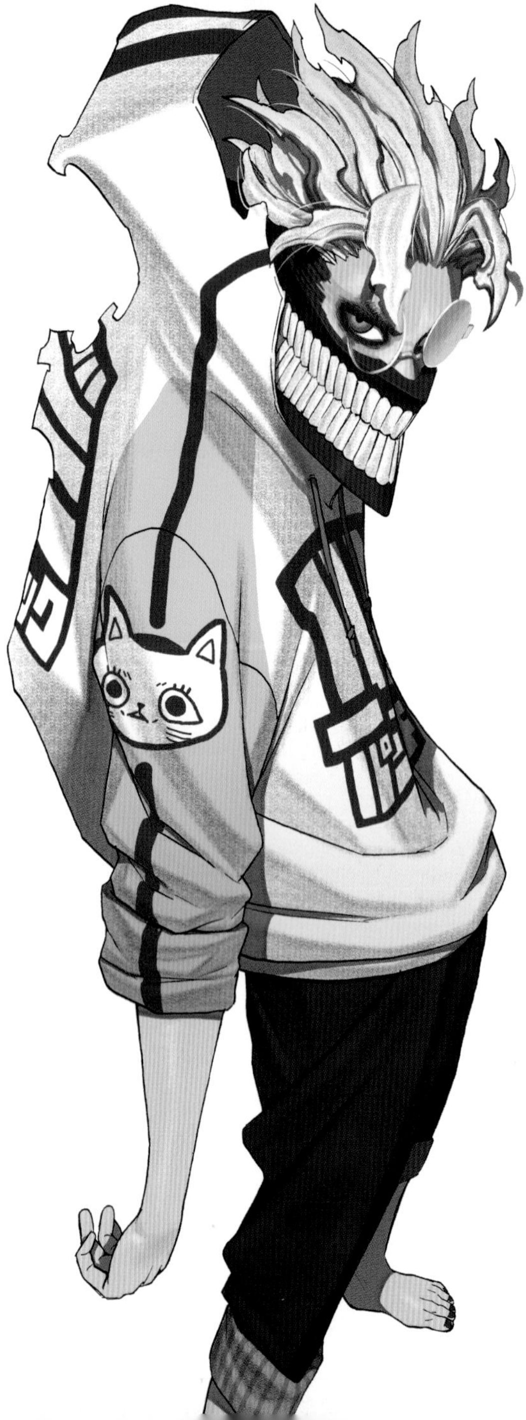

STORY AND ART BY
YUKINOBU TATSU

DANDADAN

7

CHARACTERS

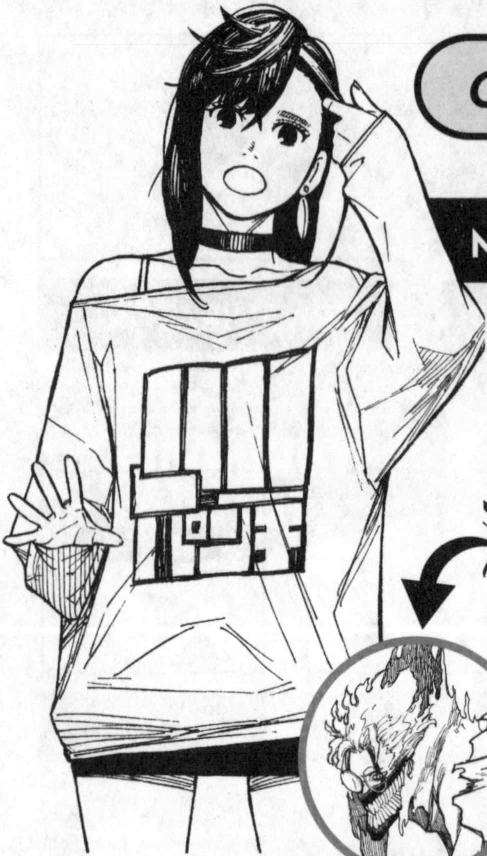

MOMO AYASE

A high school girl from a family of spirit mediums. Her powers awakened after she was abducted by aliens. Following the battle with Turbo Granny, she helps to search for Okarun's testicles.

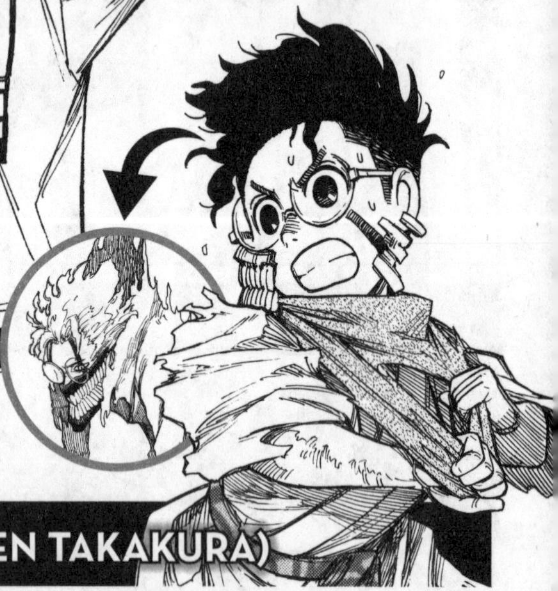

OKARUN (KEN TAKAKURA)

A geek for paranormal phenomena who lost his testicles in the fight against Turbo Granny and must now spend his time looking for them. He has developed feelings for Momo.

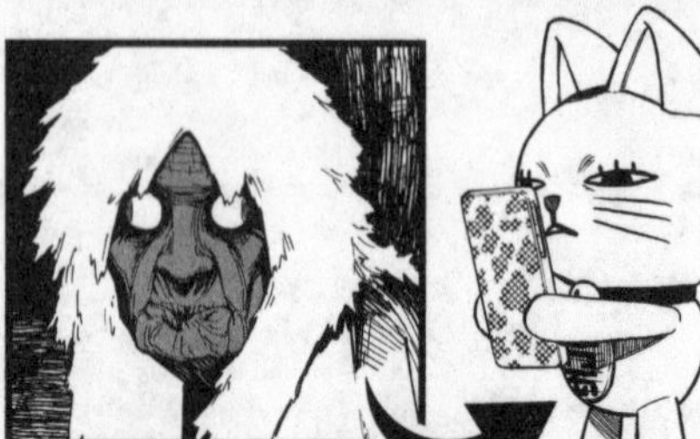

TURBO GRANNY

Appearing at unexpected times and places, she's a present-day yokai who ran riot throughout the country. Her power remains within Okarun, while her consciousness is stuck in a beckoning-cat figure that she uses to get around.

JIJI (JIN ENJOJI)

Momo's friend since childhood. He recruits Momo and Okarun to investigate and exorcise the spirits in his family's new house. But before they can, his body is possessed by the Evil Eye, a boy who'd been sacrificed under the house and became a yokai.

AIRA SHIRATORI

A popular, attractive girl at Momo's school whose powers awaken when she unknowingly picks up one of Okarun's family jewels. She ends up taking on the aura of the Acrobatic Silky.

TARO

An anatomical-model yokai who is dating anatomical model Hana. At present he has Jiji, currently possessed by the Evil Eye, trapped inside his own body.

MANJIRO

A priest at the Tsuchinoko Shrine near Jiji's home. He is also Seiko's disciple.

SEIKO

Momo's grandmother. She's active as the spirit medium Santa Dodoria. She's powerful enough to enclose their home in a mystical barrier, and she supports Momo and the others from the shadows.

STORY

Momo, a firm believer in spirits, comes to the rescue of a paranormal fanatic named Ken Takakura, aka Okarun, when he's getting bullied. After arguing about the validity of each other's interests, they decide to prove their respective beliefs, so Momo is sent to an abandoned hospital known for UFO sightings and Okarun heads to a supposedly haunted tunnel. Once there, Okarun gets cursed by a yokai called Turbo Granny! At the hospital, Momo ends up abducted by aliens called Serpoians, who are seeking a human female for reproduction. They take her aboard their ship, and Momo finds herself in big trouble. Suddenly, Okarun appears, and thanks to Turbo Granny's curse, he's able to transform. At the same time, Momo awakens to her paranormal abilities, and the two are able to escape the UFO. But Okarun's curse affects those around them, so they decide to have a showdown with Turbo Granny. Seiko sets up a barrier around Kamikoshi City, and Momo and Okarun subsequently beat Turbo Granny through a game of tag. Later, Jiji, Momo's old childhood friend and first crush, shows up troubled with supernatural problems of his own occurring in his family's new home, so Okarun and Momo head there to investigate. However, there are legends of a giant serpent in the area. In fact, the Kito clan has been secretly sacrificing humans to it under Jiji's new home, and they toss the young trio into an underground alternate reality as the latest offering. There the three find the serpent as well as a sacrificed child, now an Evil Eye yokai who goes on to possess Jiji. Suddenly, Seiko appears, sealing Jiji's possessed body inside the anatomical-model yokai Taro with a plan to exorcise it. Will Jiji get his body back, or is it too late to separate them?!

DANDADAN 7

50 Let's All Carry Around Hot Water —————— 7

51 We Can All Stay There Together! ————— 27

52 The Hayashi Perfomers Are Here ———— 47

53 We Became a Family ———————— 67

54 Get a Part-Time Job ———————— 87

55 Moe! Moe! Tri-beam! ———————107

56 Feeling Kinda Gloomy ——————— 127

57 Scary Dudes at School ——————— 149

58 Symphony No. 6 ————————— 169

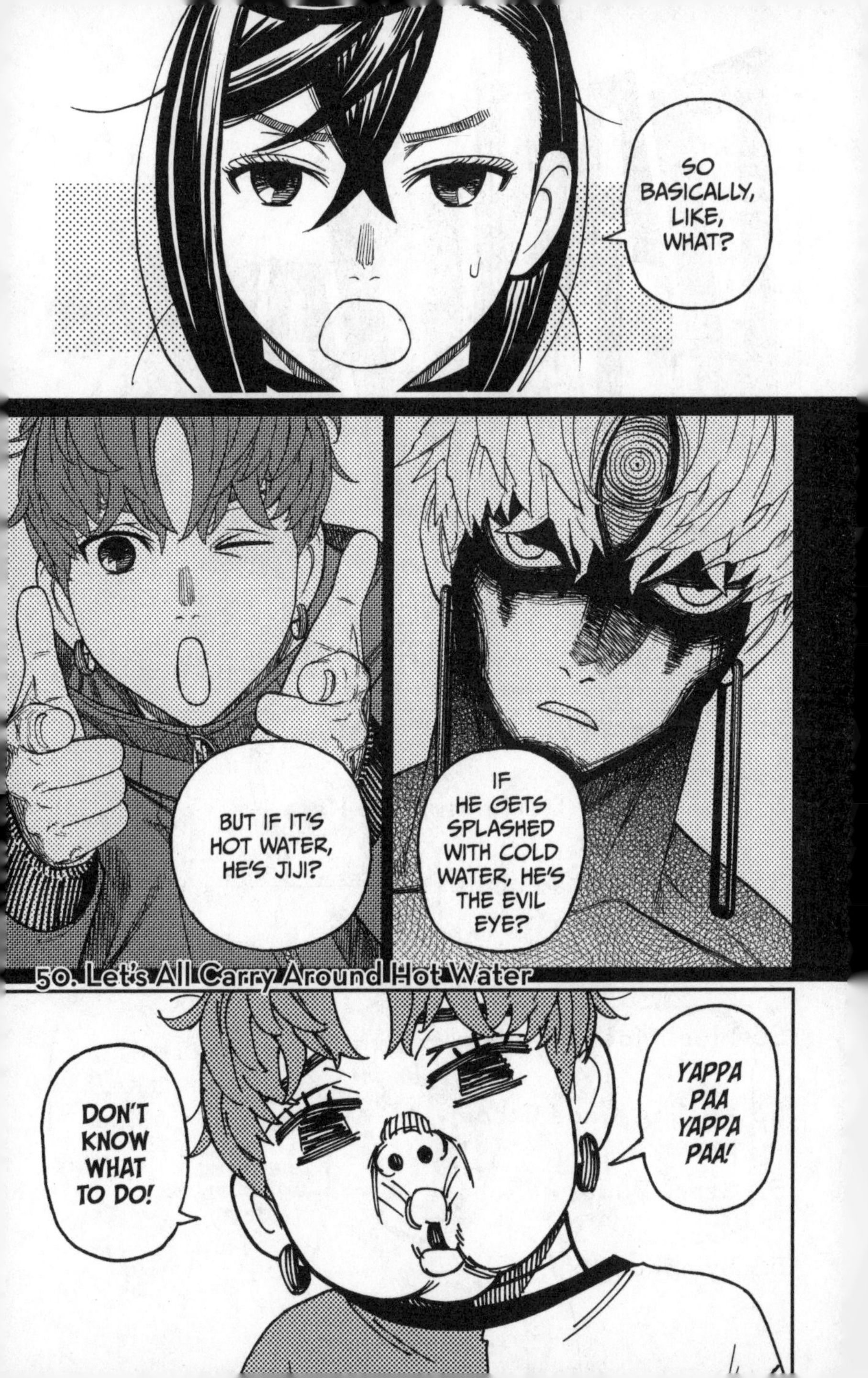
SO BASICALLY, LIKE, WHAT?
IF HE GETS SPLASHED WITH COLD WATER, HE'S THE EVIL EYE?
BUT IF IT'S HOT WATER, HE'S JIJI?
50. Let's All Carry Around Hot Water
YAPPA PAA YAPPA PAA!
DON'T KNOW WHAT TO DO!

THE EVIL EYE WAS ORIGINALLY A MOUNTAIN YOKAI.

YOU'RE ALL SO NAIVE!

...ARE SO FULL-ON THEY'RE REVERED AS GODS.

AND MOUNTAIN YOKAI...

DON'T TELL ME YOU TRULY BELIEVE YOU'VE GOT THE EVIL EYE UNDER CONTROL.

THAT'S WHY THEY ONLY GO AFTER PEOPLE WITH HIGH SPIRITUAL POWER.

...THEY LOSE THEIR MINDS, THEIR CELLS BREAK DOWN, AND THEY DIE.

IF AN ORDINARY HUMAN GETS POSSESSED BY ONE...

...JIJI IS THE ULTIMATE VESSEL.

IN THAT RESPECT...

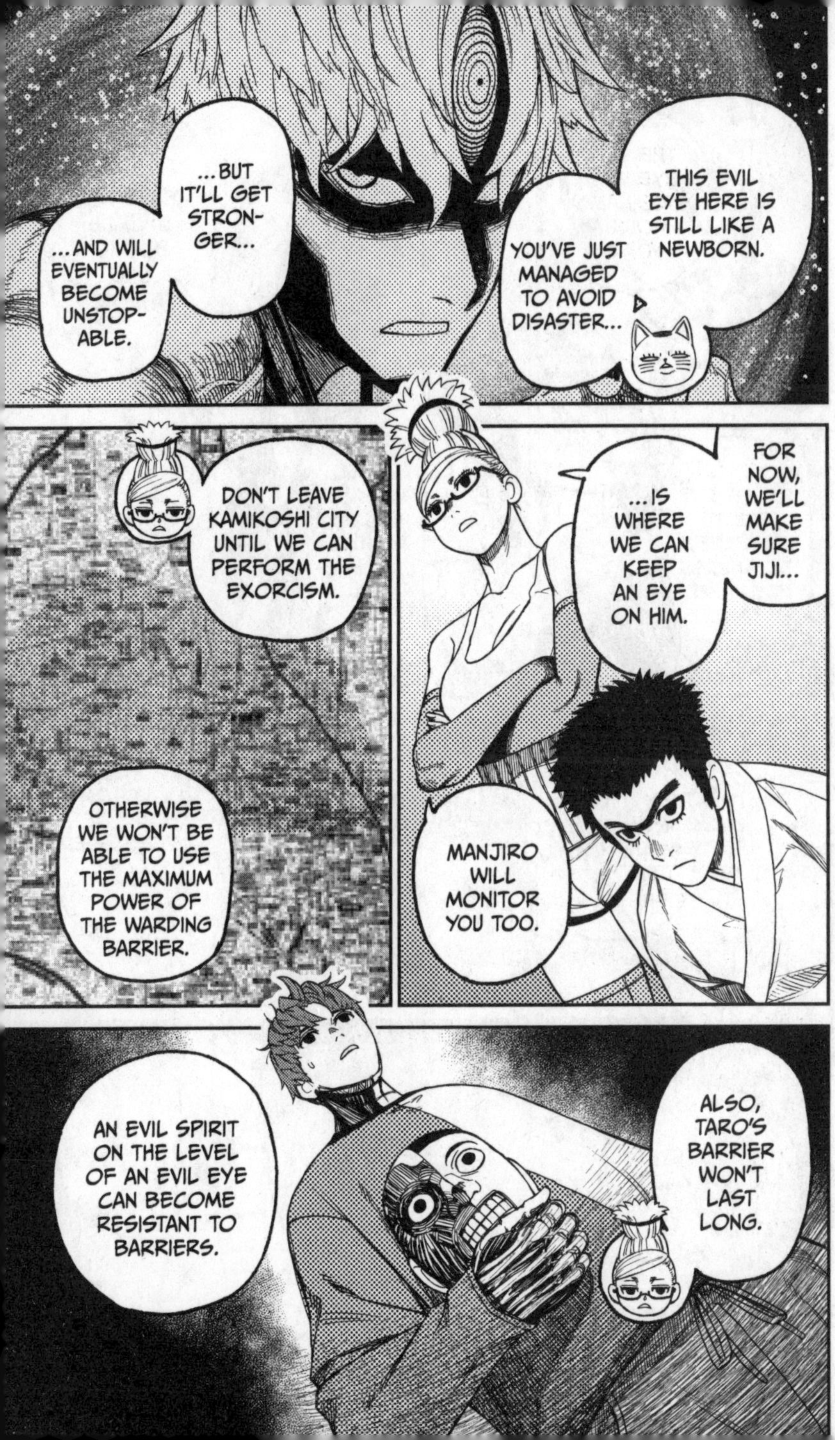
THIS EVIL EYE HERE IS STILL LIKE A NEWBORN.
YOU'VE JUST MANAGED TO AVOID DISASTER...
...BUT IT'LL GET STRONGER...
...AND WILL EVENTUALLY BECOME UNSTOPPABLE.
FOR NOW, WE'LL MAKE SURE JIJI...
...IS WHERE WE CAN KEEP AN EYE ON HIM.
MANJIRO WILL MONITOR YOU TOO.
DON'T LEAVE KAMIKOSHI CITY UNTIL WE CAN PERFORM THE EXORCISM.
OTHERWISE WE WON'T BE ABLE TO USE THE MAXIMUM POWER OF THE WARDING BARRIER.
ALSO, TARO'S BARRIER WON'T LAST LONG.
AN EVIL SPIRIT ON THE LEVEL OF AN EVIL EYE CAN BECOME RESISTANT TO BARRIERS.

EACH OF YOU...

...KEEP A HOT-WATER THERMOS ON YOU...

...SO YOU'RE PREPARED TO SPLASH HIM AT ANY TIME.

WE HAVE NO CHOICE BUT TO USE THESE.

WHEN YOU WASH YOUR HANDS, DRINK WATER, GO OUT IN THE RAIN...

YOU TAKE PLENTY OF CARE TOO, JIJI.

THE SLIGHTEST BIT OF COLD WATER WILL CAUSE YOU TO TRANSFORM.

YOU GOT THAT RIGHT.

I DON'T EVER WANT TO DEAL WITH IT AGAIN.

WE'VE GOTTA BE VIGILANT...

...UNTIL WE CAN COMPLETE THE EXORCISM!

WHERE WILL YOU LIVE, SHRIMP ALIEN?

I'LL BE LIVING AND WORKING AT A NEARBY DAIRY FARM.

THANKS TO MISS SEIKO.

HOW DOES THAT UFO ACTUALLY FLY?!

IS IT AN ANTI-GRAVITY PROPULSION SYSTEM?!

IT'S 🔧🔩⚙️!

IF ANYTHING COMES UP, FEEL FREE TO CALL ON ME AGAIN.

THANKS FOR COMING TO OUR RESCUE!

HOOH! HOOH!

BY THE WAY, SHRIMP, SIR...

ER...

WHAT'S YOUR NAME?

ON EARTH IT WOULD BE PRO-NOUNCED...

UM, MR. SHRIMP?!

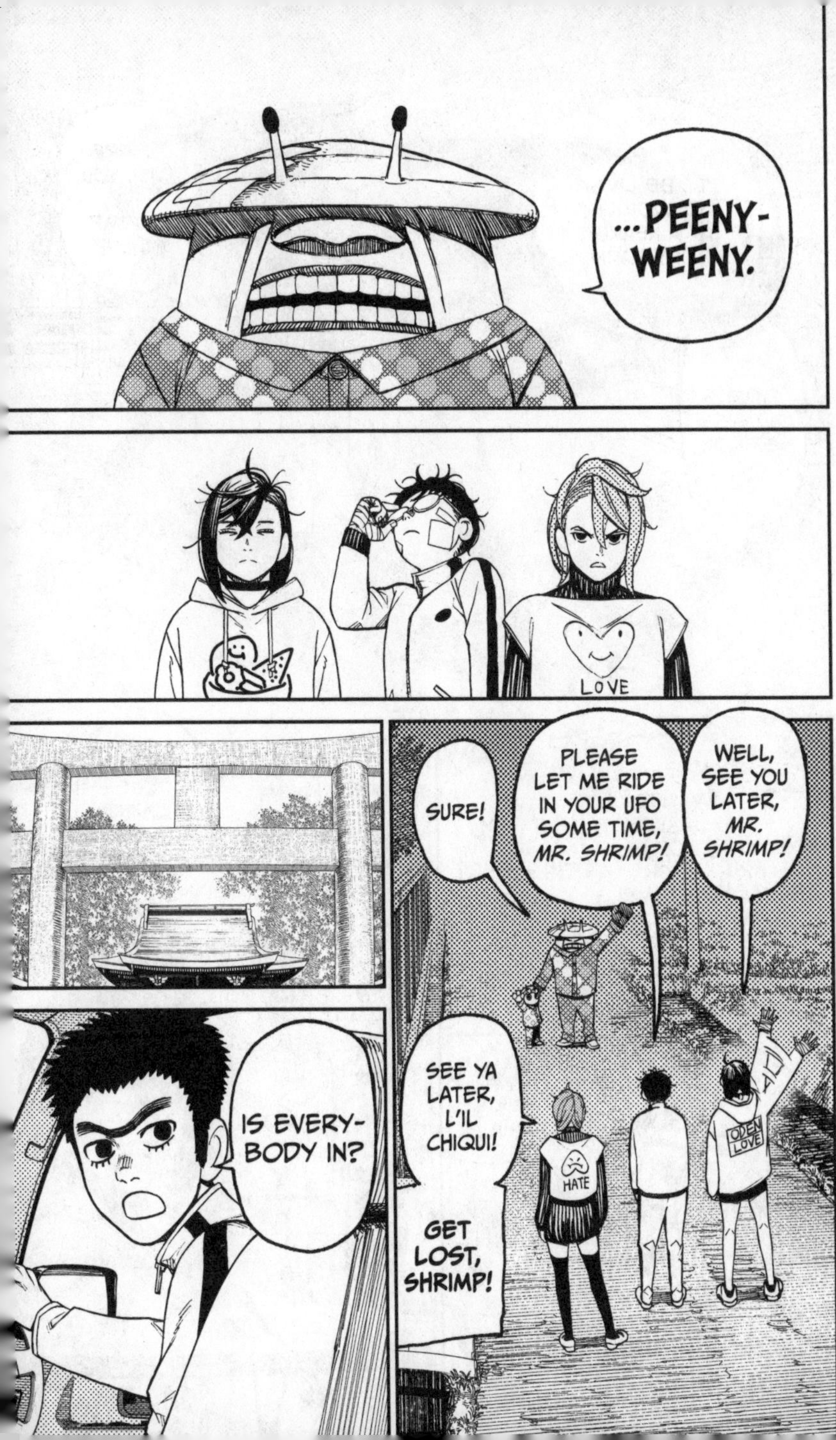
...PEENY-WEENY.
LOVE
WELL, SEE YOU LATER, MR. SHRIMP!
PLEASE LET ME RIDE IN YOUR UFO SOME TIME, MR. SHRIMP!
SURE!
ODEN LOVE
HATE
SEE YA LATER, L'IL CHIQUI!
GET LOST, SHRIMP!
IS EVERY-BODY IN?

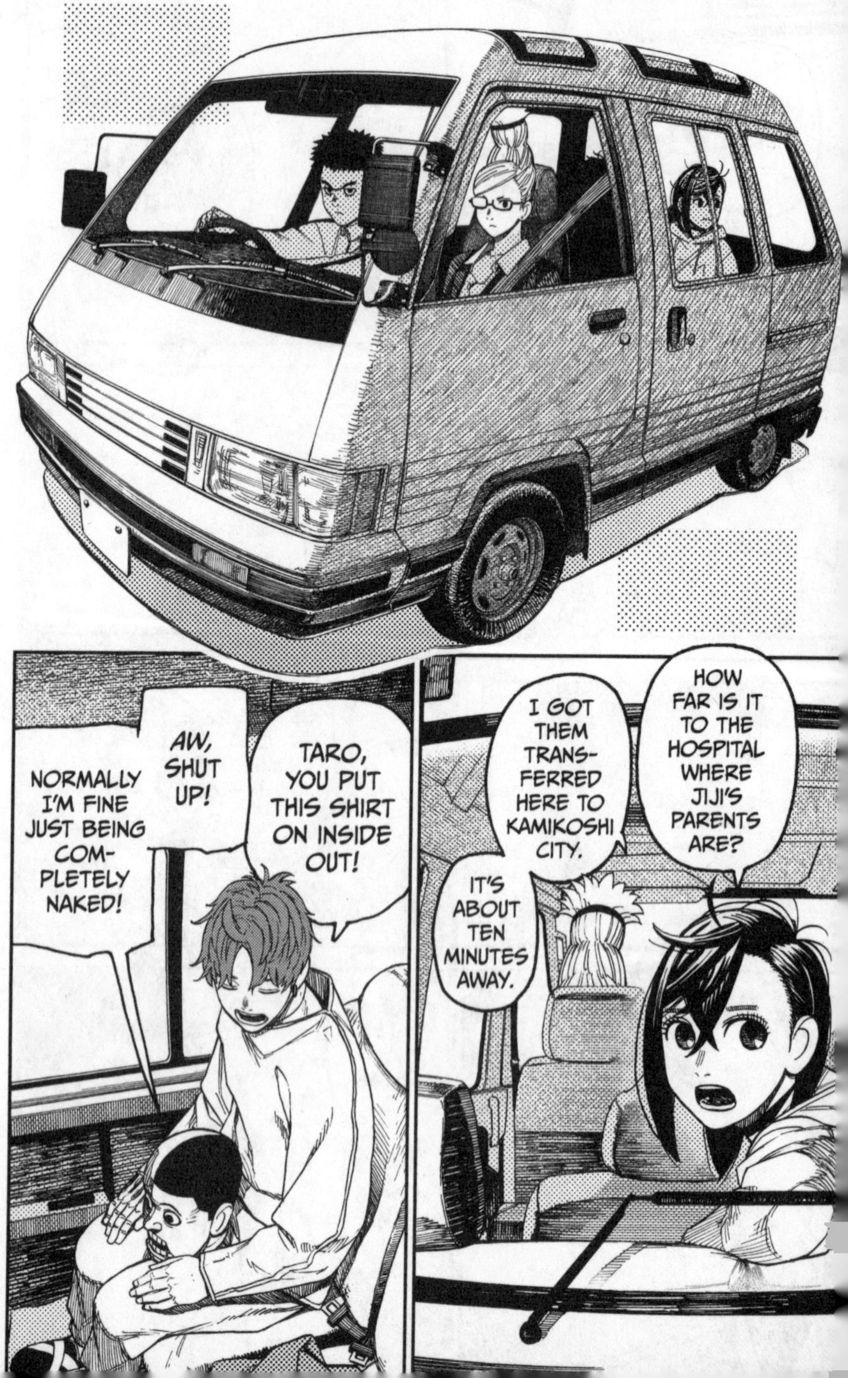
HOW FAR IS IT TO THE HOSPITAL WHERE JIJI'S PARENTS ARE?
I GOT THEM TRANSFERRED HERE TO KAMIKOSHI CITY.
IT'S ABOUT TEN MINUTES AWAY.
TARO, YOU PUT THIS SHIRT ON INSIDE OUT!
AW, SHUT UP!
NORMALLY I'M FINE JUST BEING COMPLETELY NAKED!

RIGHT HERE!

OKARUN!

GOT MINE!

DO YOU ALL HAVE YOUR THERMOSES?!

AND HOT WATER?!

NICE AND FULL!

COOL.

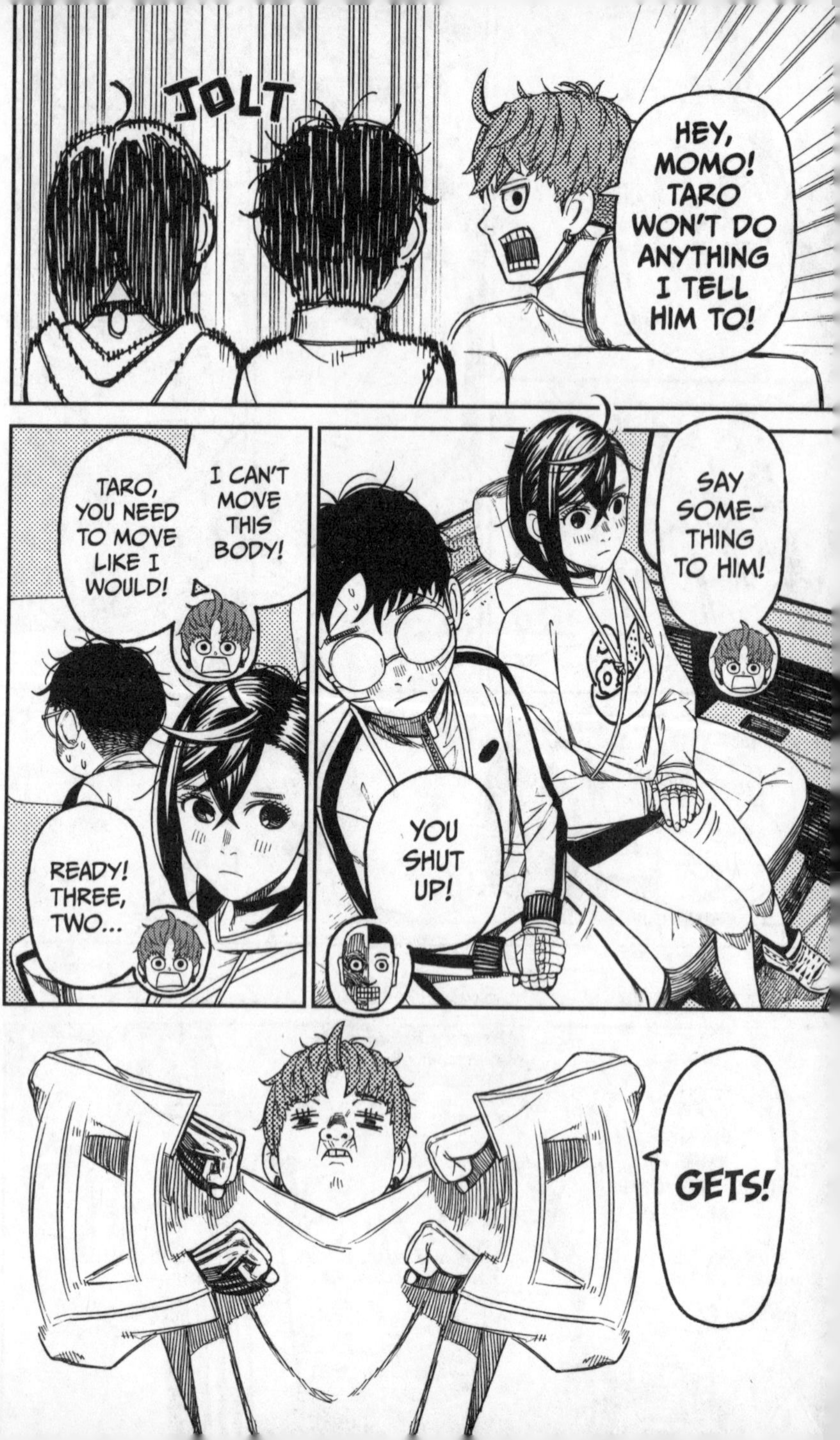
JOLT
HEY, MOMO! TARO WON'T DO ANYTHING I TELL HIM TO!
SAY SOME-THING TO HIM!
YOU SHUT UP!
I CAN'T MOVE THIS BODY!
TARO, YOU NEED TO MOVE LIKE I WOULD!
READY! THREE, TWO...
GETS!

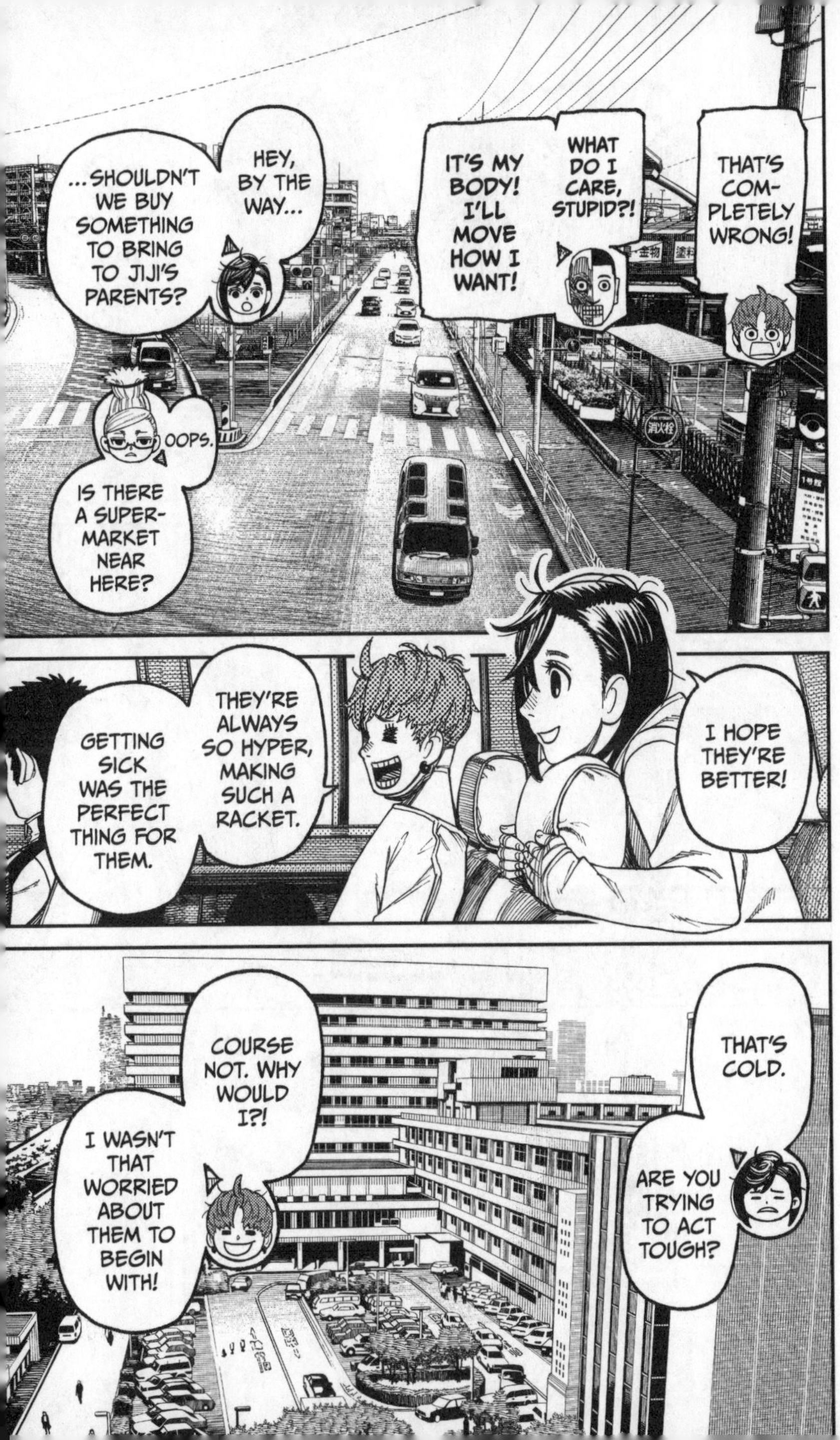
THAT'S COM-PLETELY WRONG!
WHAT DO I CARE, STUPID?!
IT'S MY BODY! I'LL MOVE HOW I WANT!
HEY, BY THE WAY...
...SHOULDN'T WE BUY SOMETHING TO BRING TO JIJI'S PARENTS?
OOPS.
IS THERE A SUPER-MARKET NEAR HERE?
I HOPE THEY'RE BETTER!
THEY'RE ALWAYS SO HYPER, MAKING SUCH A RACKET.
GETTING SICK WAS THE PERFECT THING FOR THEM.
THAT'S COLD.
ARE YOU TRYING TO ACT TOUGH?
COURSE NOT. WHY WOULD I?!
I WASN'T THAT WORRIED ABOUT THEM TO BEGIN WITH!

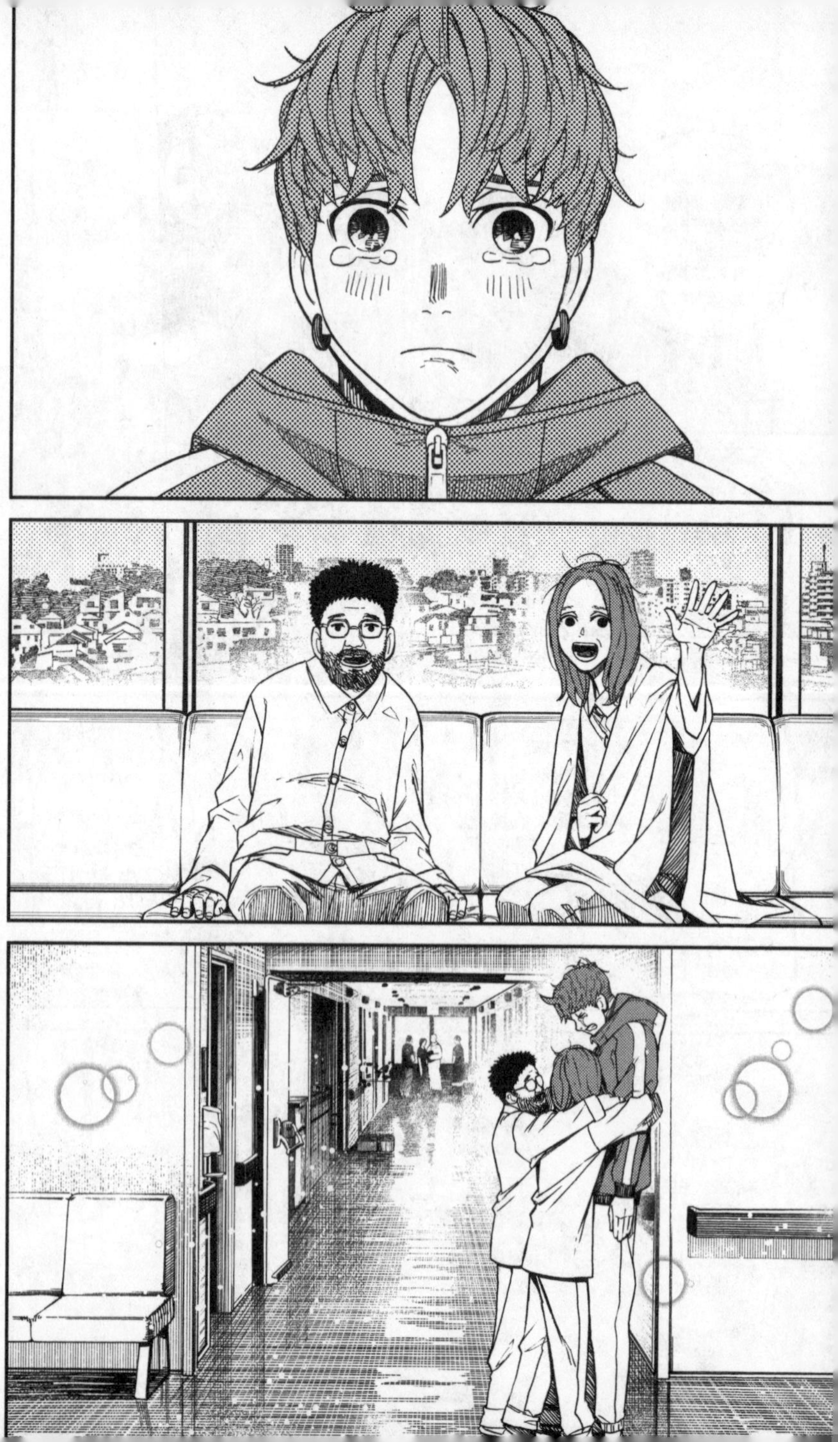

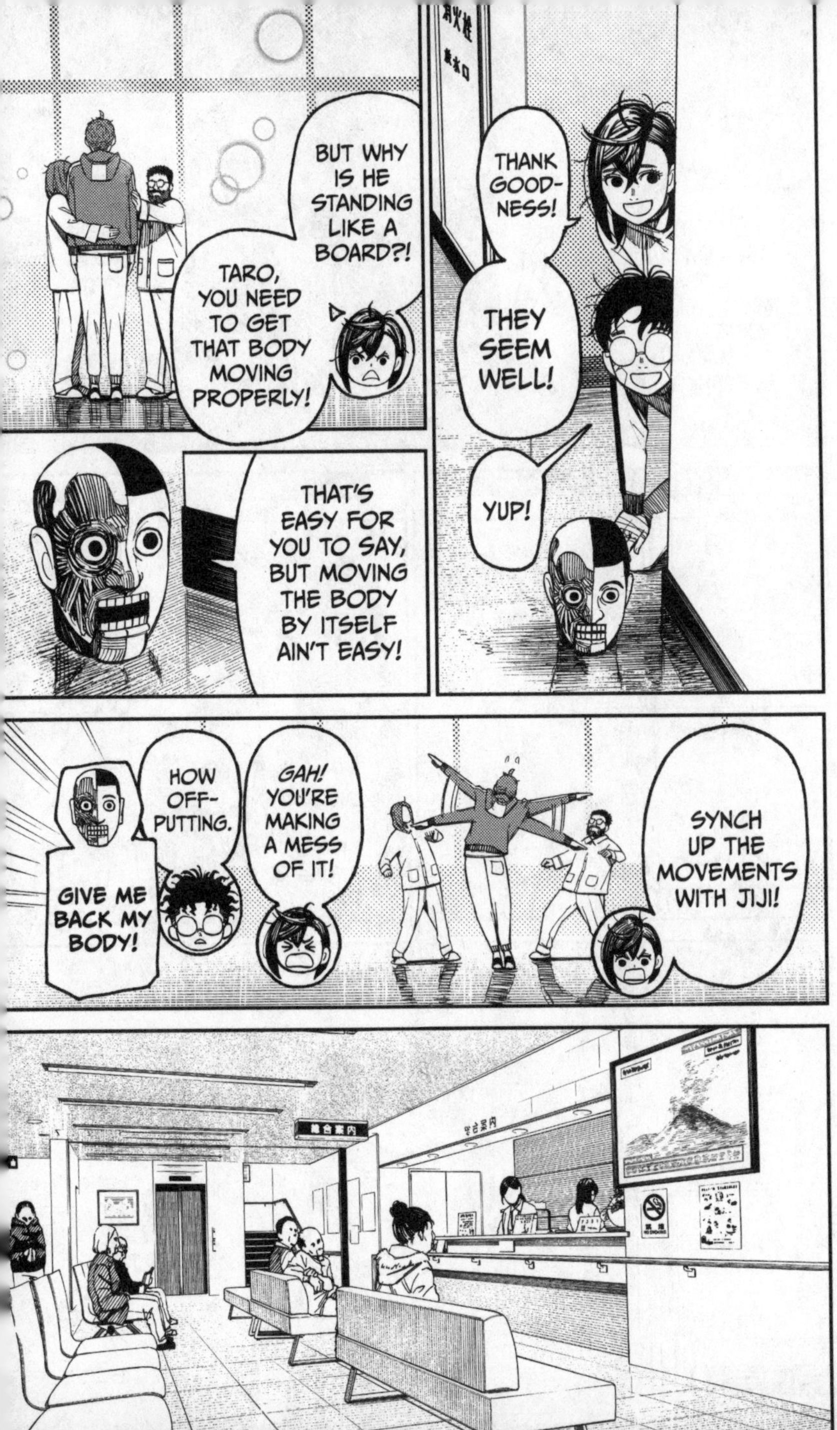
THANK GOODNESS!
THEY SEEM WELL!
YUP!
BUT WHY IS HE STANDING LIKE A BOARD?!
TARO, YOU NEED TO GET THAT BODY MOVING PROPERLY!
THAT'S EASY FOR YOU TO SAY, BUT MOVING THE BODY BY ITSELF AIN'T EASY!
SYNCH UP THE MOVEMENTS WITH JIJI!
GAH! YOU'RE MAKING A MESS OF IT!
HOW OFF-PUTTING.
GIVE ME BACK MY BODY!

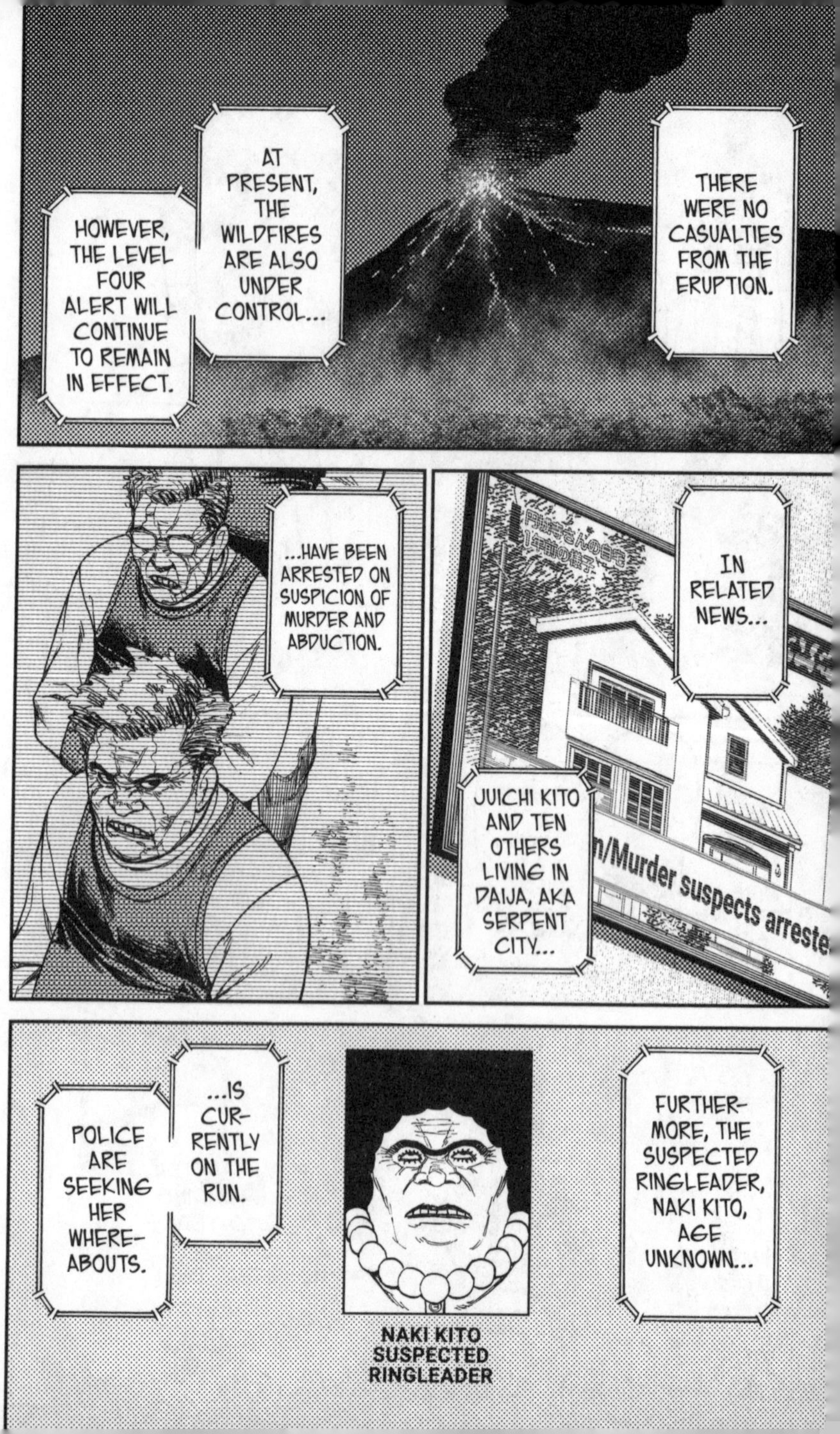
THERE WERE NO CASUALTIES FROM THE ERUPTION.
AT PRESENT, THE WILDFIRES ARE ALSO UNDER CONTROL...
HOWEVER, THE LEVEL FOUR ALERT WILL CONTINUE TO REMAIN IN EFFECT.
IN RELATED NEWS...
JUICHI KITO AND TEN OTHERS LIVING IN DAIJA, AKA SERPENT CITY...
...HAVE BEEN ARRESTED ON SUSPICION OF MURDER AND ABDUCTION.
FURTHER-MORE, THE SUSPECTED RINGLEADER, NAKI KITO, AGE UNKNOWN...
NAKI KITO SUSPECTED RINGLEADER
...IS CUR-RENTLY ON THE RUN.
POLICE ARE SEEKING HER WHERE-ABOUTS.

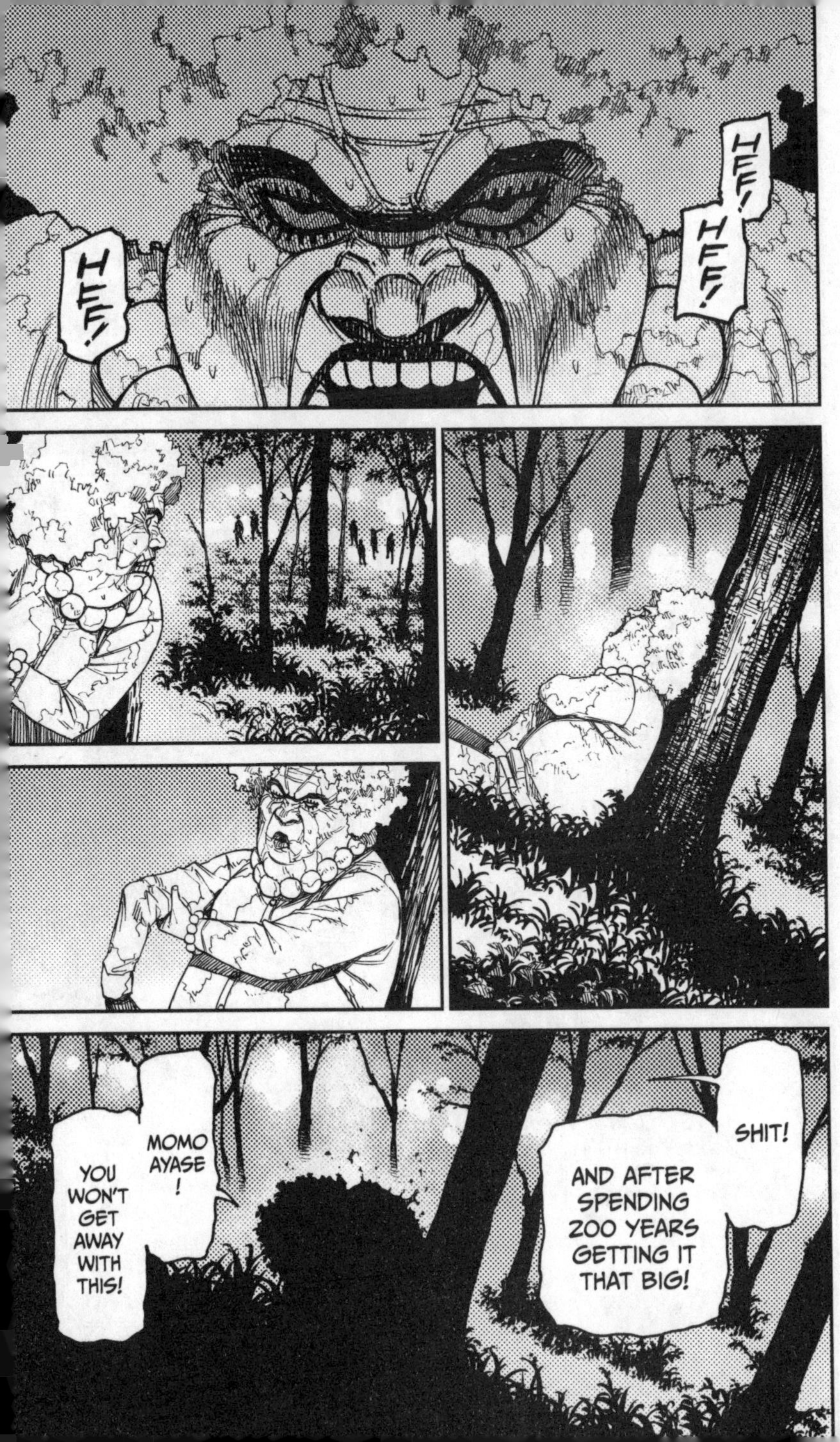
HFF! HFF!
HFF!
SHIT!
AND AFTER SPENDING 200 YEARS GETTING IT THAT BIG!
MOMO AYASE!
YOU WON'T GET AWAY WITH THIS!

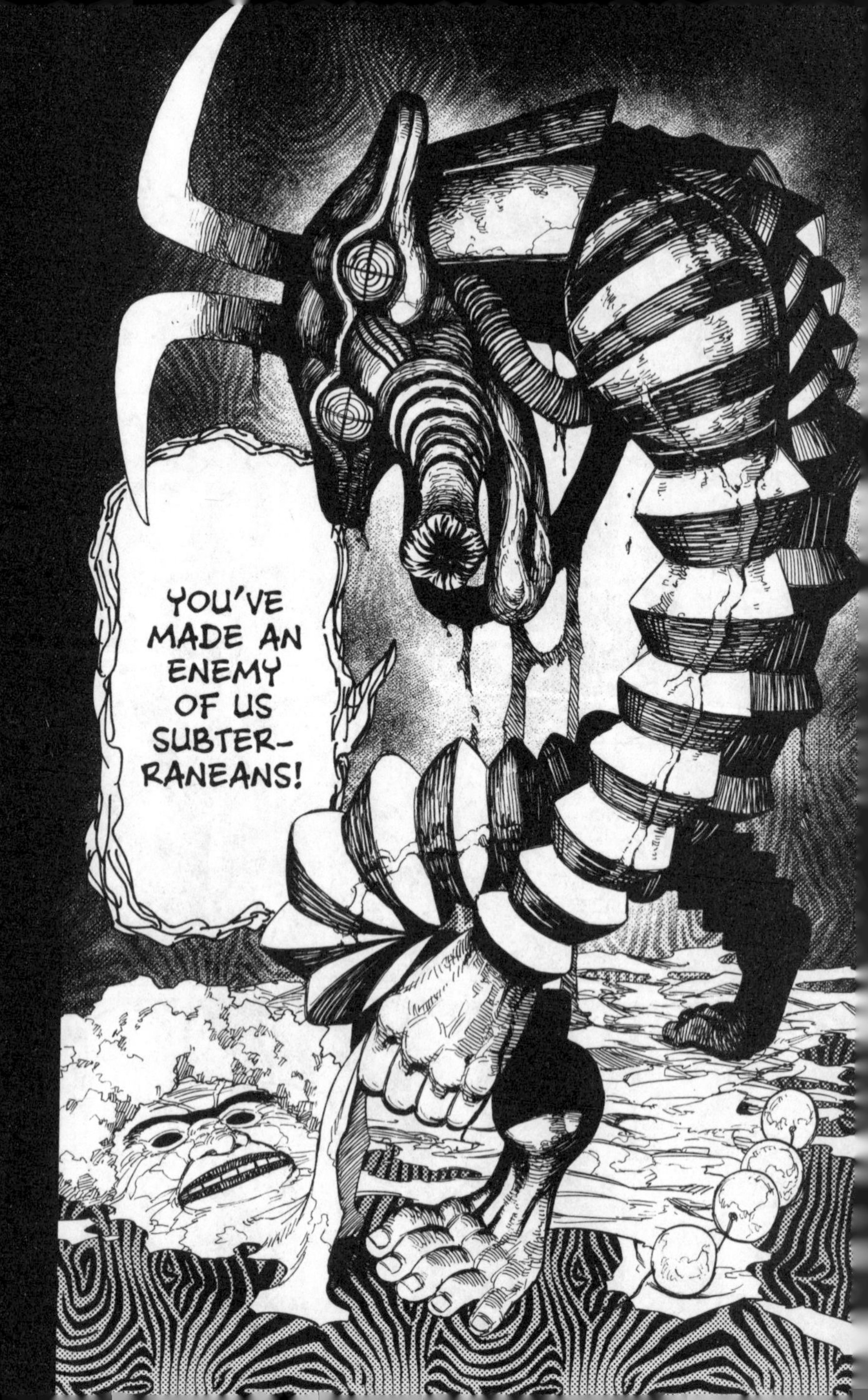
YOU'VE MADE AN ENEMY OF US SUBTER-RANEANS!

51. We Can All Stay There Together!

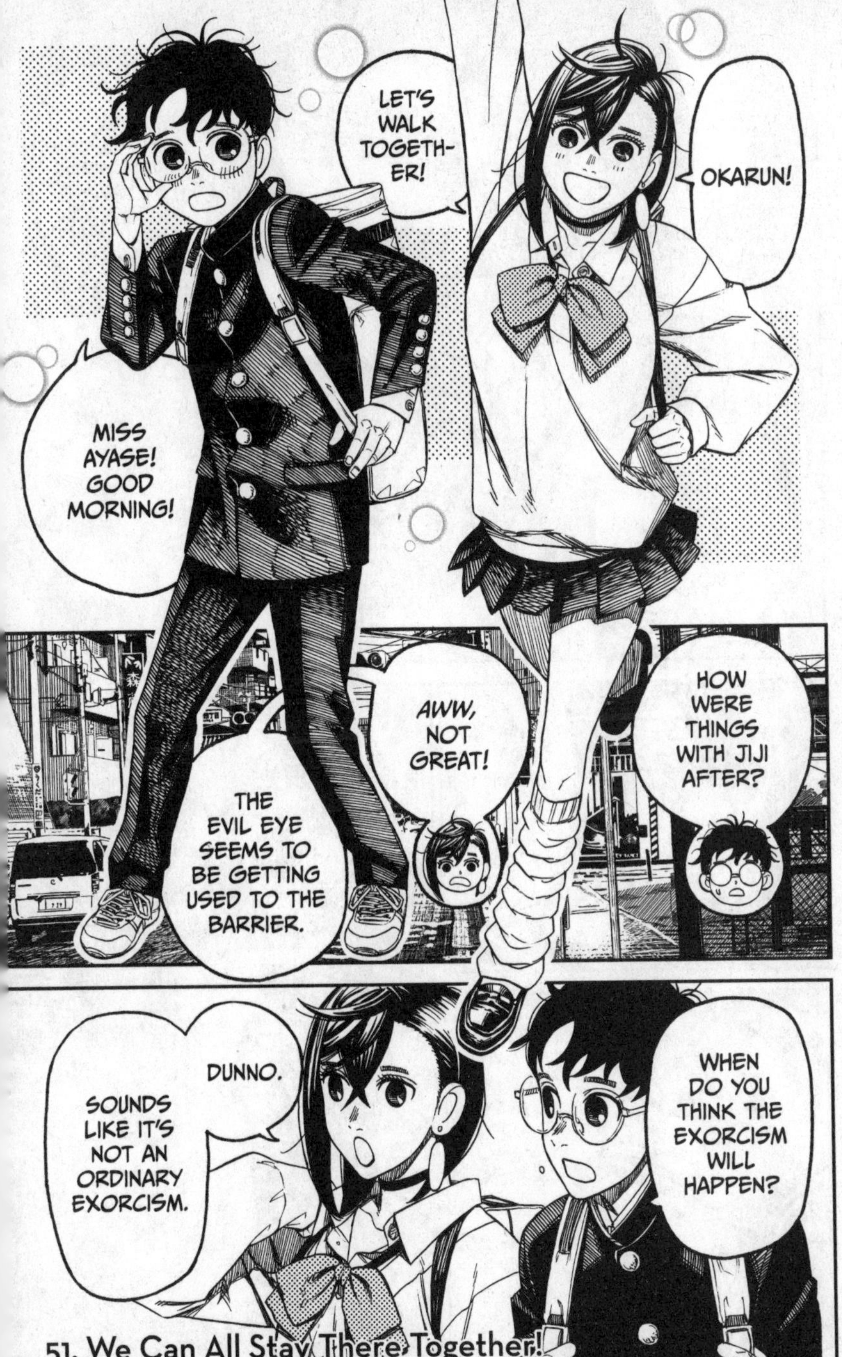
OKARUN!
LET'S WALK TOGETH-ER!
MISS AYASE! GOOD MORNING!
HOW WERE THINGS WITH JIJI AFTER?
AWW, NOT GREAT!
THE EVIL EYE SEEMS TO BE GETTING USED TO THE BARRIER.
WHEN DO YOU THINK THE EXORCISM WILL HAPPEN?
DUNNO.
SOUNDS LIKE IT'S NOT AN ORDINARY EXORCISM.

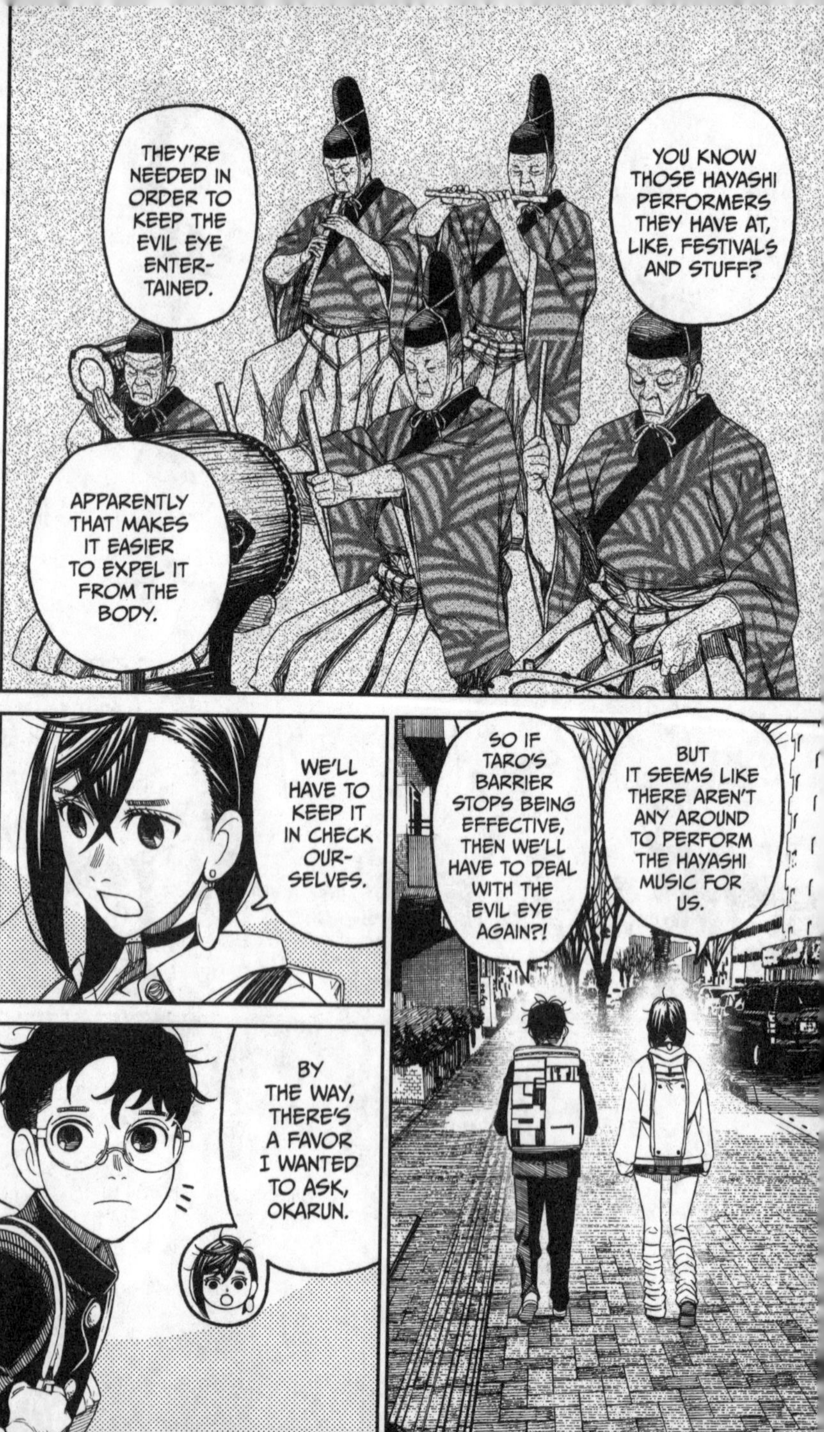
YOU KNOW THOSE HAYASHI PERFORMERS THEY HAVE AT, LIKE, FESTIVALS AND STUFF?
THEY'RE NEEDED IN ORDER TO KEEP THE EVIL EYE ENTER-TAINED.
APPARENTLY THAT MAKES IT EASIER TO EXPEL IT FROM THE BODY.
BUT IT SEEMS LIKE THERE AREN'T ANY AROUND TO PERFORM THE HAYASHI MUSIC FOR US.
SO IF TARO'S BARRIER STOPS BEING EFFECTIVE, THEN WE'LL HAVE TO DEAL WITH THE EVIL EYE AGAIN?!
WE'LL HAVE TO KEEP IT IN CHECK OUR-SELVES.
BY THE WAY, THERE'S A FAVOR I WANTED TO ASK, OKARUN.

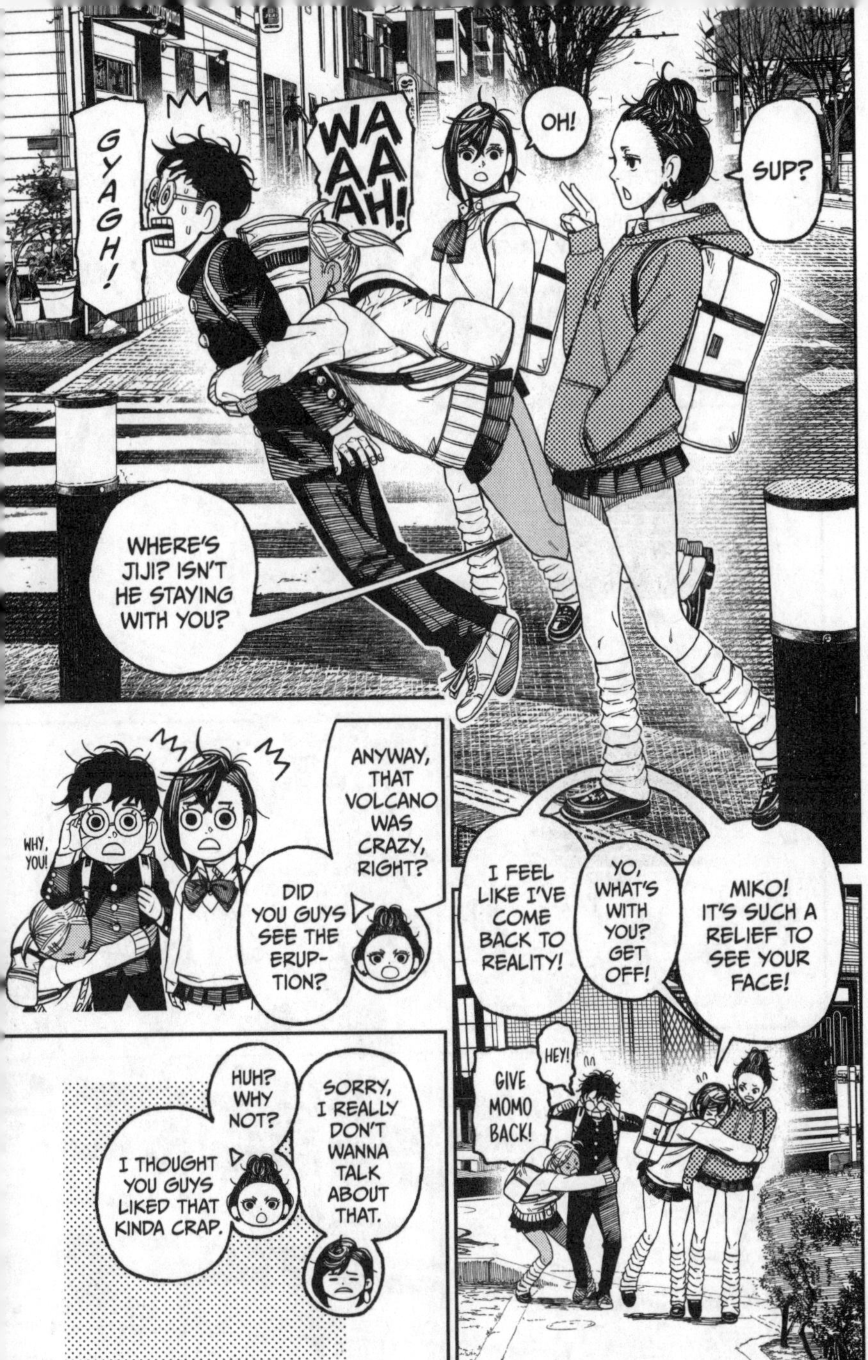
SUP?
OH!
WAAAAH!
GYAGH!
WHERE'S JIJI? ISN'T HE STAYING WITH YOU?
MIKO! IT'S SUCH A RELIEF TO SEE YOUR FACE!
YO, WHAT'S WITH YOU? GET OFF!
I FEEL LIKE I'VE COME BACK TO REALITY!
HEY!
GIVE MOMO BACK!
ANYWAY, THAT VOLCANO WAS CRAZY, RIGHT?
DID YOU GUYS SEE THE ERUP-TION?
WHY, YOU!
SORRY, I REALLY DON'T WANNA TALK ABOUT THAT.
HUH? WHY NOT?
I THOUGHT YOU GUYS LIKED THAT KINDA CRAP.

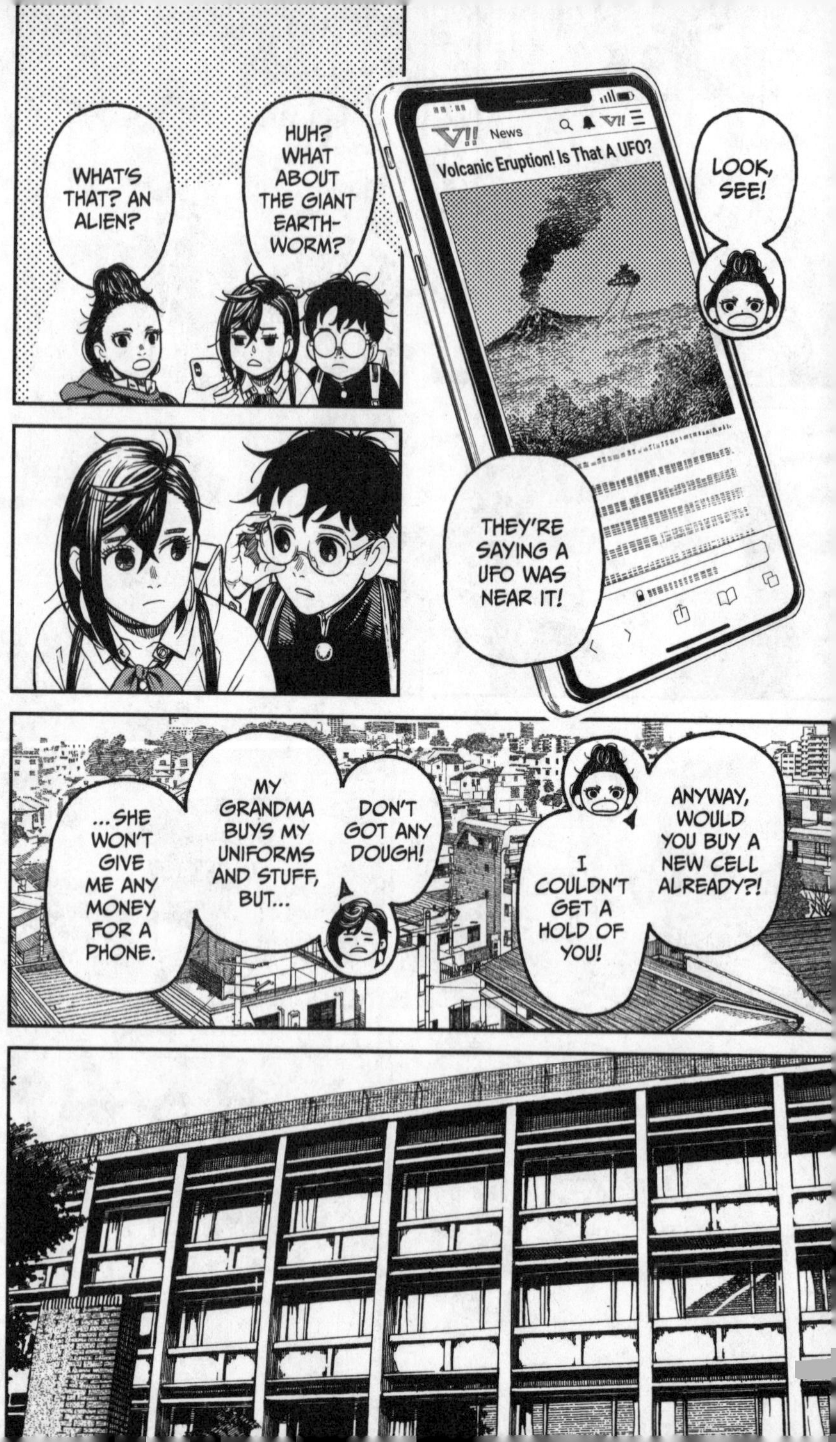
LOOK, SEE!
V!! News
Volcanic Eruption! Is That A UFO?
THEY'RE SAYING A UFO WAS NEAR IT!
HUH? WHAT ABOUT THE GIANT EARTH-WORM?
WHAT'S THAT? AN ALIEN?
ANYWAY, WOULD YOU BUY A NEW CELL ALREADY?!
I COULDN'T GET A HOLD OF YOU!
DON'T GOT ANY DOUGH!
MY GRANDMA BUYS MY UNIFORMS AND STUFF, BUT...
...SHE WON'T GIVE ME ANY MONEY FOR A PHONE.

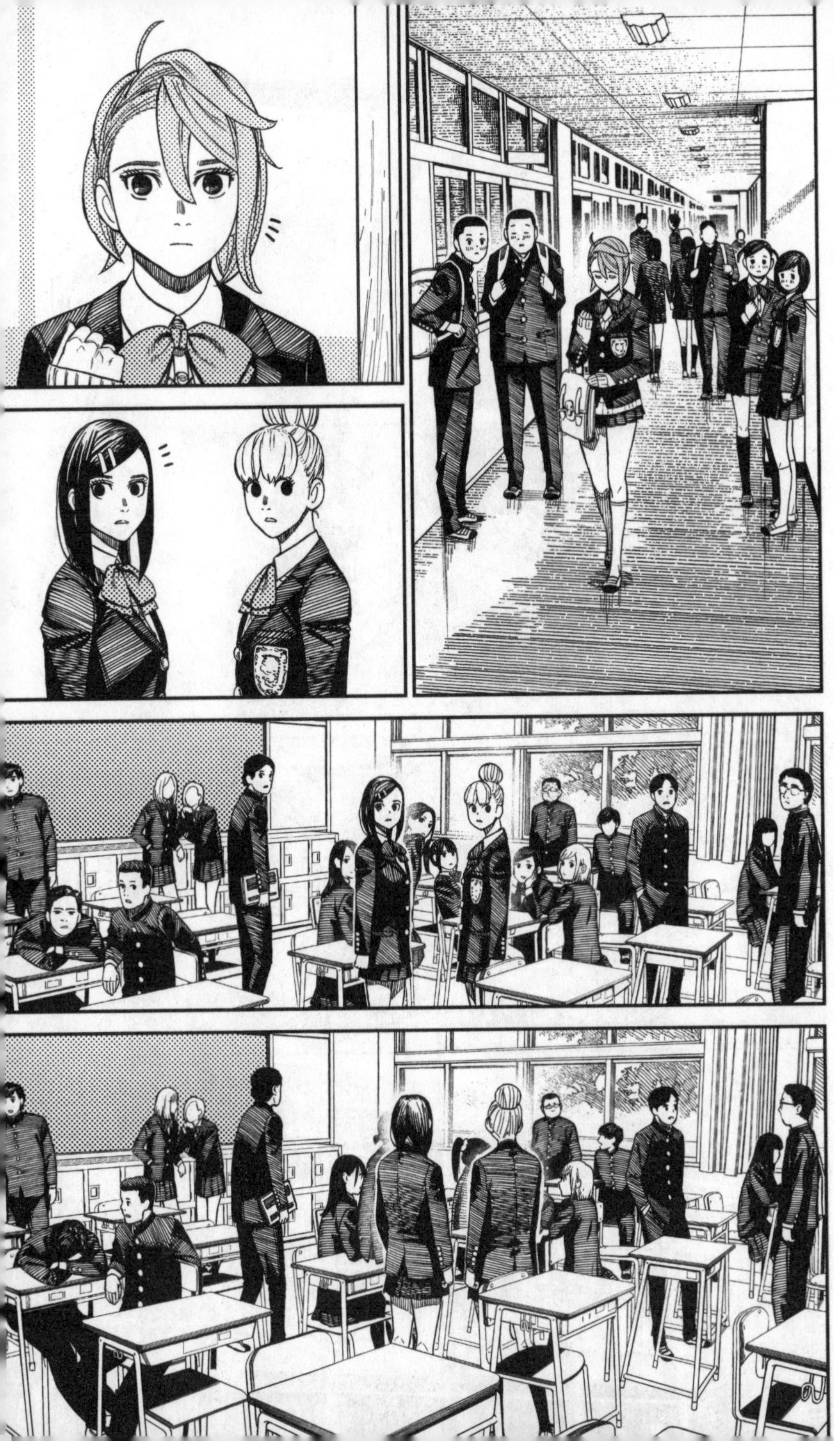

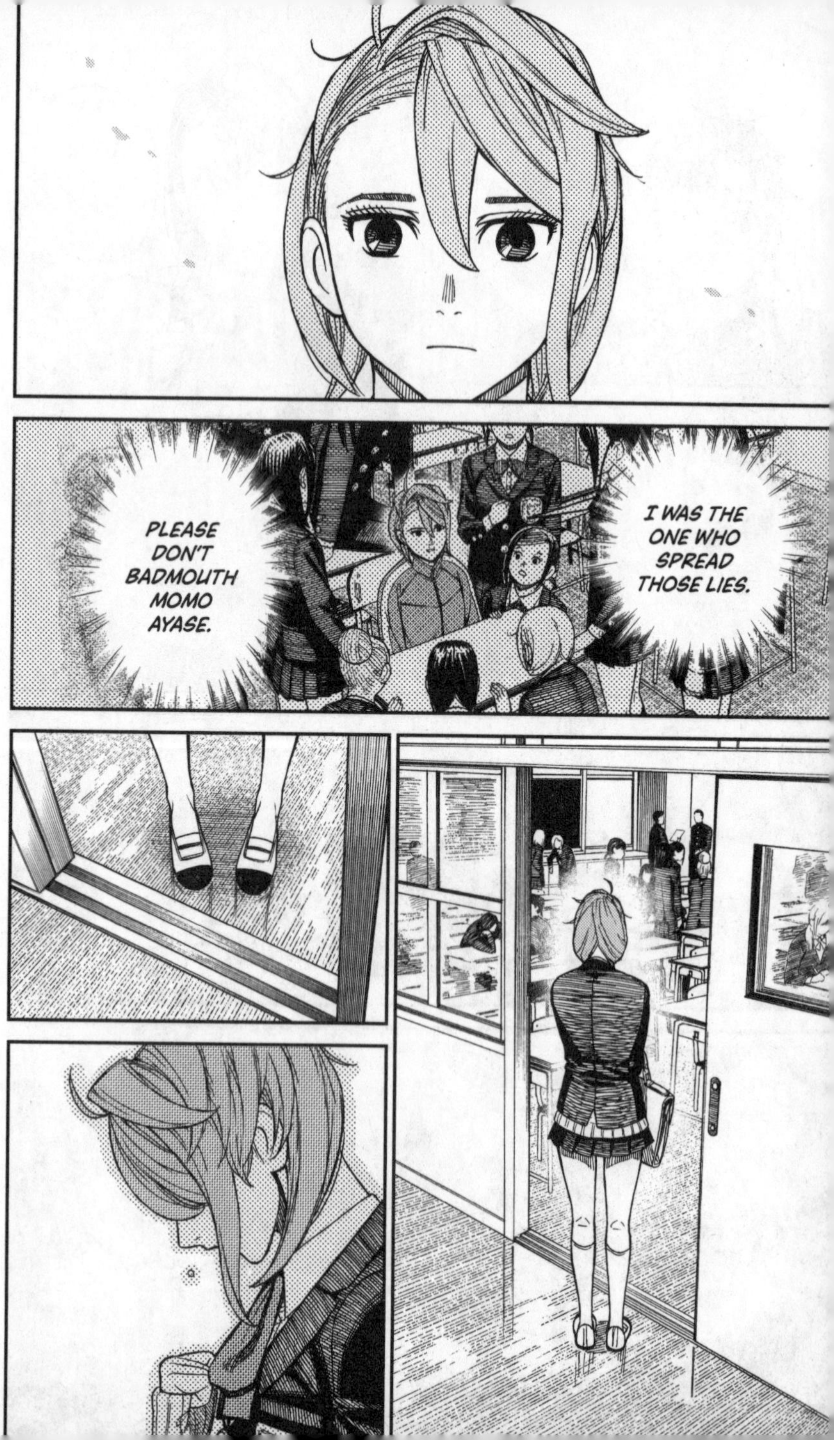
I WAS THE ONE WHO SPREAD THOSE LIES.
PLEASE DON'T BADMOUTH MOMO AYASE.

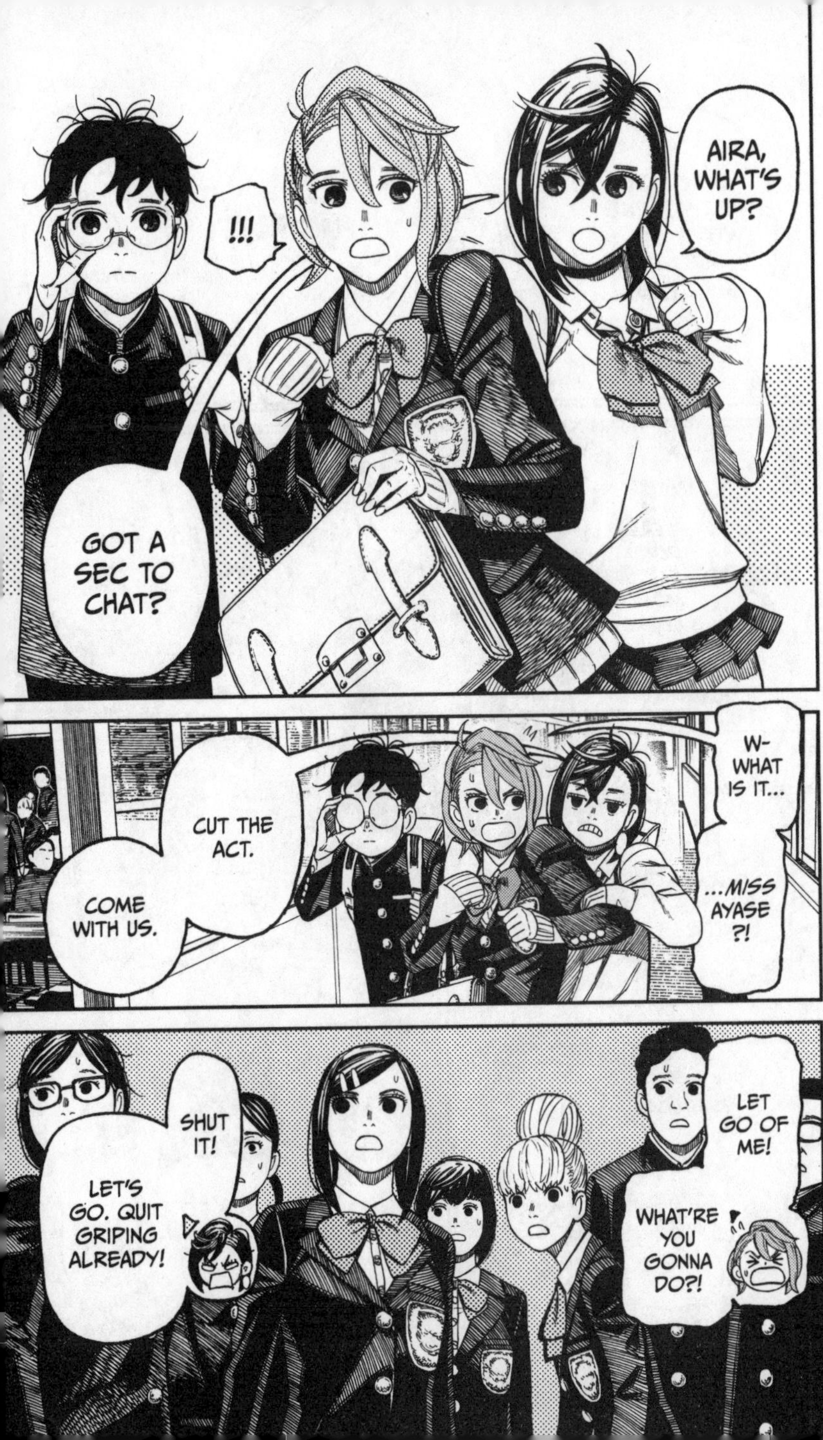
AIRA, WHAT'S UP?
!!!
GOT A SEC TO CHAT?
W- WHAT IS IT...
...MISS AYASE ?!
CUT THE ACT.
COME WITH US.
LET GO OF ME!
WHAT'RE YOU GONNA DO?!
SHUT IT!
LET'S GO. QUIT GRIPING ALREADY!

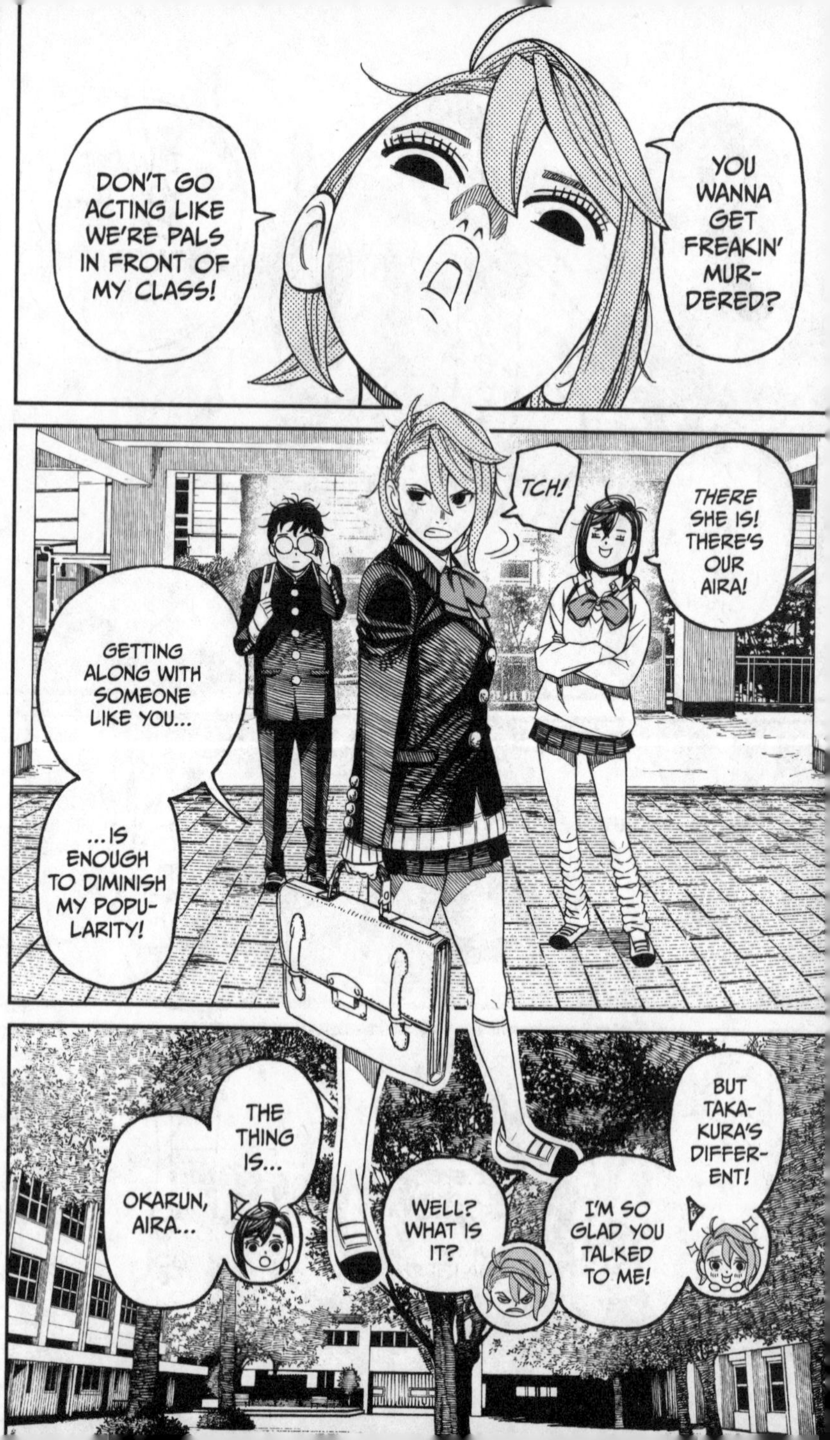
YOU WANNA GET FREAKIN' MURDERED?
DON'T GO ACTING LIKE WE'RE PALS IN FRONT OF MY CLASS!
THERE SHE IS! THERE'S OUR AIRA!
TCH!
GETTING ALONG WITH SOMEONE LIKE YOU...
...IS ENOUGH TO DIMINISH MY POPULARITY!
BUT TAKAKURA'S DIFFERENT!
I'M SO GLAD YOU TALKED TO ME!
WELL? WHAT IS IT?
OKARUN, AIRA...
THE THING IS...

I MEAN, JUST THE THOUGHT OF IT ...

THIS IS THE WORST!

... MAKES ME SICK.

WELL, I GUESS THERE'S NO OTHER WAY...

CAN'T BE HELPED.

THIS TOTALLY SUCKS!

WHY HAS IT COME TO THIS?!

AGH! NO, NO, NO!

I GUESS IT'S UNAVOID-ABLE, HUH?

C'EST LA VIE, AS THEY SAY...

WE'LL DO IT!

IF YOU CAN'T, THAT'S FINE. I'LL—

AIRA, IF YOU'VE GOT PLANS WITH FRIENDS, YOU CAN COME OVER WHENEVER.

TO-NIGHT ?!

HOW ABOUT STARTING TONIGHT?

COOL!

HUH?! WHAT DO I DO?!

HUH?

...YOU DON'T HAVE TO FORCE YOURSELF TO HANG OUT WITH ME.

AIRA. IF SOMETHING'S GOING ON BETWEEN YOU AND YOUR FRIENDS BECAUSE OF ME...

NO...

I DON'T NEED TO HEAR THAT FROM YOU.

NOTHING LIKE THAT.

...

IT'S MY FAULT...

YOU'VE GOT NOTHING TO DO WITH IT.

AH!

THE ARM'S COME OFF.

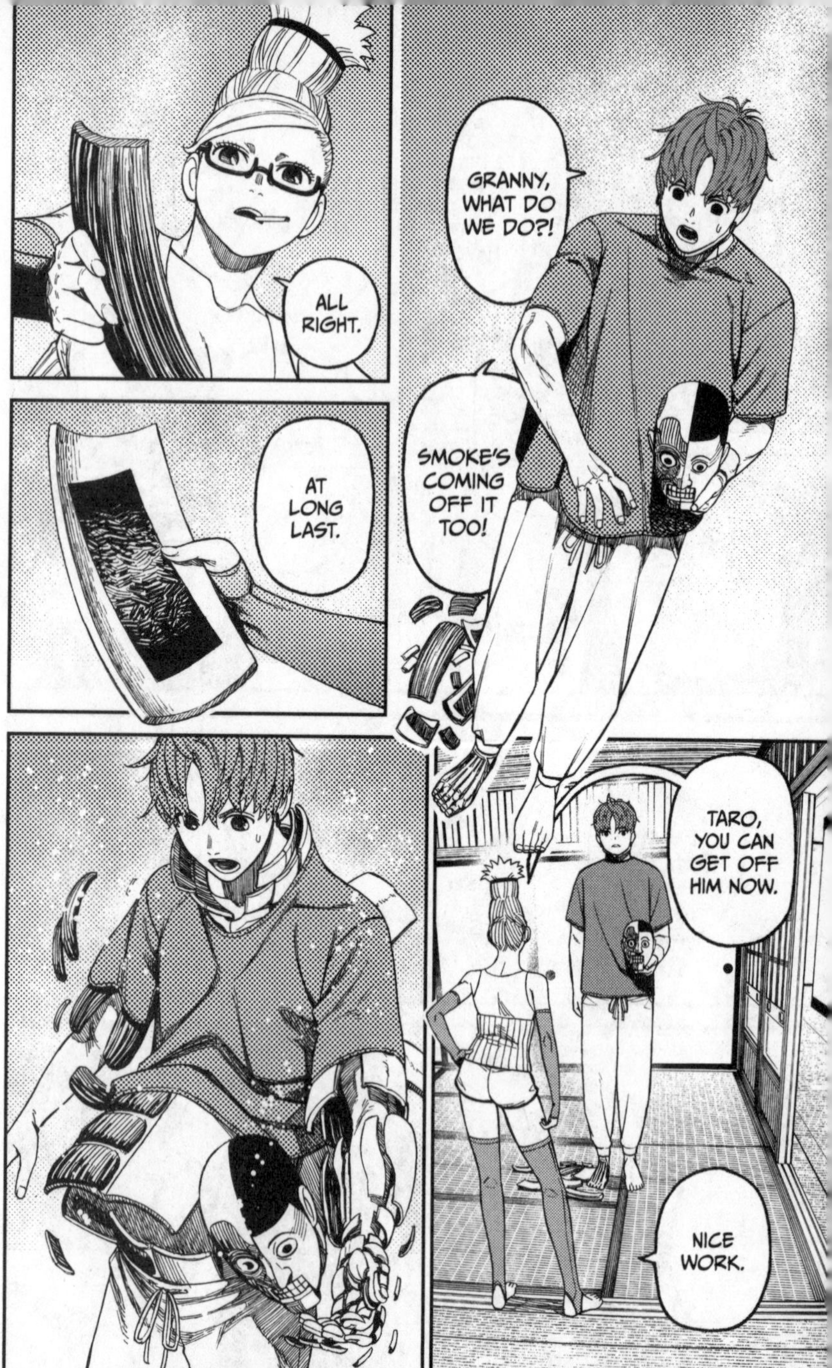
GRANNY, WHAT DO WE DO?!
SMOKE'S COMING OFF IT TOO!
ALL RIGHT.
AT LONG LAST.
TARO, YOU CAN GET OFF HIM NOW.
NICE WORK.

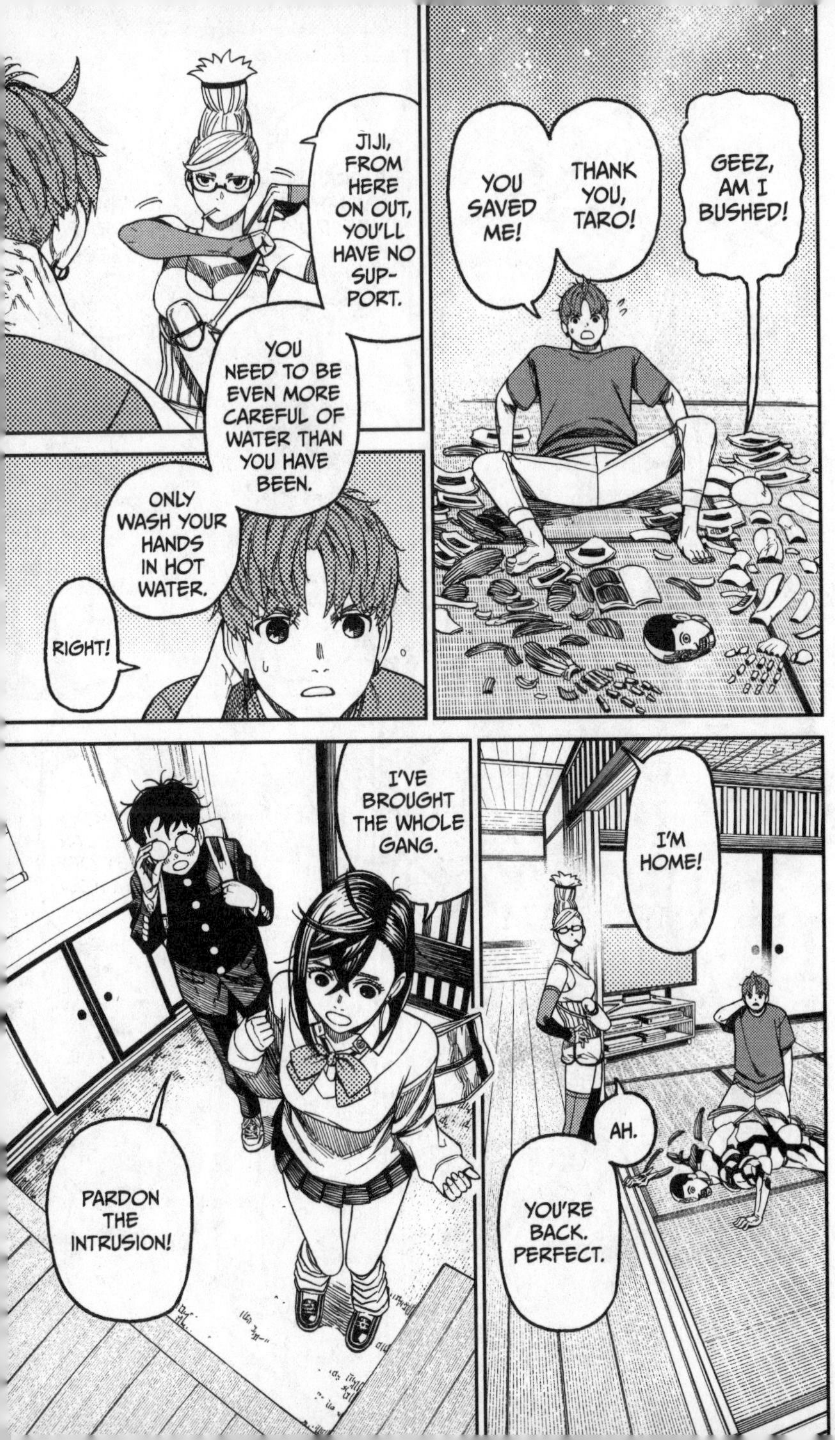
GEEZ, AM I BUSHED!
THANK YOU, TARO!
YOU SAVED ME!
JIJI, FROM HERE ON OUT, YOU'LL HAVE NO SUP-PORT.
YOU NEED TO BE EVEN MORE CAREFUL OF WATER THAN YOU HAVE BEEN.
ONLY WASH YOUR HANDS IN HOT WATER.
RIGHT!
I'M HOME!
AH.
YOU'RE BACK. PERFECT.
I'VE BROUGHT THE WHOLE GANG.
PARDON THE INTRUSION!

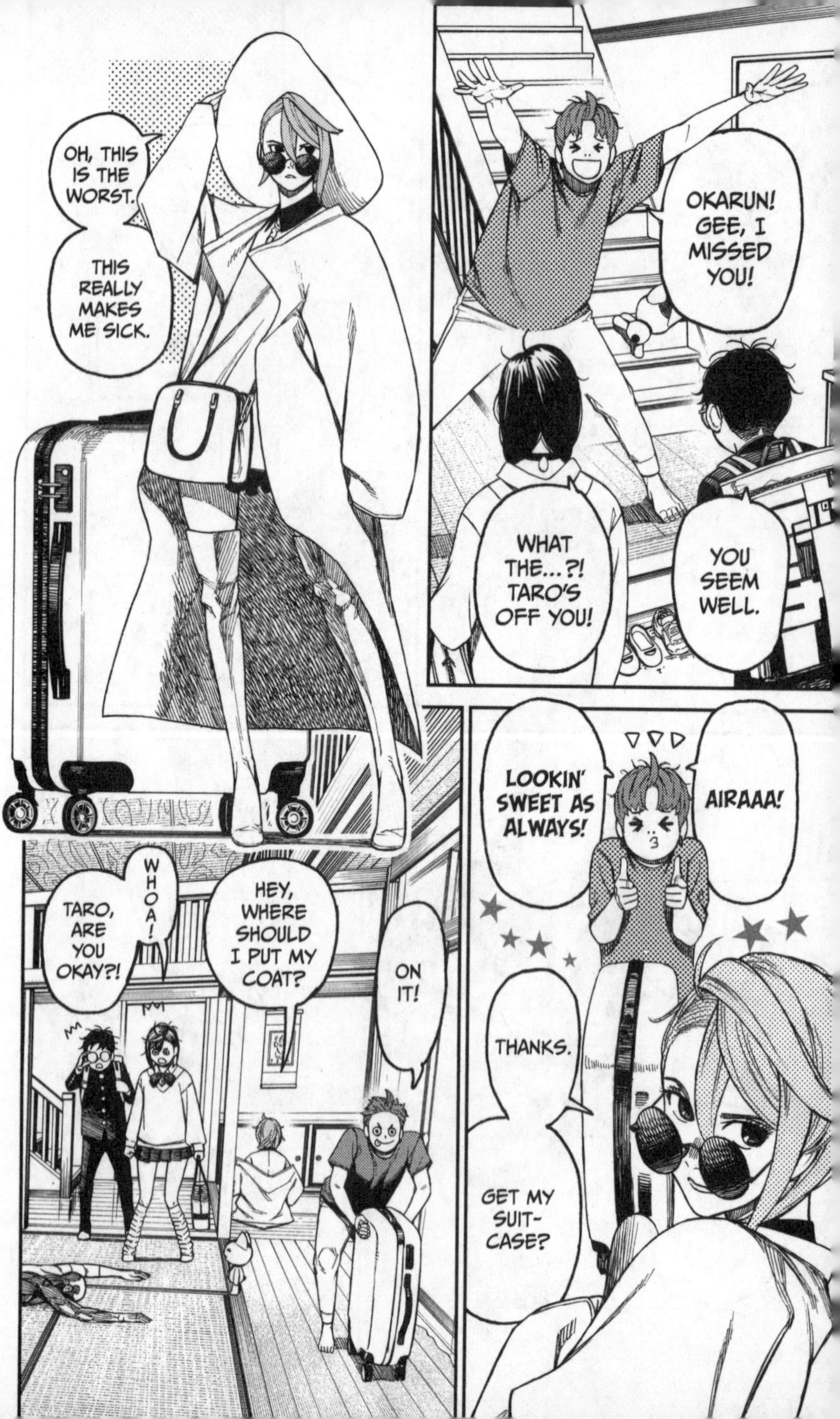
OKARUN! GEE, I MISSED YOU!
YOU SEEM WELL.
WHAT THE...?! TARO'S OFF YOU!
OH, THIS IS THE WORST.
THIS REALLY MAKES ME SICK.
AIRAAA!
LOOKIN' SWEET AS ALWAYS!
THANKS.
GET MY SUIT-CASE?
ON IT!
HEY, WHERE SHOULD I PUT MY COAT?
WHOA!
TARO, ARE YOU OKAY?!

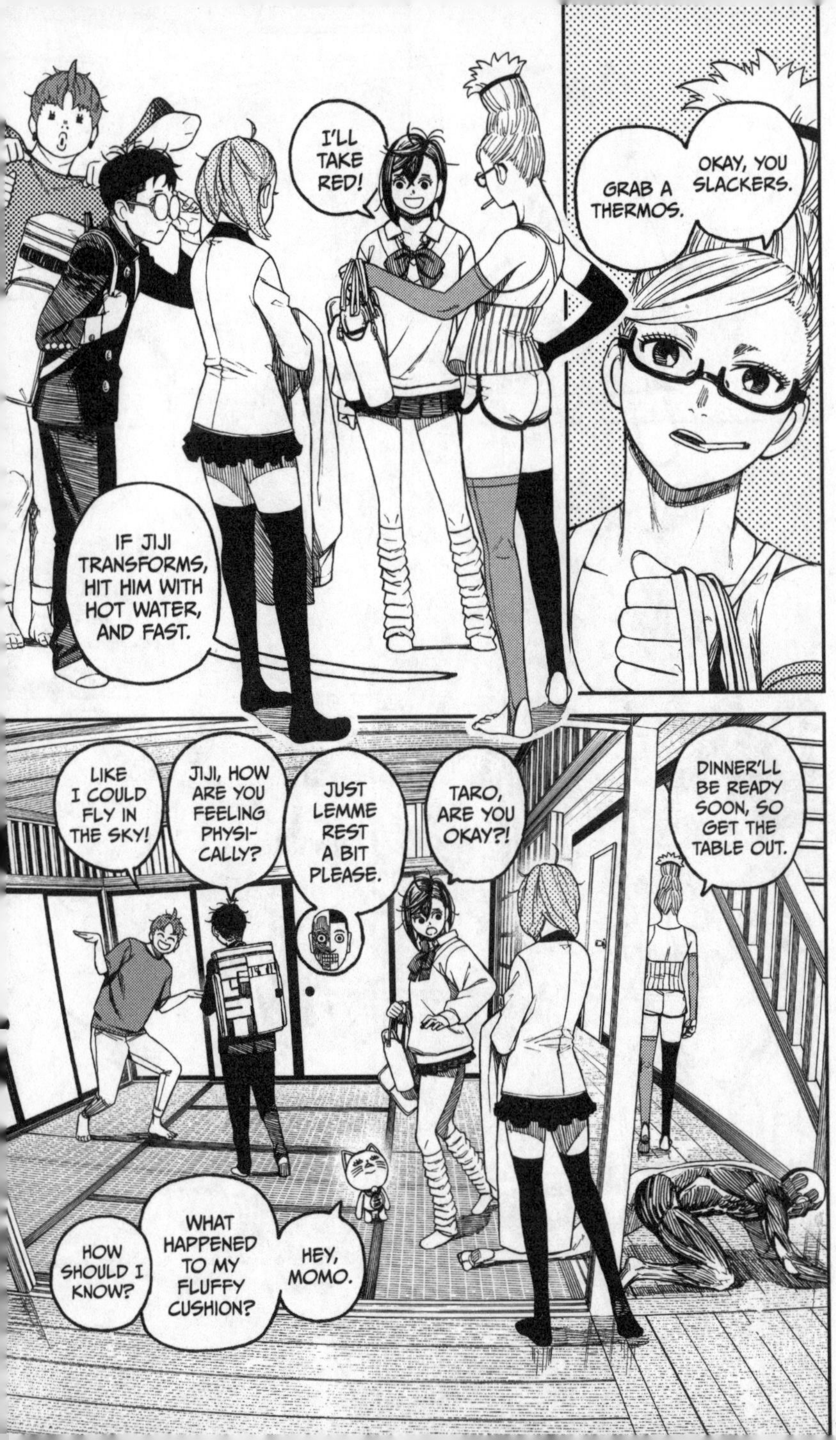

OKAY, YOU SLACKERS.
GRAB A THERMOS.
I'LL TAKE RED!
IF JIJI TRANSFORMS, HIT HIM WITH HOT WATER, AND FAST.
DINNER'LL BE READY SOON, SO GET THE TABLE OUT.
TARO, ARE YOU OKAY?!
JUST LEMME REST A BIT PLEASE.
JIJI, HOW ARE YOU FEELING PHYSI-CALLY?
LIKE I COULD FLY IN THE SKY!
HEY, MOMO.
WHAT HAPPENED TO MY FLUFFY CUSHION?
HOW SHOULD I KNOW?

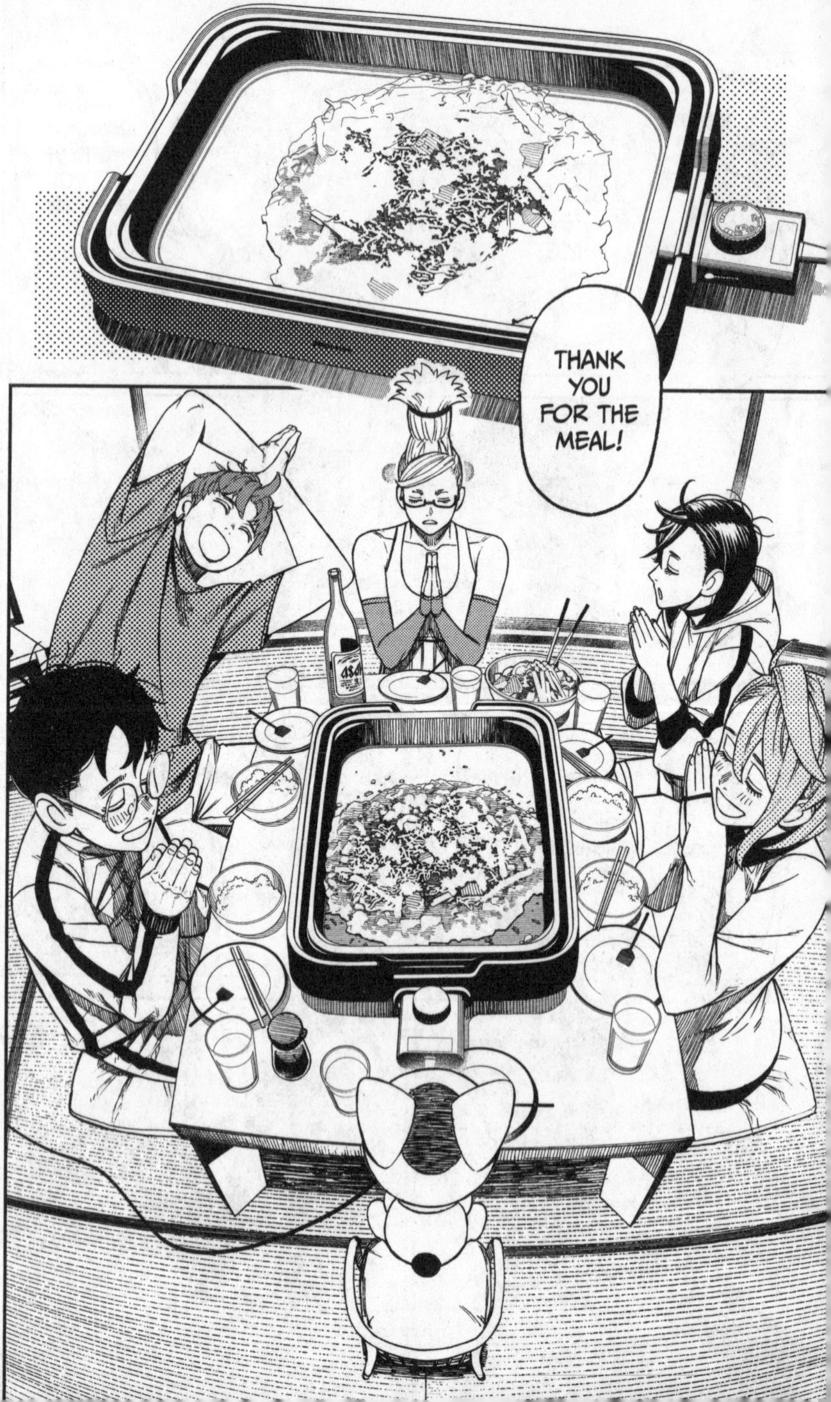
THANK YOU FOR THE MEAL!

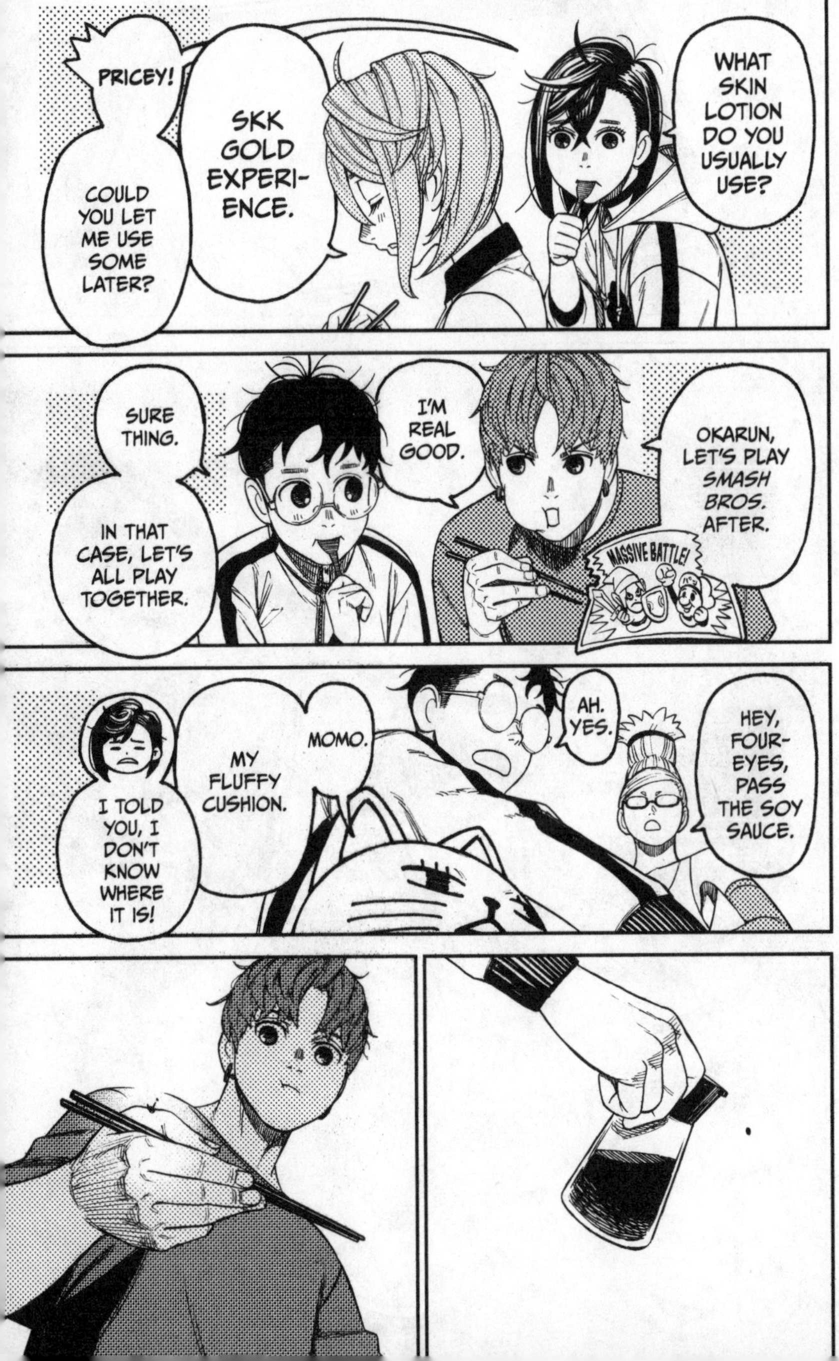
WHAT SKIN LOTION DO YOU USUALLY USE?
SKK GOLD EXPERI-ENCE.
PRICEY!
COULD YOU LET ME USE SOME LATER?
OKARUN, LET'S PLAY SMASH BROS. AFTER.
MASSIVE BATTLE!
I'M REAL GOOD.
SURE THING.
IN THAT CASE, LET'S ALL PLAY TOGETHER.
HEY, FOUR-EYES, PASS THE SOY SAUCE.
AH. YES.
MOMO.
MY FLUFFY CUSHION.
I TOLD YOU, I DON'T KNOW WHERE IT IS!

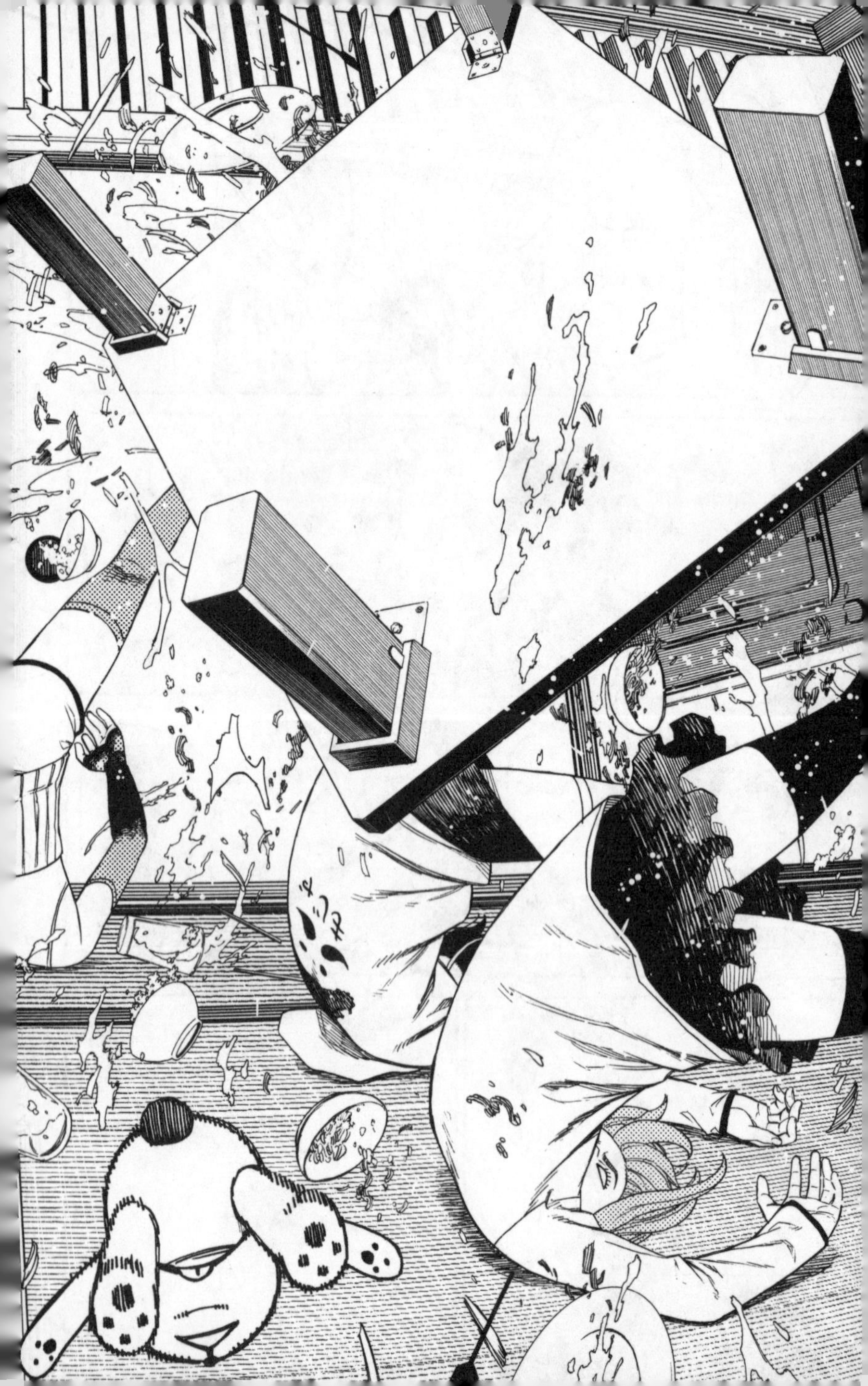

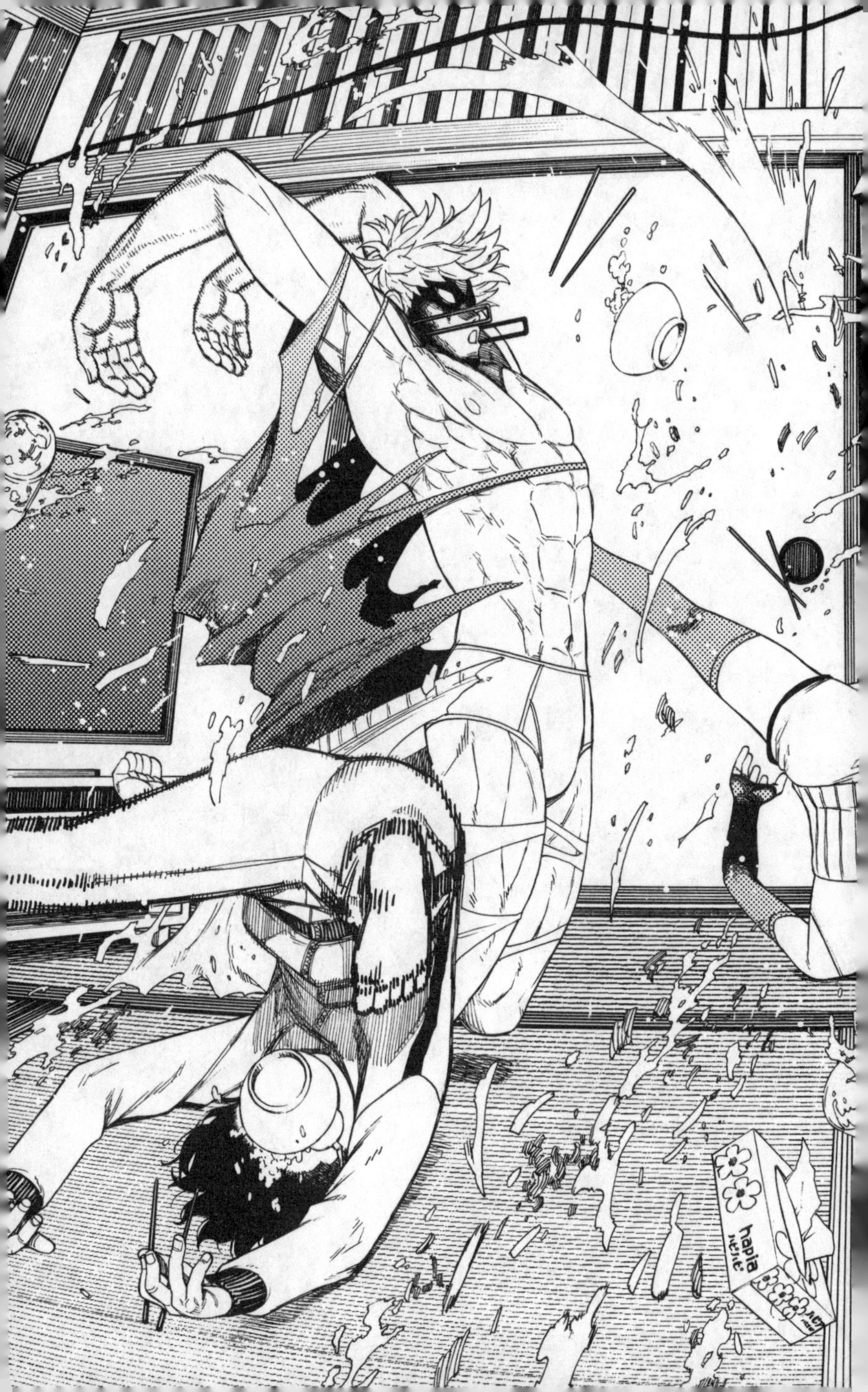
hapia

DAN DA DAN

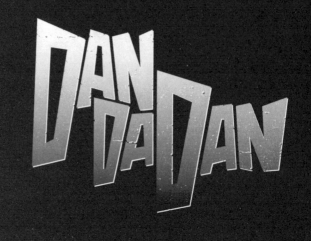

52. The Hayashi Performers Are Here

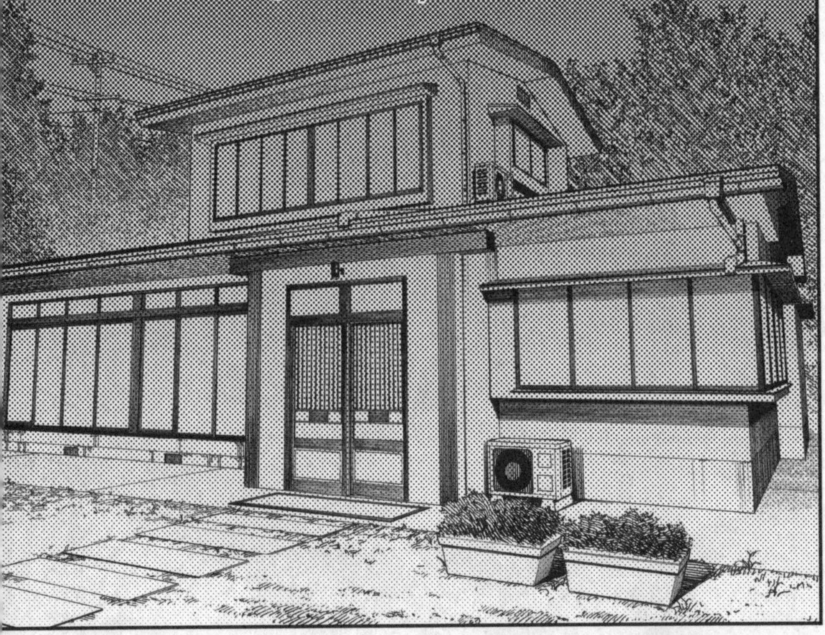

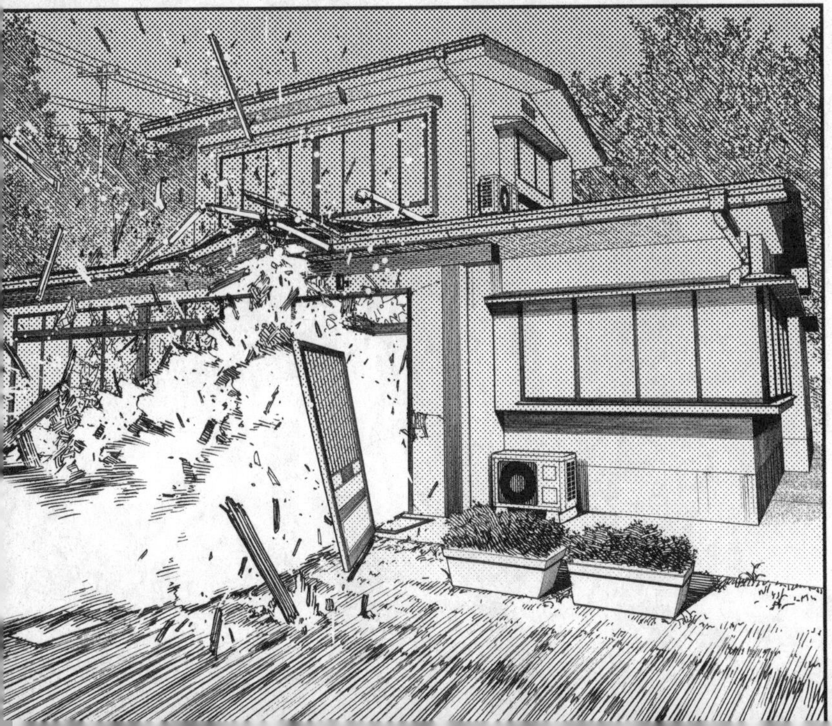

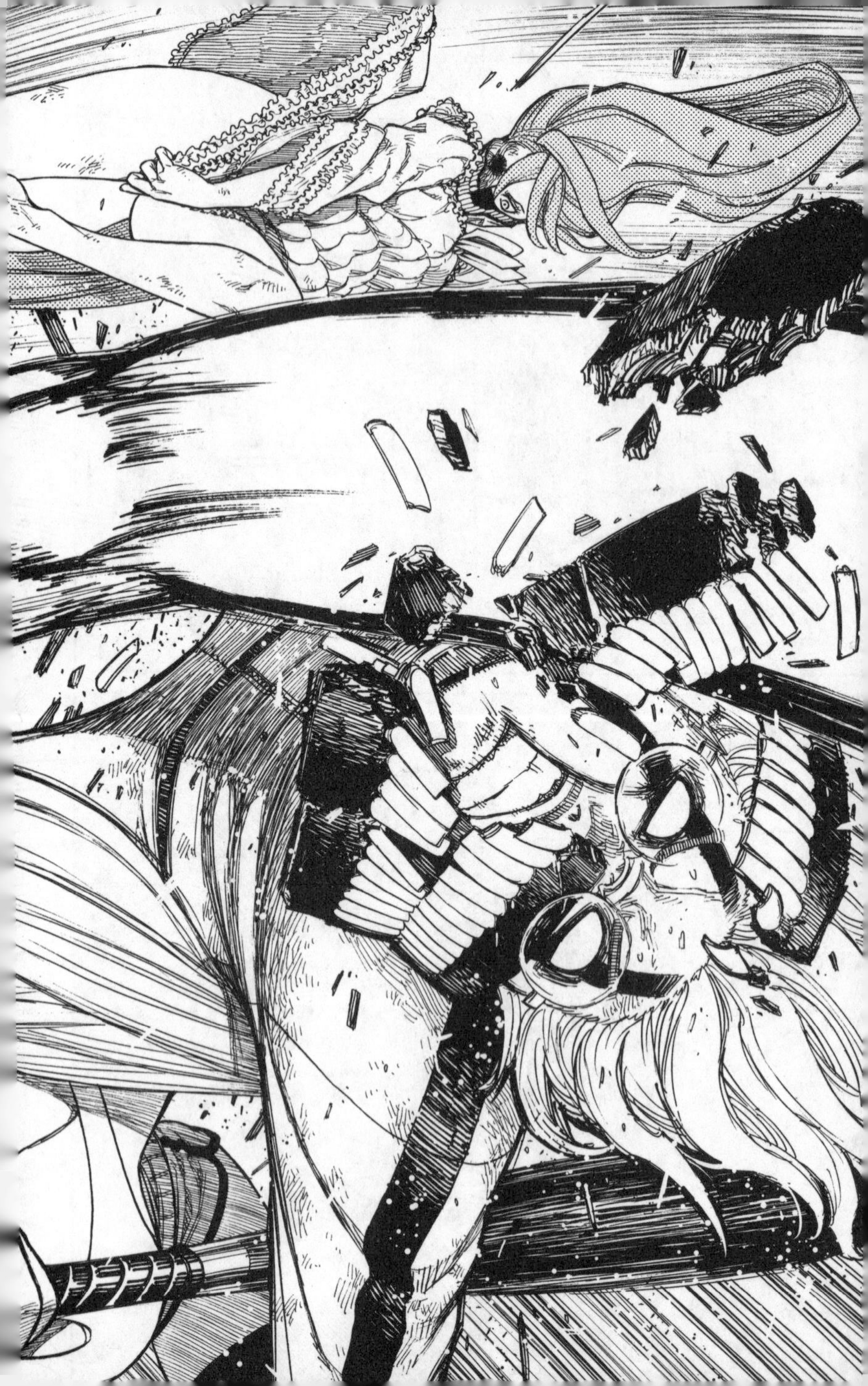

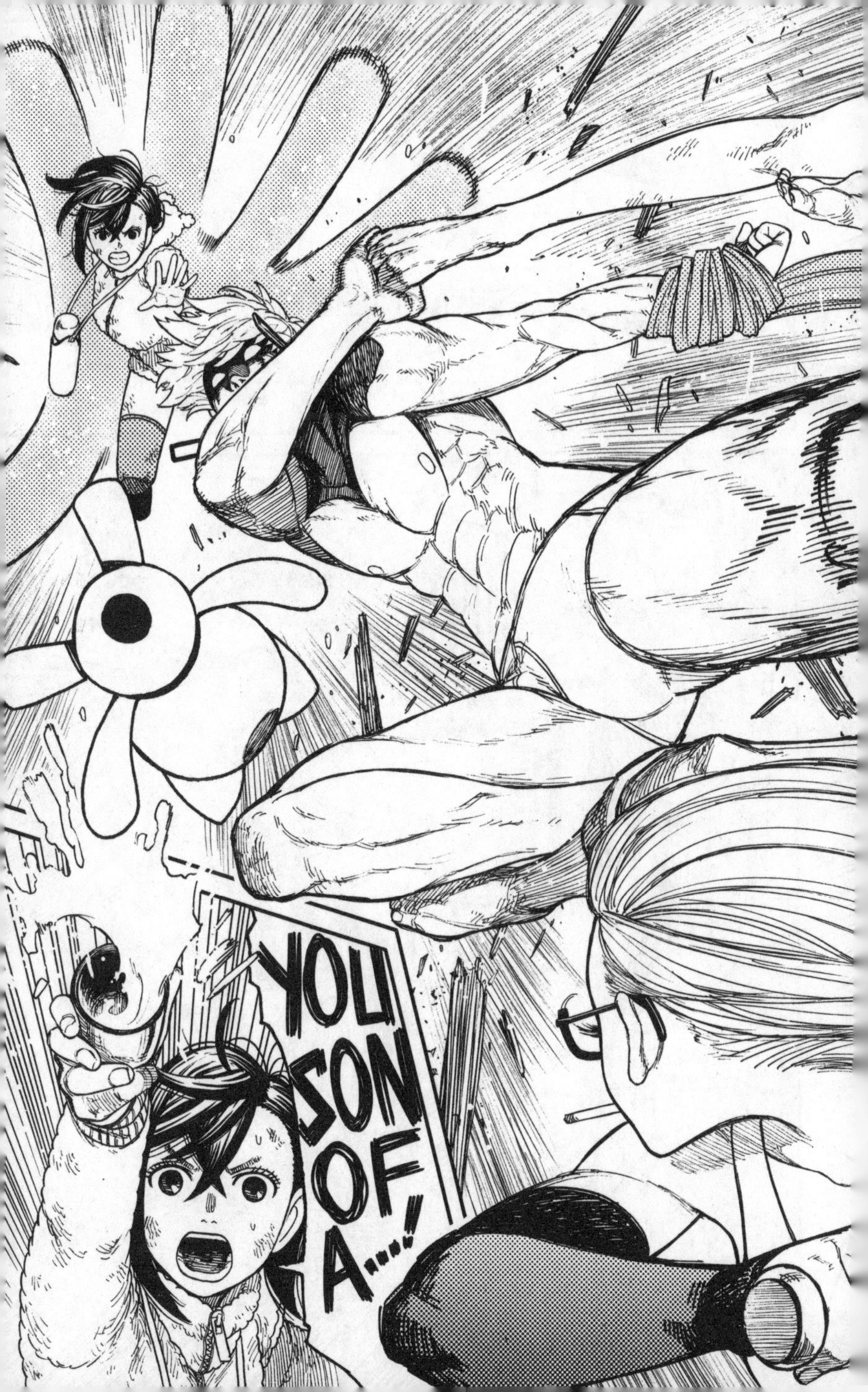
YOU SON OF A...!

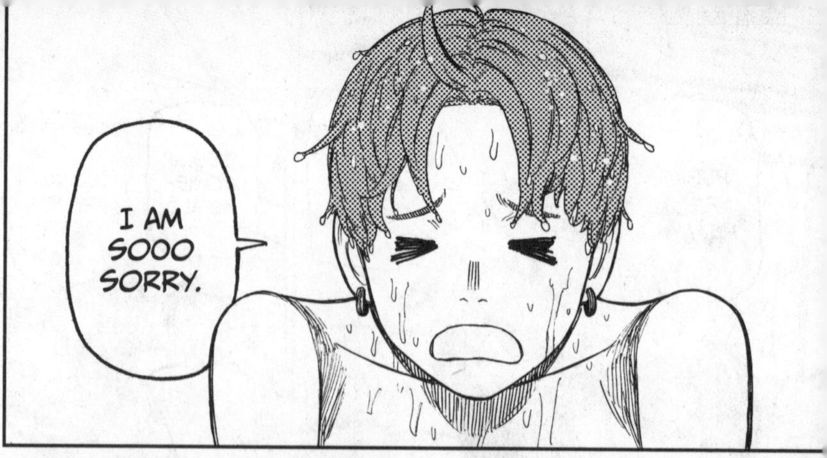
I AM SOOO SORRY.

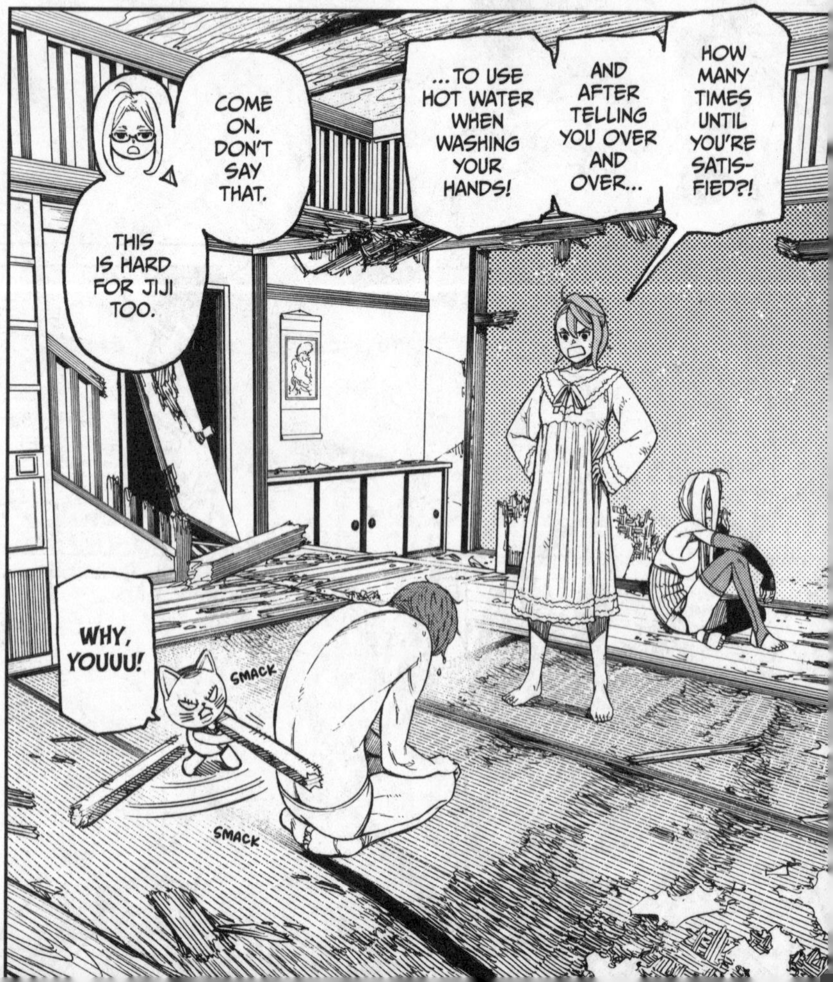
HOW MANY TIMES UNTIL YOU'RE SATIS-FIED?!
AND AFTER TELLING YOU OVER AND OVER...
...TO USE HOT WATER WHEN WASHING YOUR HANDS!
COME ON. DON'T SAY THAT.
THIS IS HARD FOR JIJI TOO.
WHY, YOUUU!
SMACK
SMACK

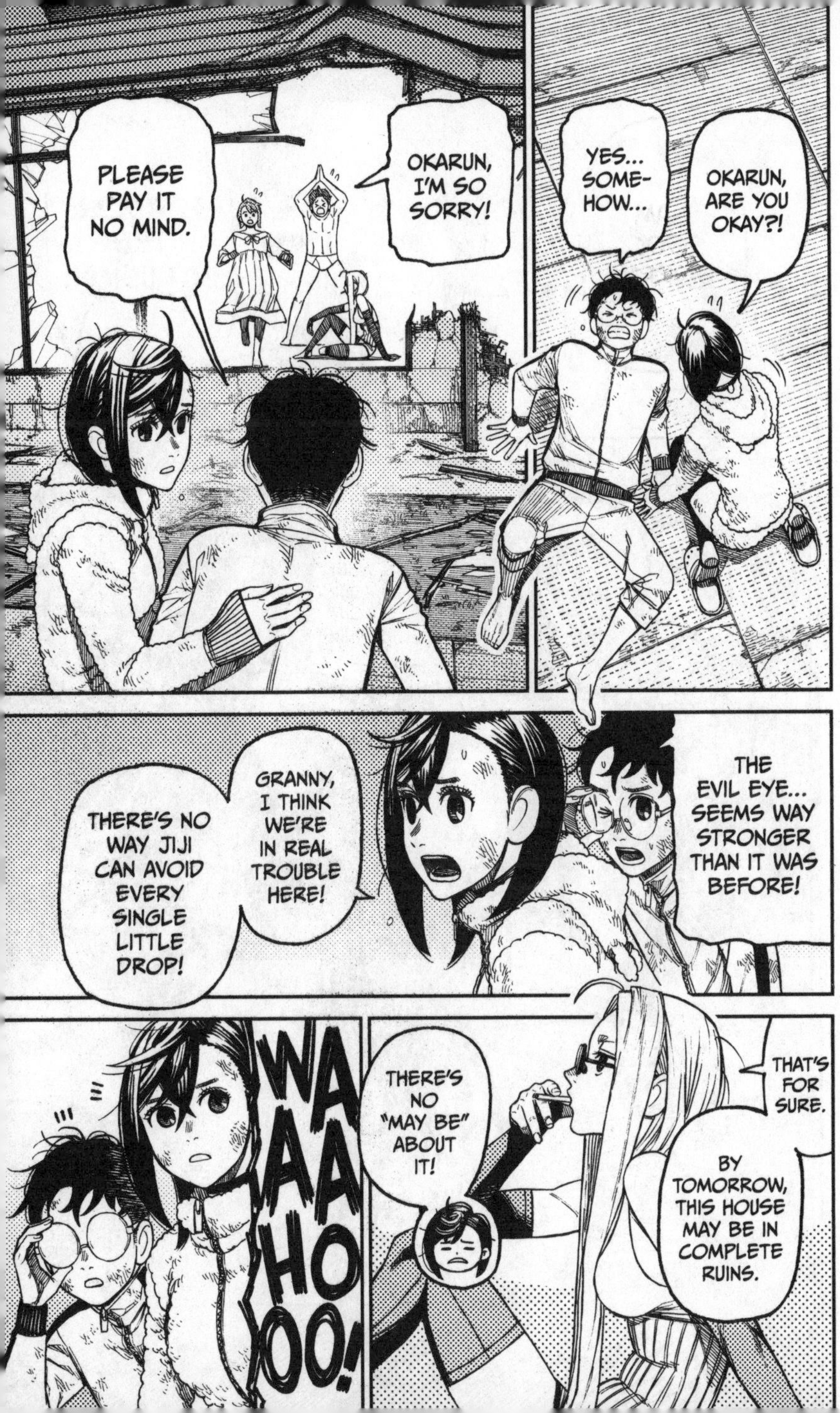
OKARUN, ARE YOU OKAY?!
YES... SOME-HOW...
OKARUN, I'M SO SORRY!
PLEASE PAY IT NO MIND.
THE EVIL EYE... SEEMS WAY STRONGER THAN IT WAS BEFORE!
GRANNY, I THINK WE'RE IN REAL TROUBLE HERE!
THERE'S NO WAY JIJI CAN AVOID EVERY SINGLE LITTLE DROP!
THAT'S FOR SURE.
BY TOMORROW, THIS HOUSE MAY BE IN COMPLETE RUINS.
THERE'S NO "MAY BE" ABOUT IT!
WAAAHOOO!

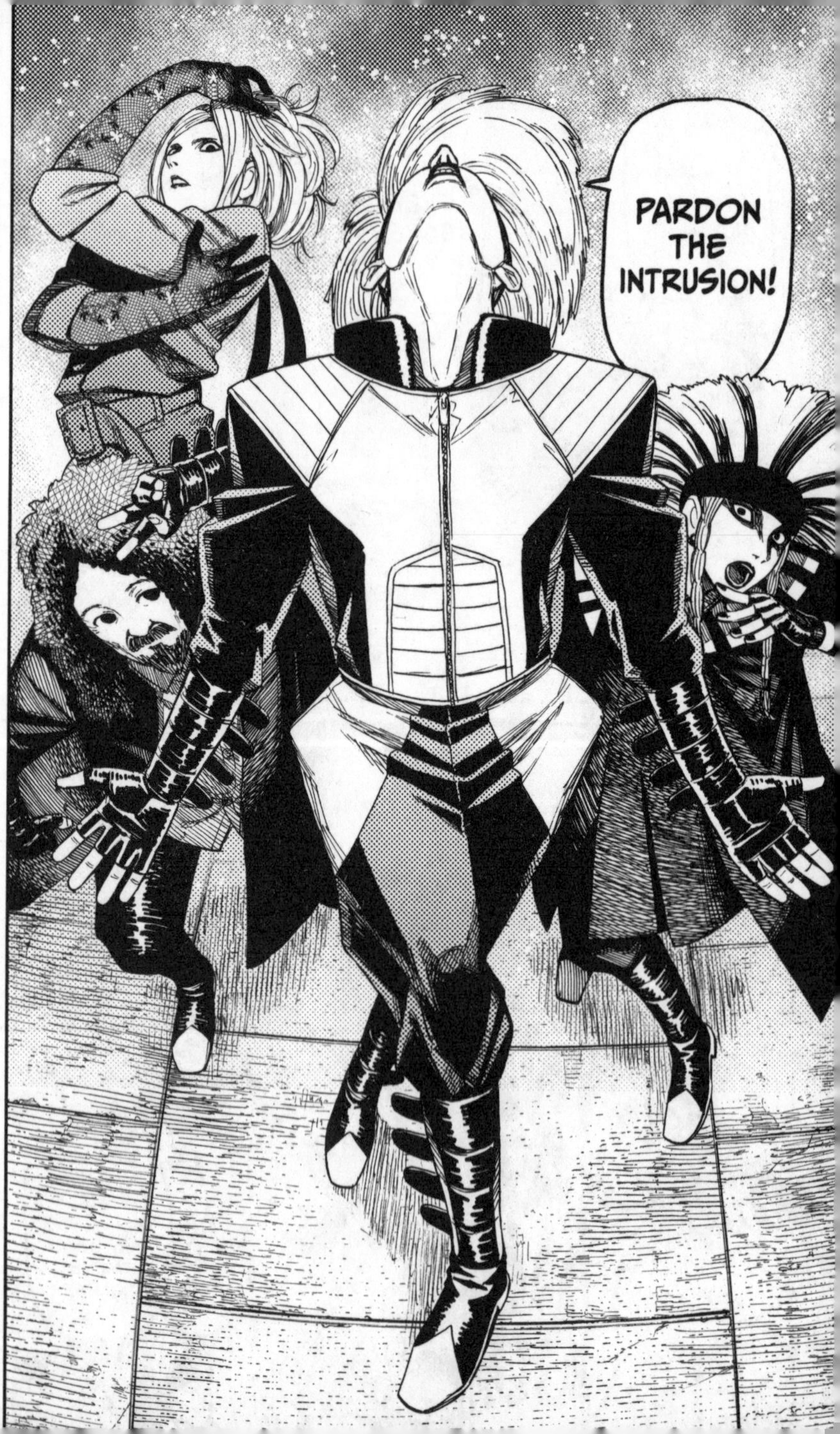
PARDON THE INTRUSION!

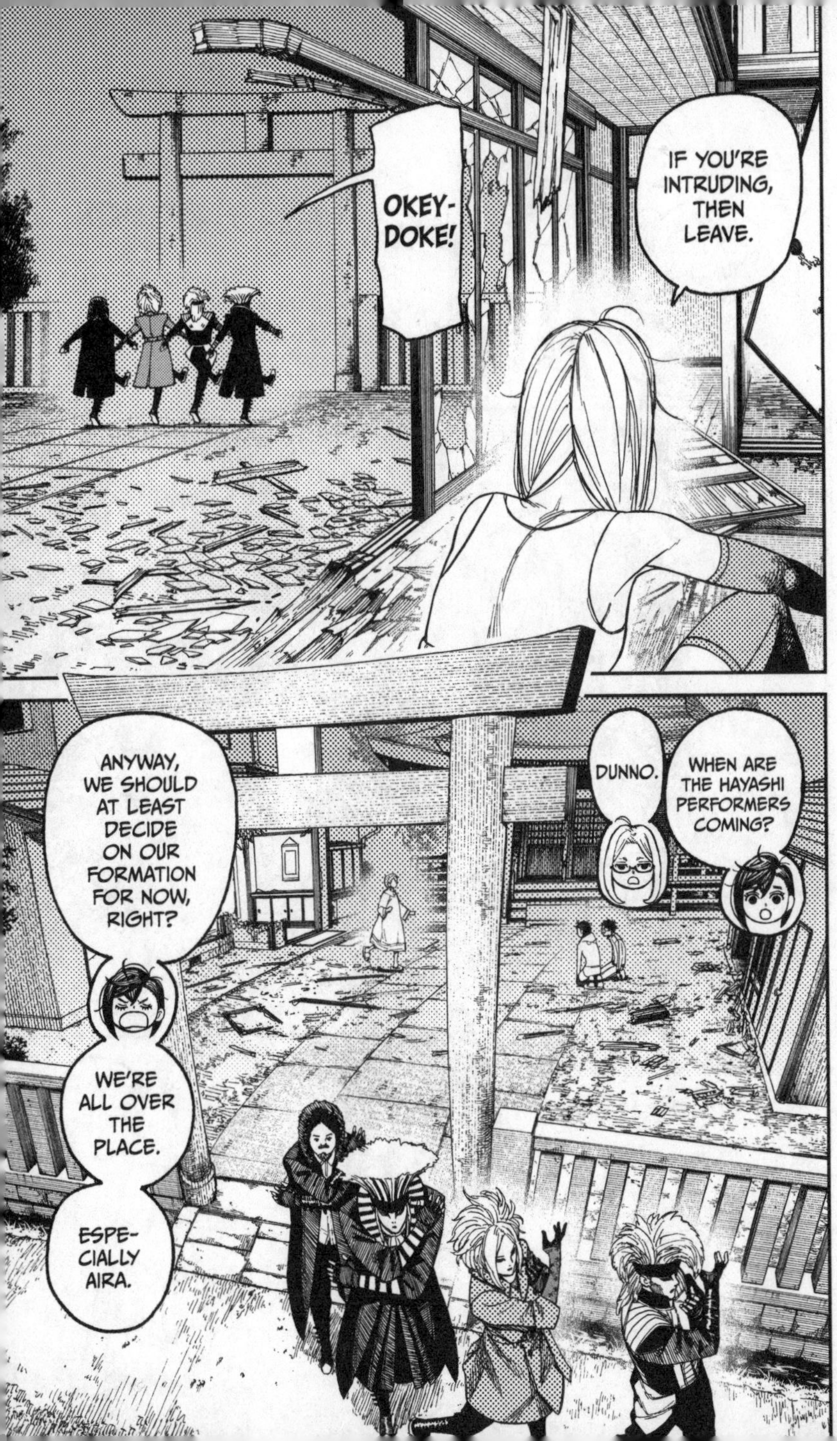
IF YOU'RE INTRUDING, THEN LEAVE.
OKEY-DOKE!
WHEN ARE THE HAYASHI PERFORMERS COMING?
DUNNO.
ANYWAY, WE SHOULD AT LEAST DECIDE ON OUR FORMATION FOR NOW, RIGHT?
WE'RE ALL OVER THE PLACE.
ESPE-CIALLY AIRA.

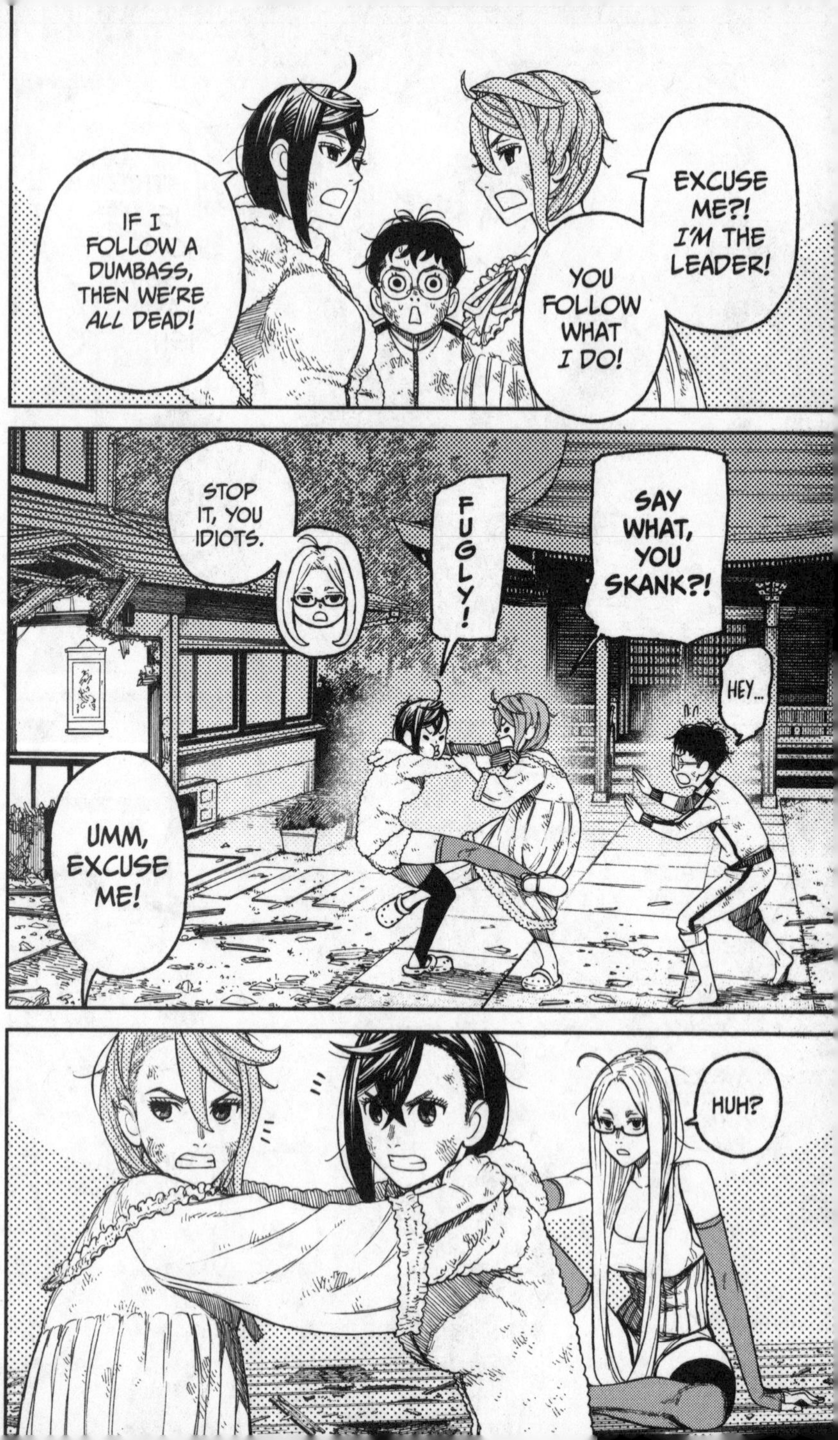
EXCUSE ME?! I'M THE LEADER!
YOU FOLLOW WHAT I DO!
IF I FOLLOW A DUMBASS, THEN WE'RE ALL DEAD!
SAY WHAT, YOU SKANK?!
HEY...
FUGLY!
STOP IT, YOU IDIOTS.
UMM, EXCUSE ME!
HUH?

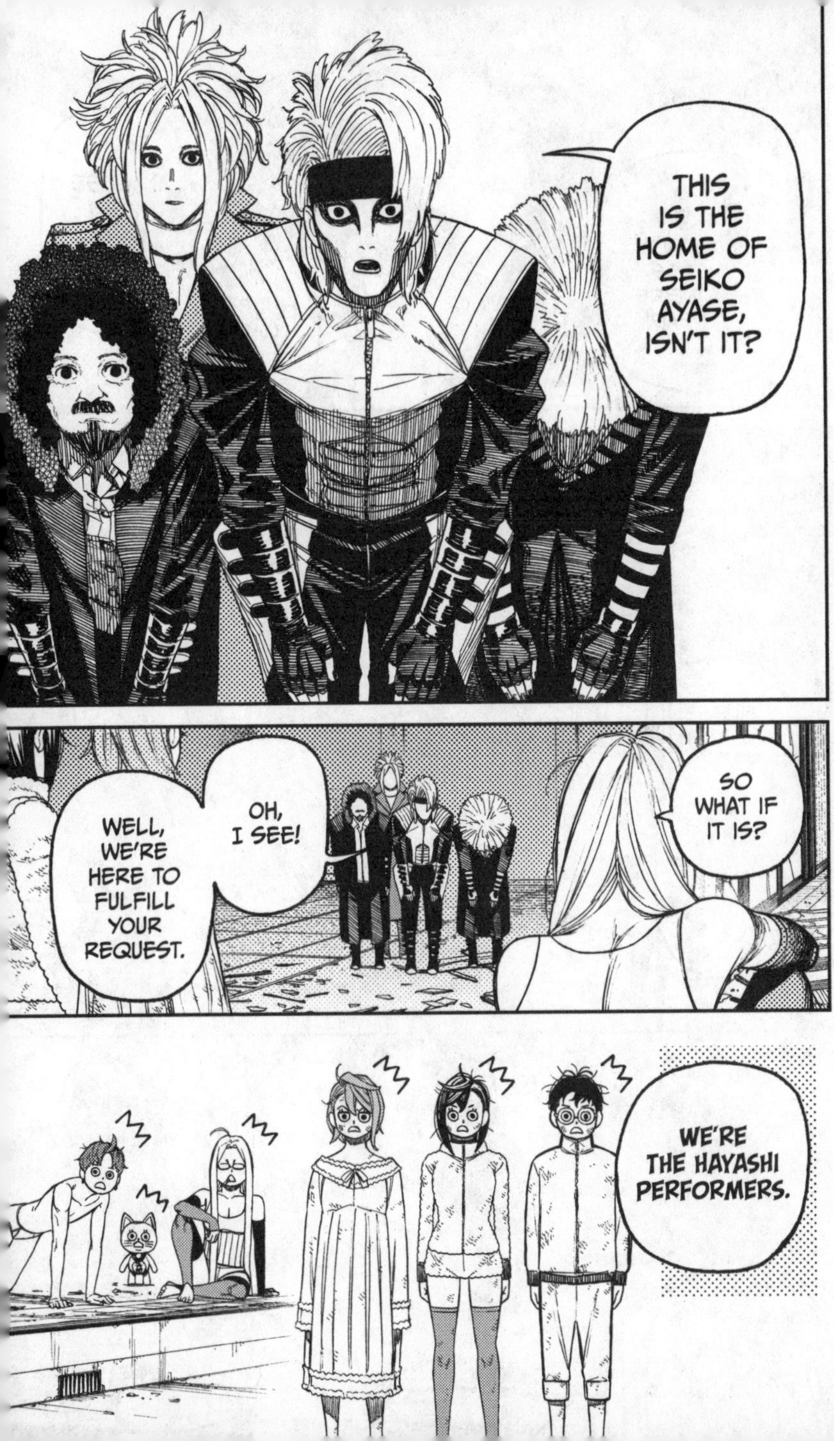
THIS IS THE HOME OF SEIKO AYASE, ISN'T IT?
SO WHAT IF IT IS?
OH, I SEE!
WELL, WE'RE HERE TO FULFILL YOUR REQUEST.
WE'RE THE HAYASHI PERFORMERS.

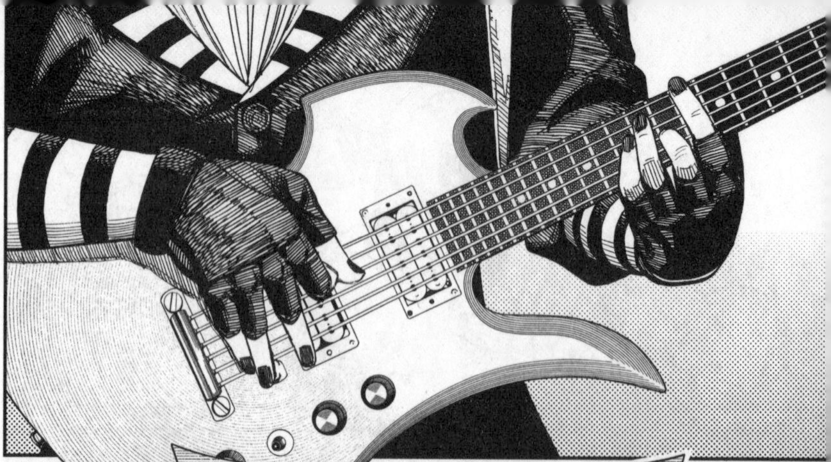

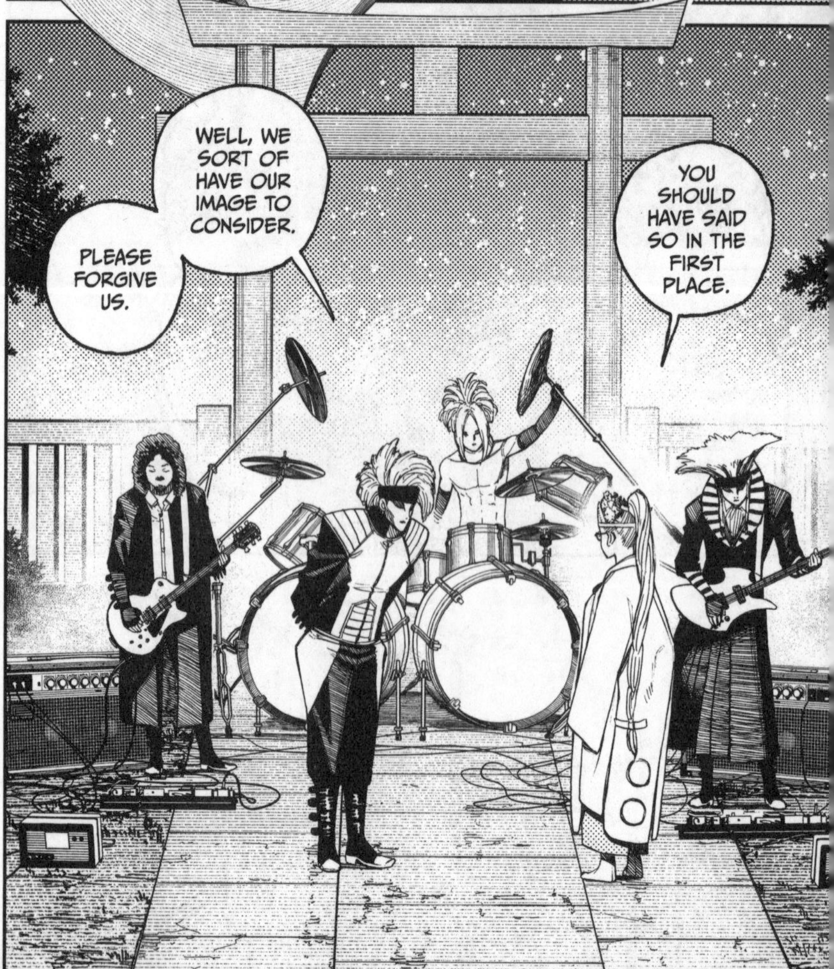
YOU SHOULD HAVE SAID SO IN THE FIRST PLACE.
WELL, WE SORT OF HAVE OUR IMAGE TO CONSIDER.
PLEASE FORGIVE US.

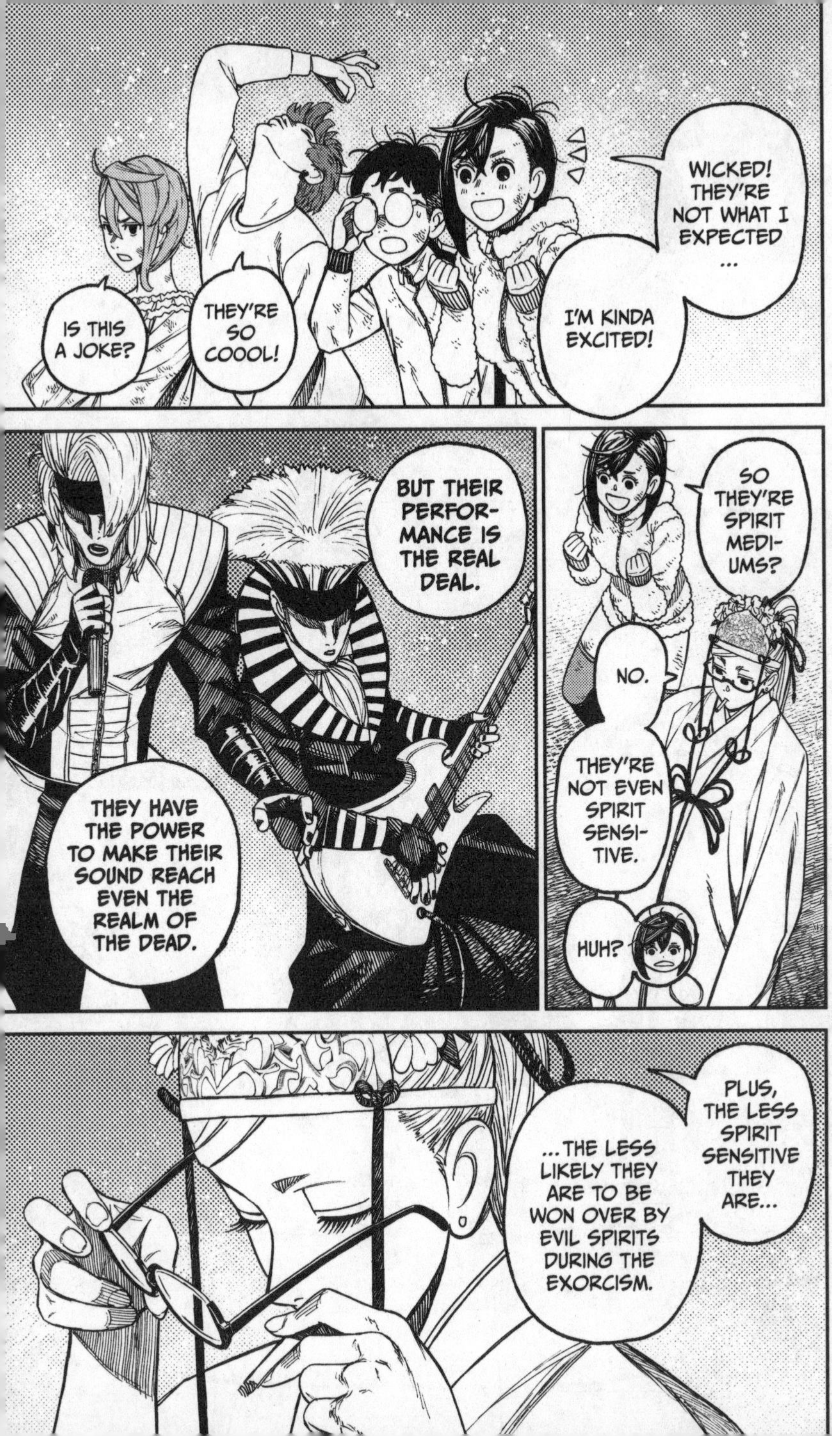
WICKED! THEY'RE NOT WHAT I EXPECTED ...
I'M KINDA EXCITED!
THEY'RE SO COOOL!
IS THIS A JOKE?
SO THEY'RE SPIRIT MEDI-UMS?
NO.
THEY'RE NOT EVEN SPIRIT SENSI-TIVE.
HUH?
BUT THEIR PERFORM-ANCE IS THE REAL DEAL.
THEY HAVE THE POWER TO MAKE THEIR SOUND REACH EVEN THE REALM OF THE DEAD.
PLUS, THE LESS SPIRIT SENSITIVE THEY ARE...
...THE LESS LIKELY THEY ARE TO BE WON OVER BY EVIL SPIRITS DURING THE EXORCISM.

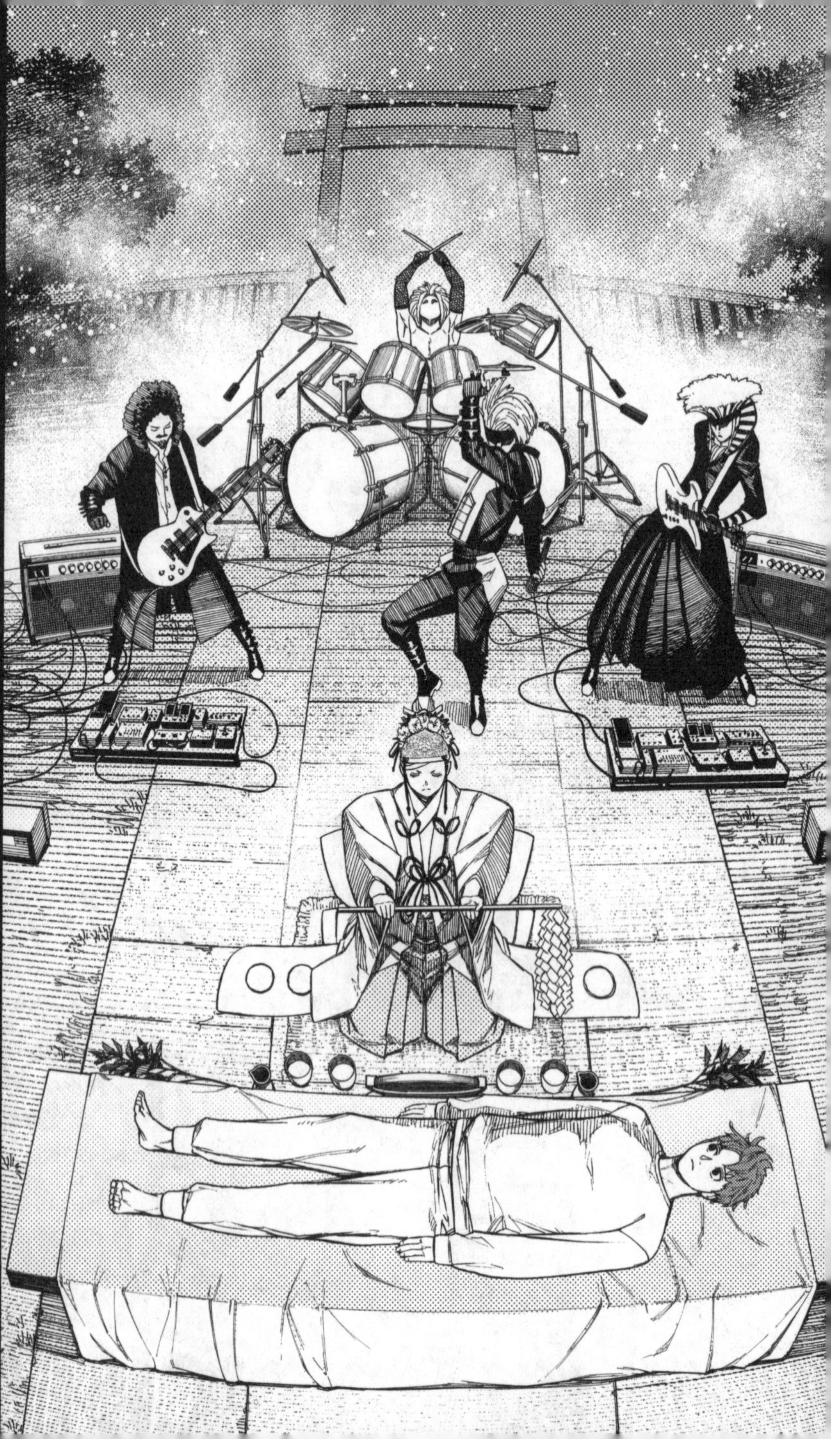

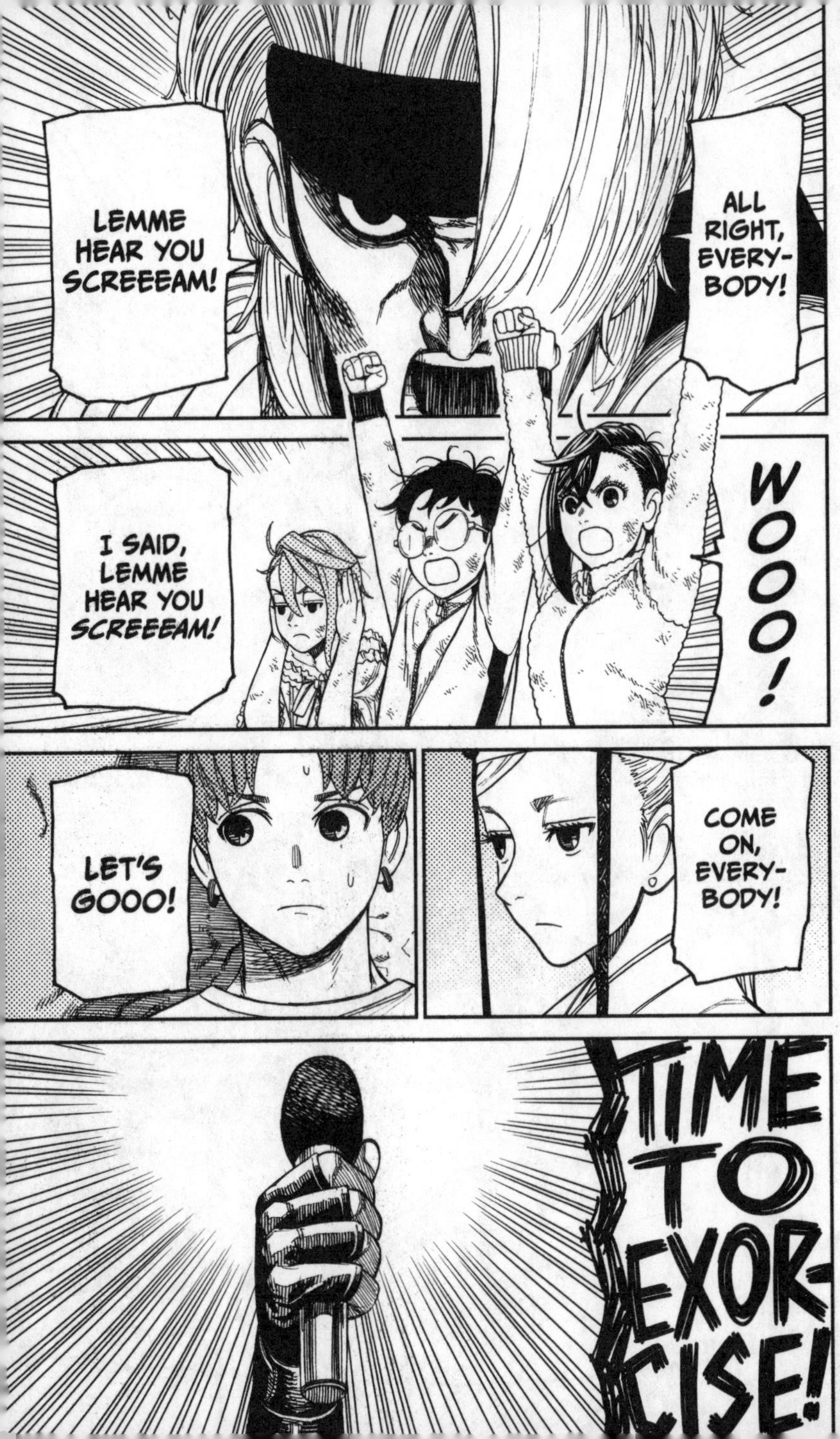
ALL RIGHT, EVERY-BODY!
LEMME HEAR YOU SCREEEAM!
WOOOO!
I SAID, LEMME HEAR YOU SCREEEAM!
COME ON, EVERY-BODY!
LET'S GOOO!
TIME TO EXOR-CISE!

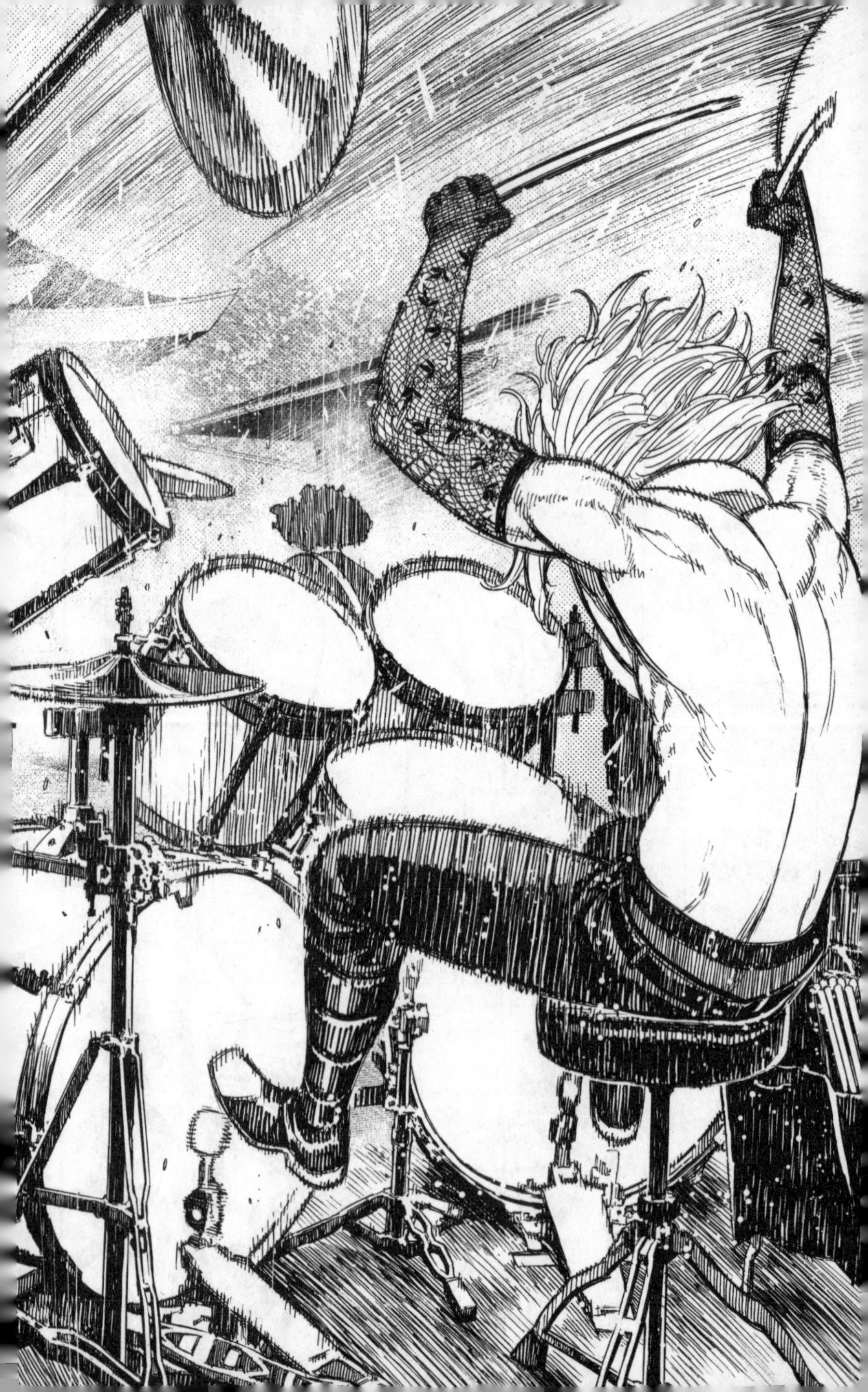

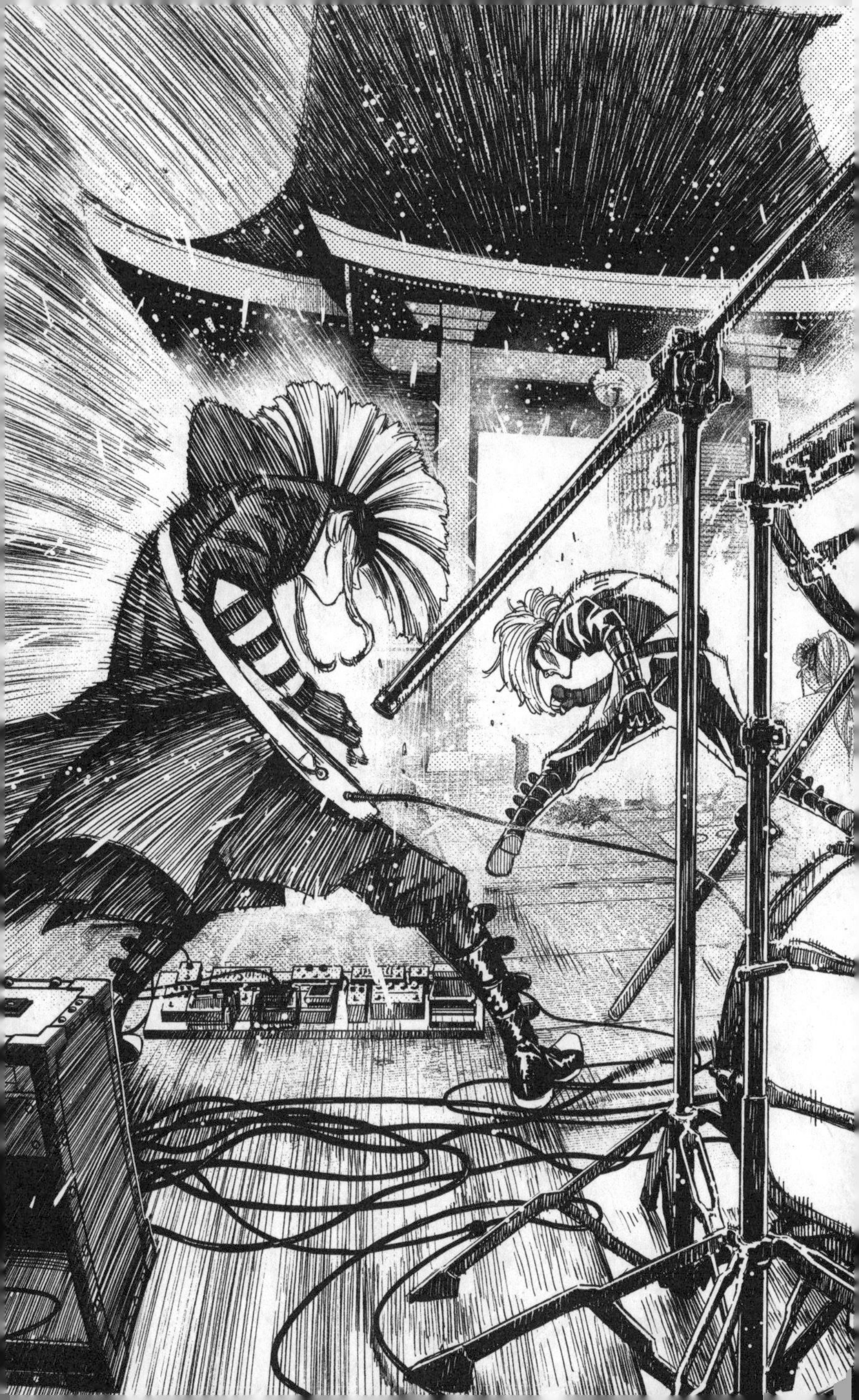

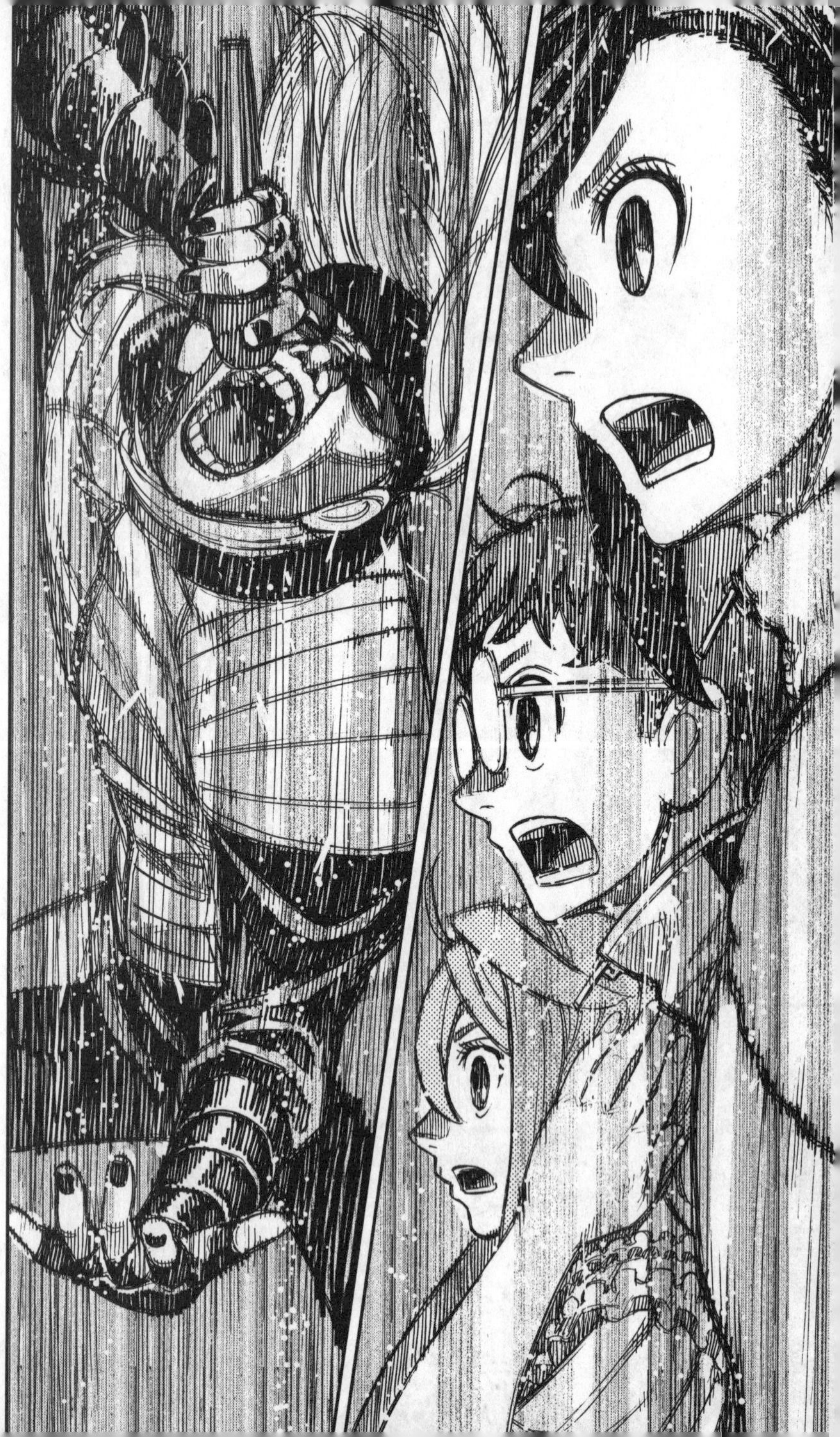

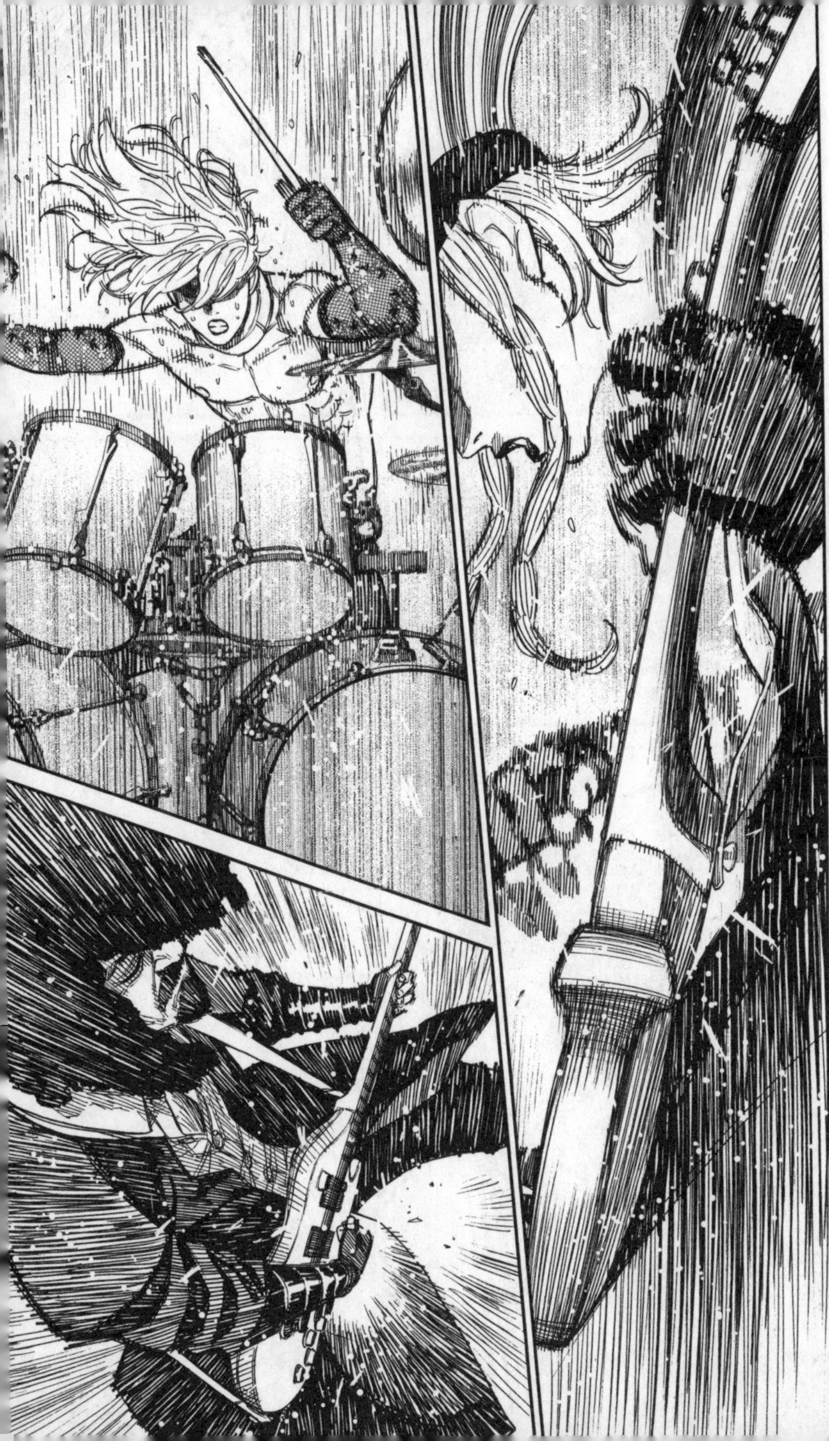

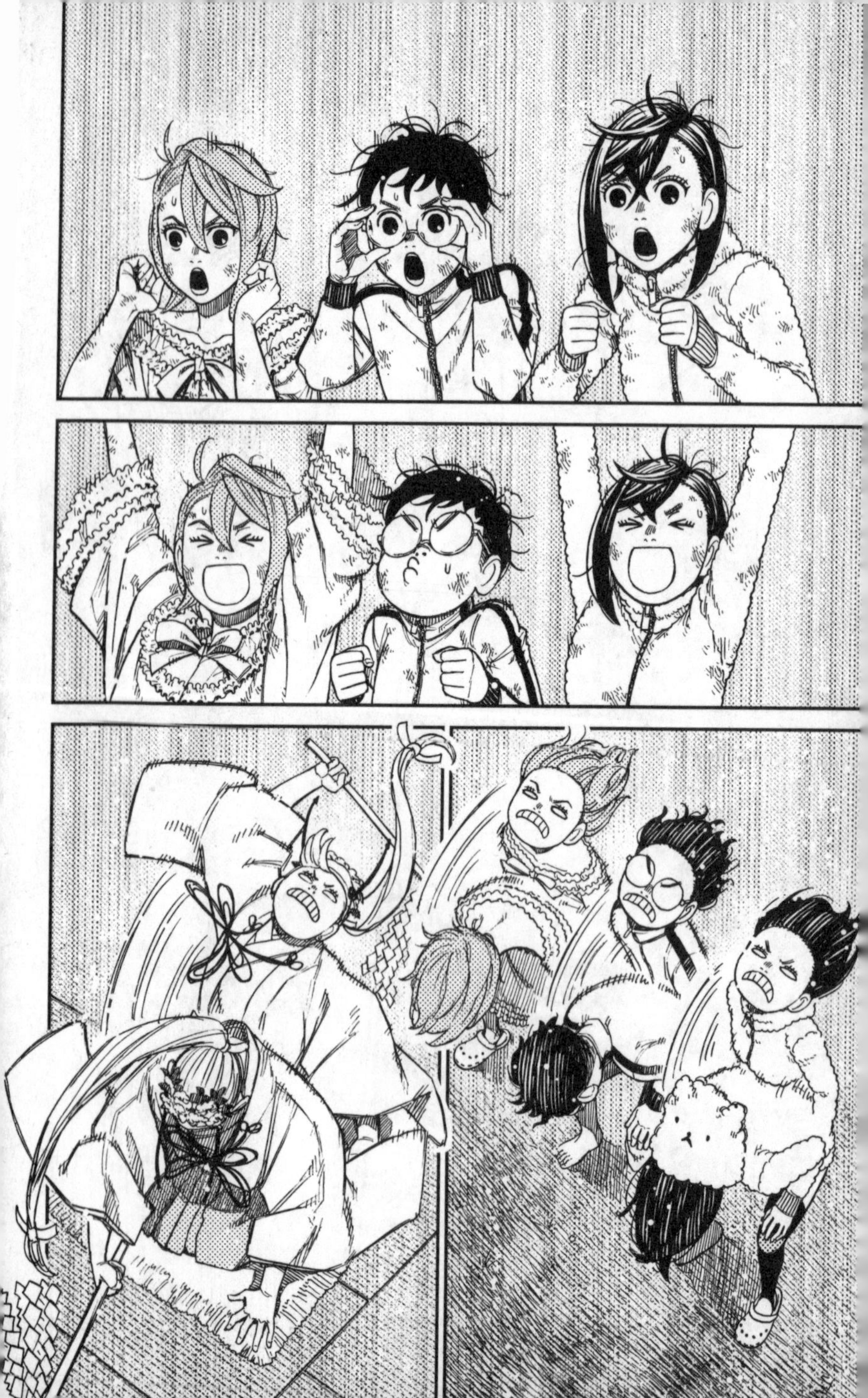

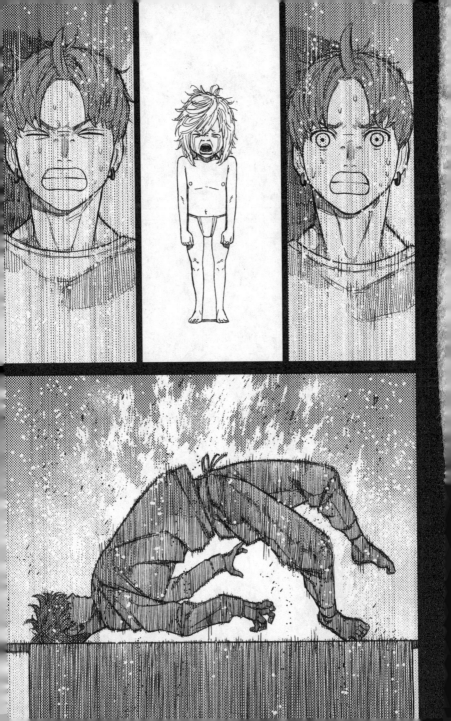

DAN DA DAN

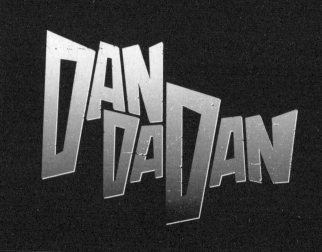

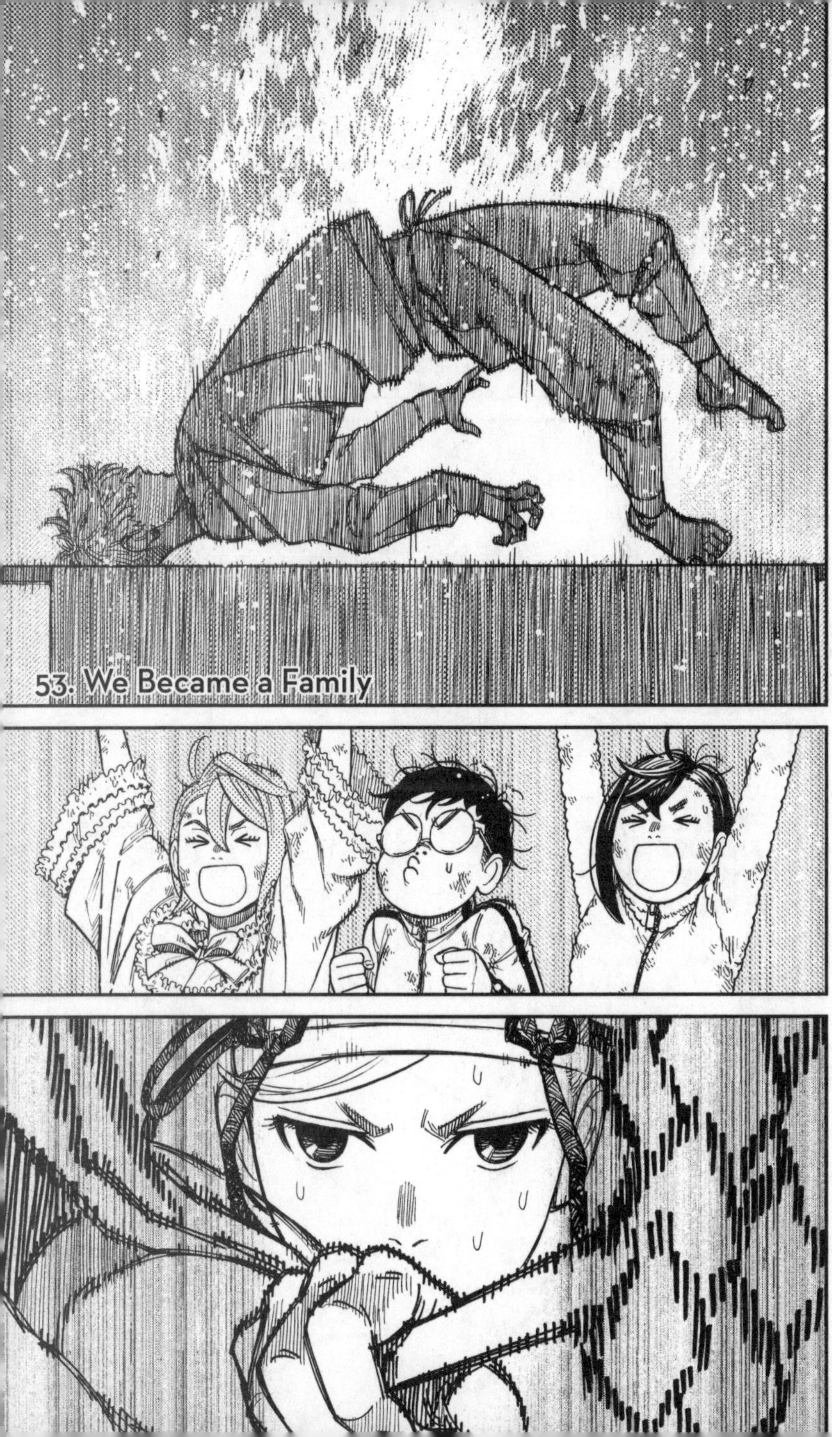
53. We Became a Family

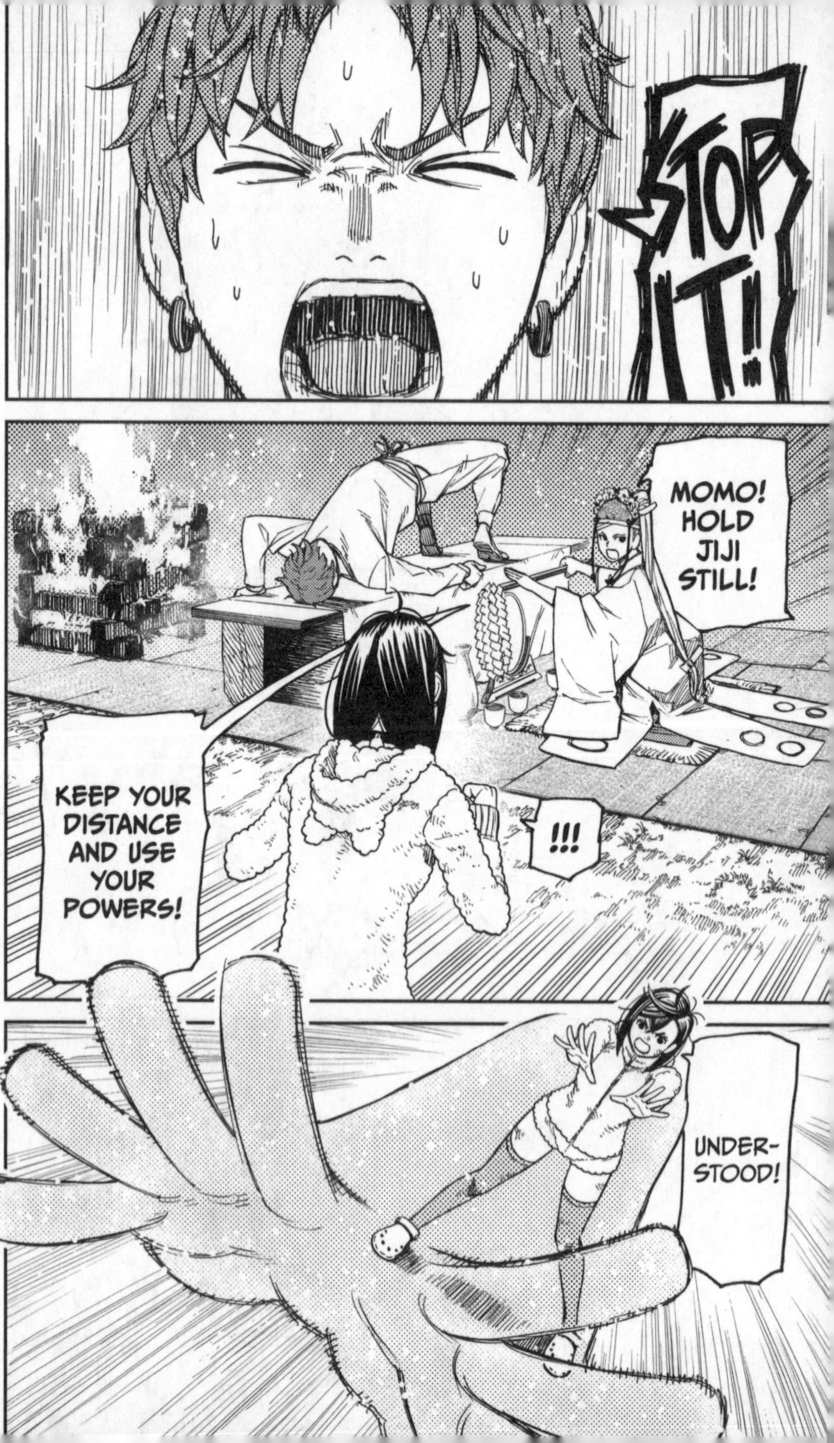
STOP IT!!
MOMO! HOLD JIJI STILL!
KEEP YOUR DISTANCE AND USE YOUR POWERS!
!!!
UNDER-STOOD!

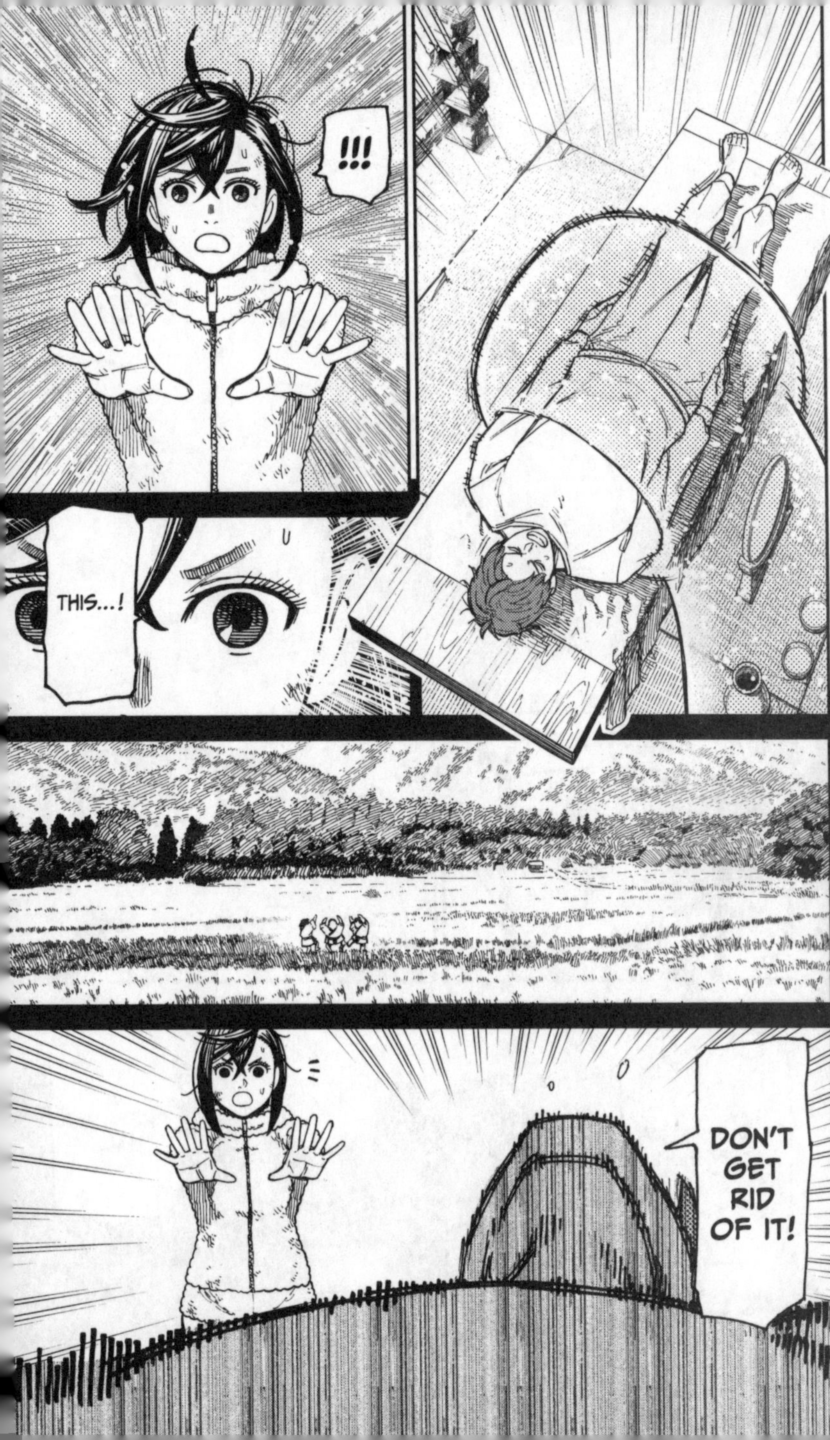
!!!
THIS...!
DON'T GET RID OF IT!

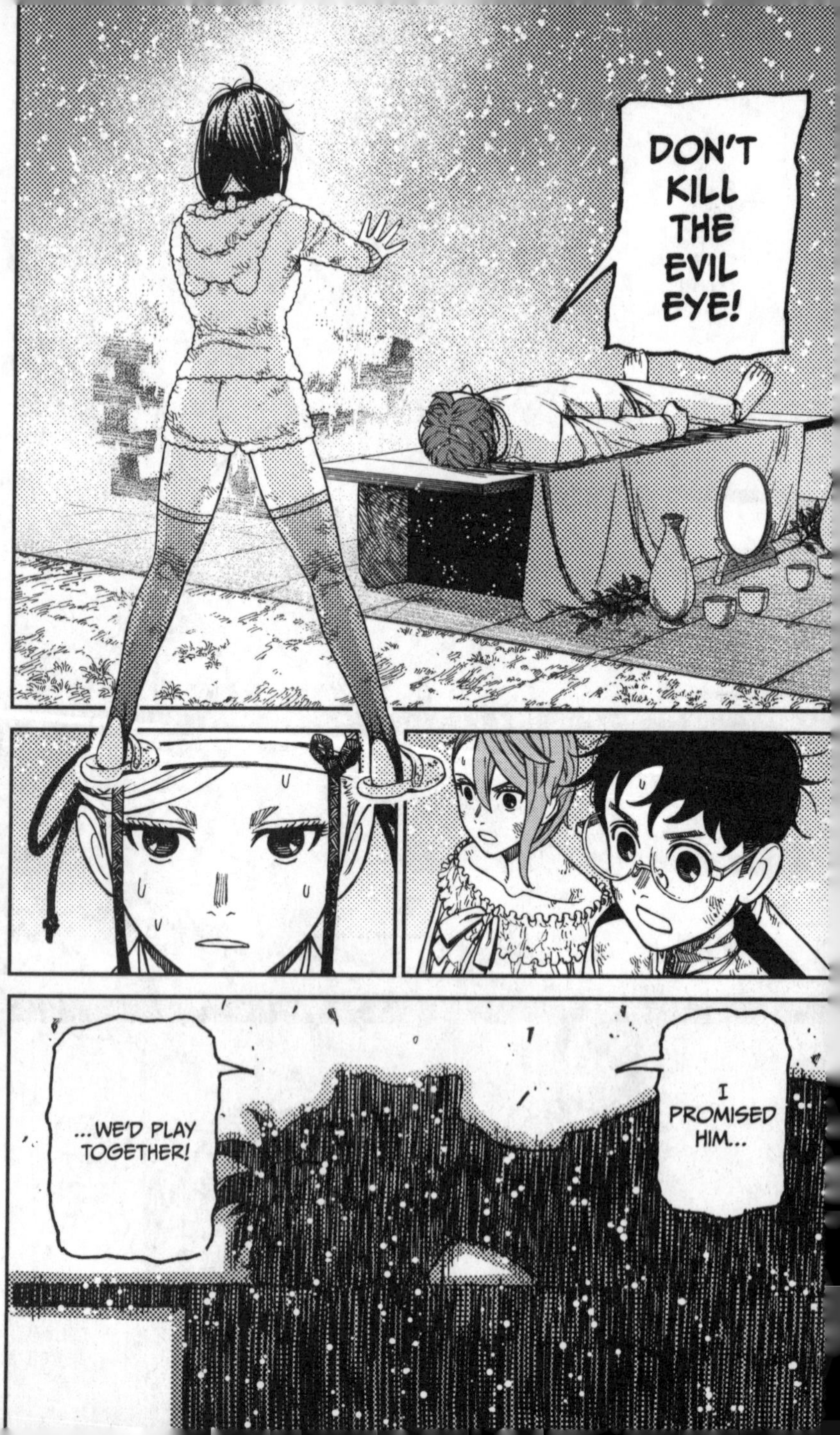
DON'T KILL THE EVIL EYE!
I PROMISED HIM...
...WE'D PLAY TOGETHER!

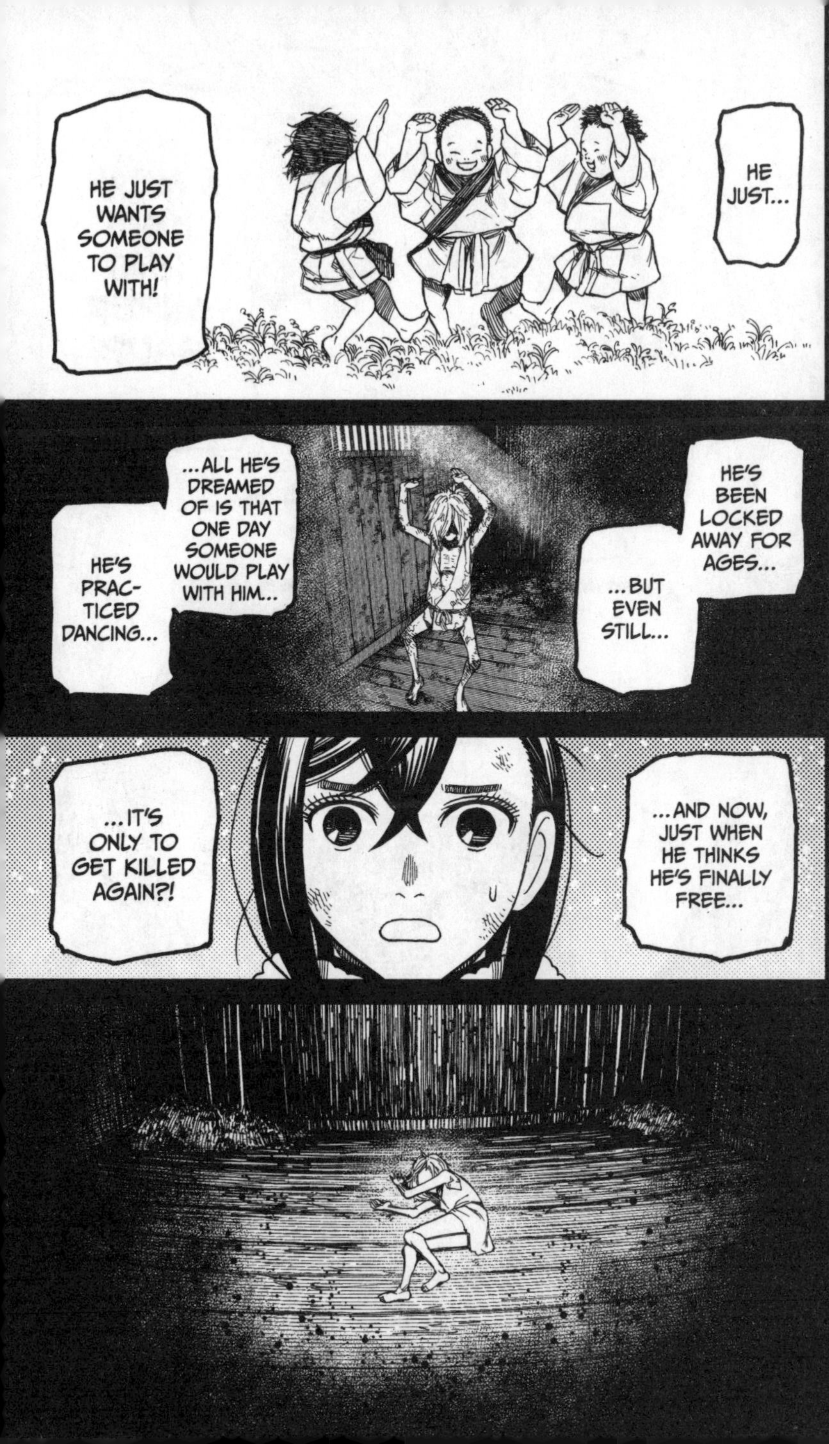
HE JUST...
HE JUST WANTS SOMEONE TO PLAY WITH!
HE'S BEEN LOCKED AWAY FOR AGES...
...BUT EVEN STILL...
HE'S PRAC-TICED DANCING...
...ALL HE'S DREAMED OF IS THAT ONE DAY SOMEONE WOULD PLAY WITH HIM...
...AND NOW, JUST WHEN HE THINKS HE'S FINALLY FREE...
...IT'S ONLY TO GET KILLED AGAIN?!

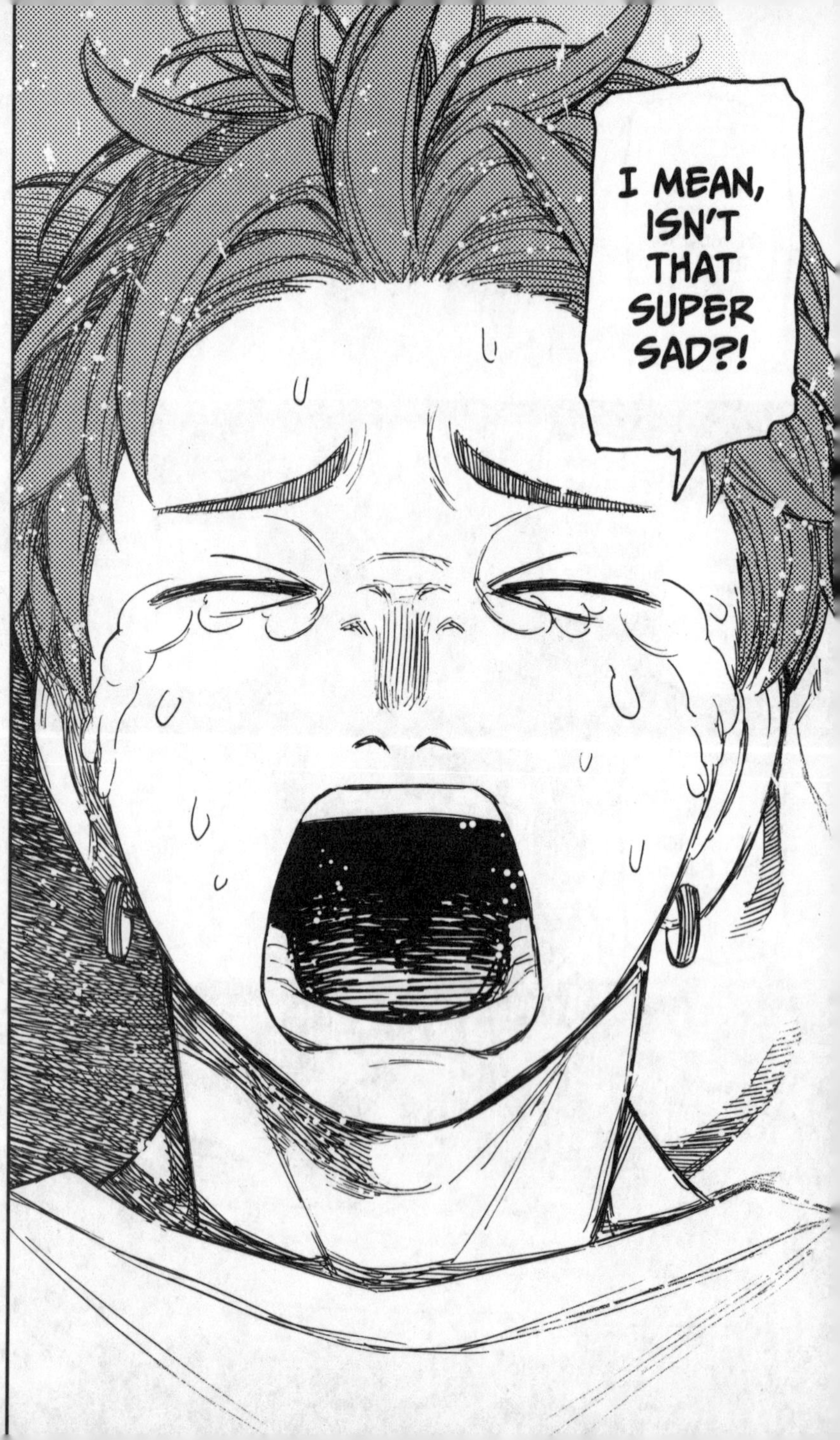
I MEAN, ISN'T THAT SUPER SAD?!

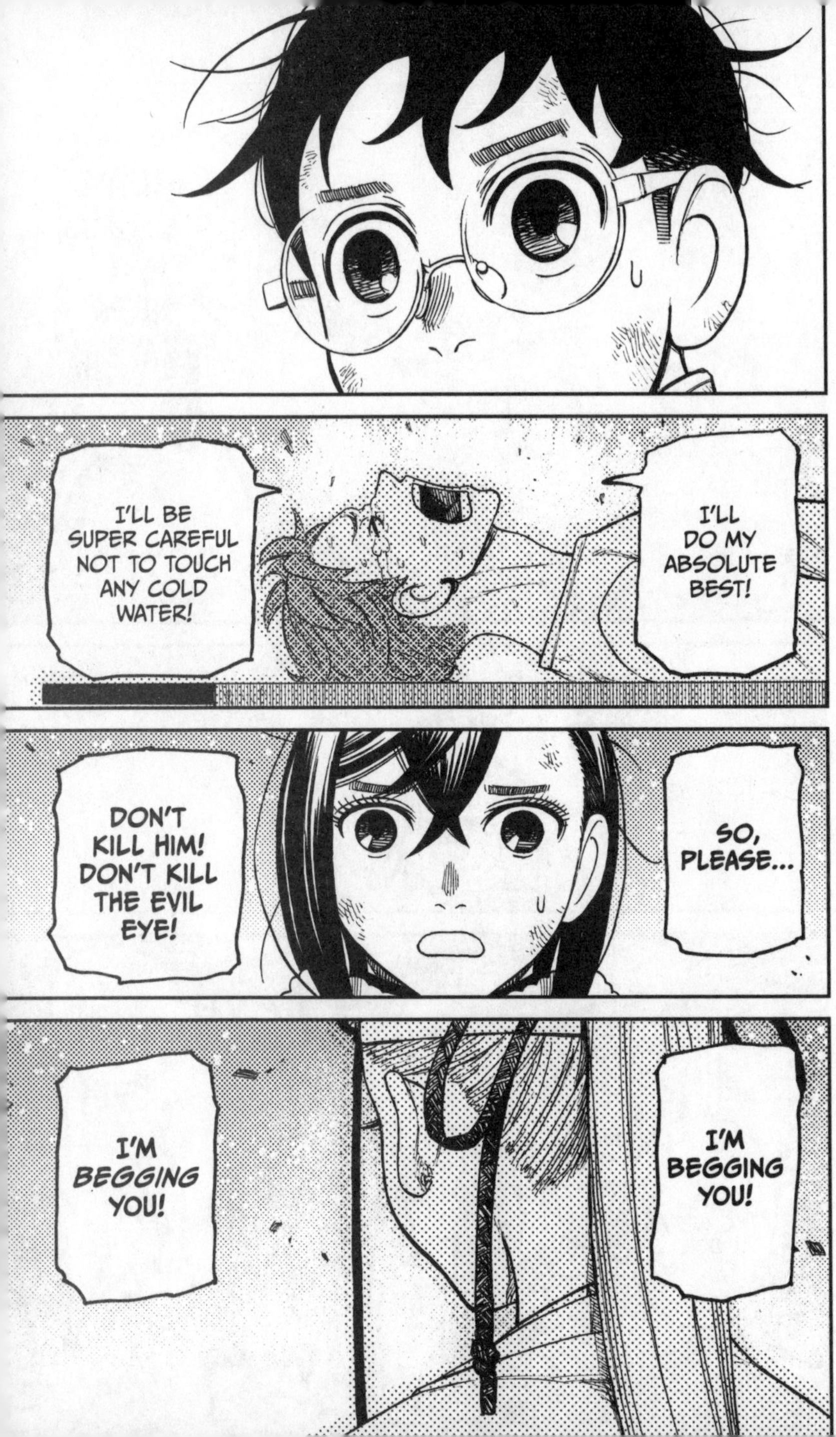
I'LL DO MY ABSOLUTE BEST!
I'LL BE SUPER CAREFUL NOT TO TOUCH ANY COLD WATER!
SO, PLEASE...
DON'T KILL HIM! DON'T KILL THE EVIL EYE!
I'M BEGGING YOU!
I'M BEGGING YOU!

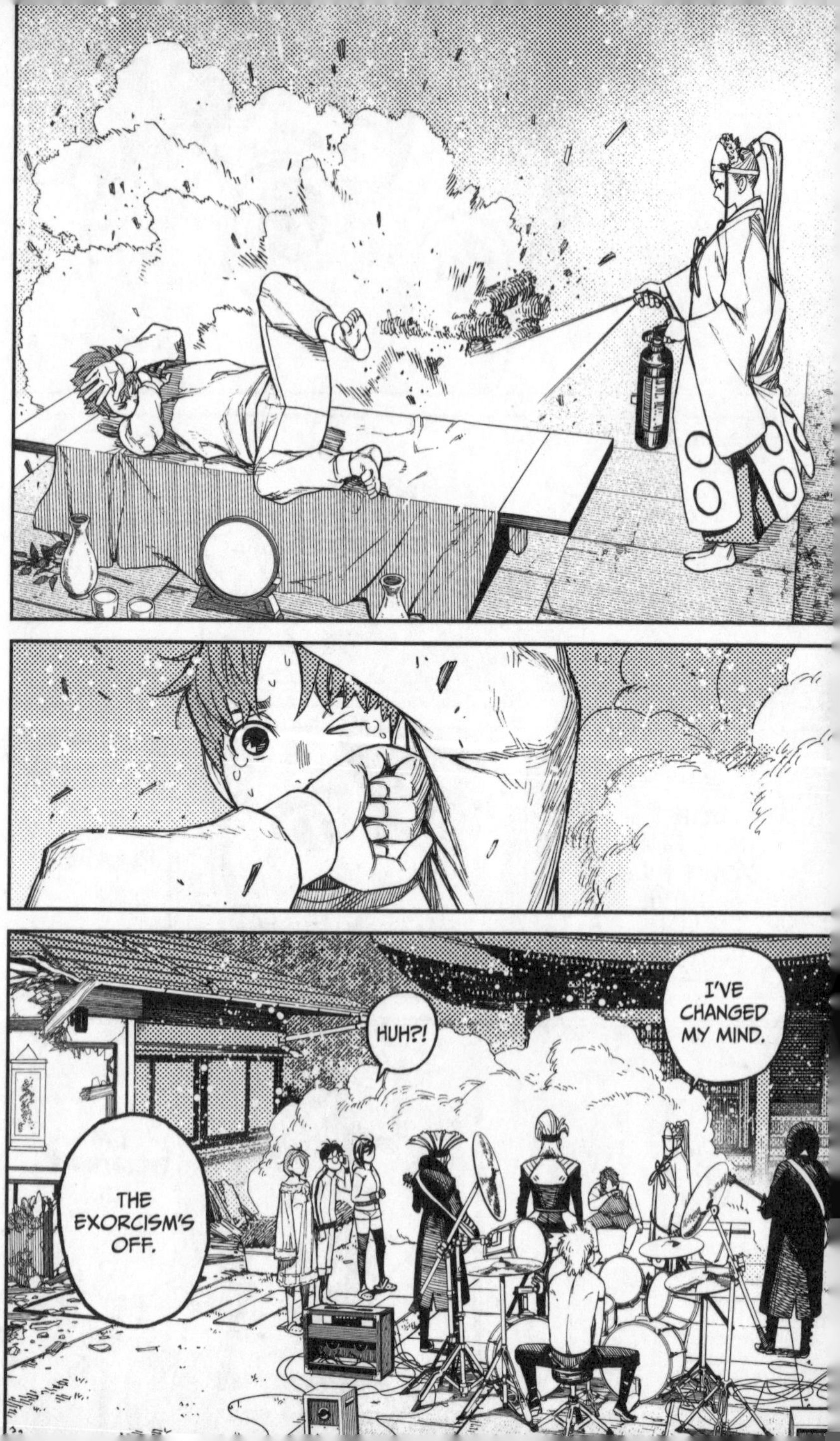
I'VE CHANGED MY MIND.
HUH?!
THE EXORCISM'S OFF.

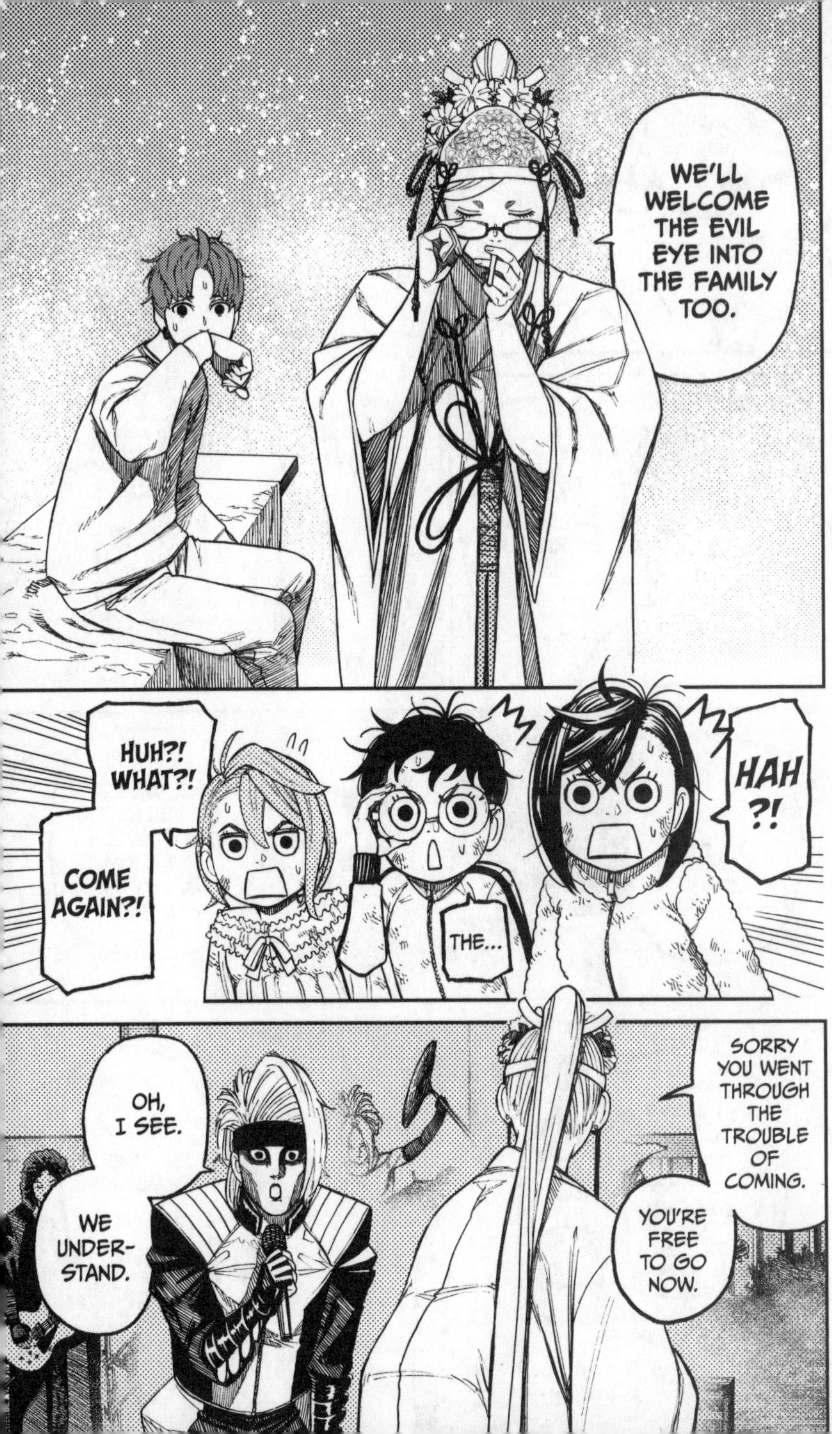
WE'LL WELCOME THE EVIL EYE INTO THE FAMILY TOO.
HAH?!
THE...
HUH?! WHAT?!
COME AGAIN?!
SORRY YOU WENT THROUGH THE TROUBLE OF COMING.
YOU'RE FREE TO GO NOW.
OH, I SEE.
WE UNDER-STAND.

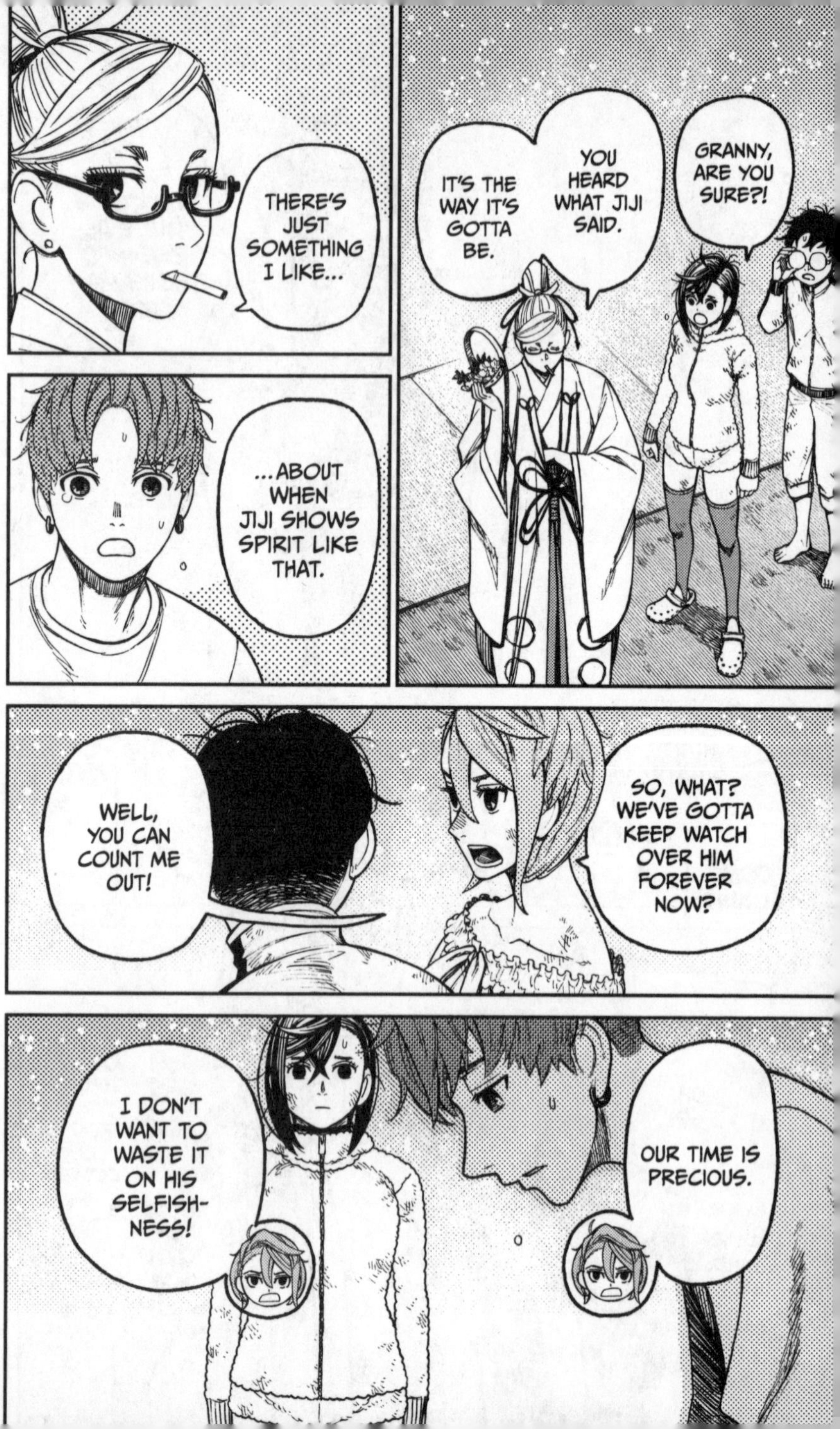
GRANNY, ARE YOU SURE?!
YOU HEARD WHAT JIJI SAID.
IT'S THE WAY IT'S GOTTA BE.
THERE'S JUST SOMETHING I LIKE...
...ABOUT WHEN JIJI SHOWS SPIRIT LIKE THAT.
SO, WHAT? WE'VE GOTTA KEEP WATCH OVER HIM FOREVER NOW?
WELL, YOU CAN COUNT ME OUT!
OUR TIME IS PRECIOUS.
I DON'T WANT TO WASTE IT ON HIS SELFISH-NESS!

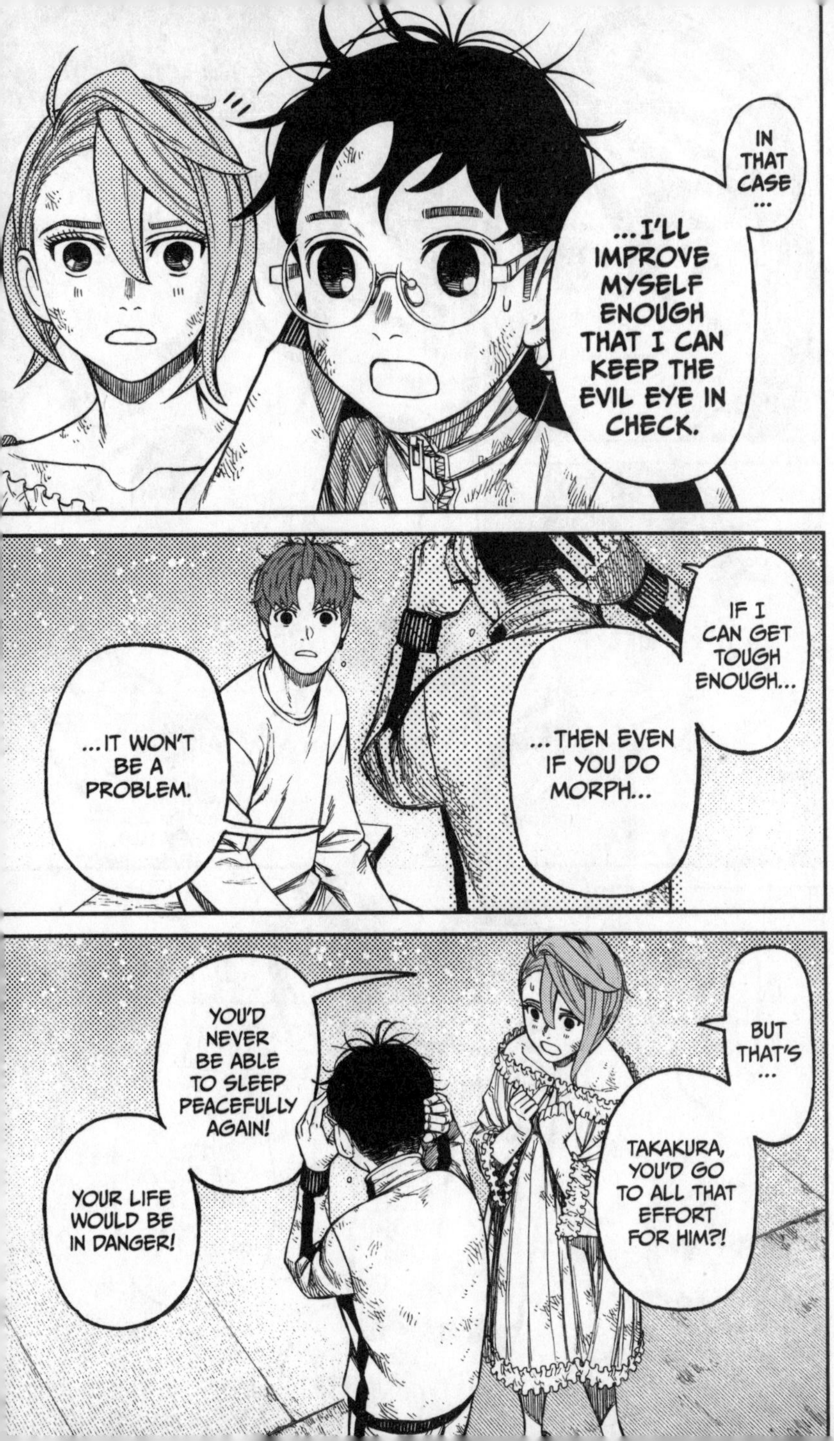
IN THAT CASE...
...I'LL IMPROVE MYSELF ENOUGH THAT I CAN KEEP THE EVIL EYE IN CHECK.
IF I CAN GET TOUGH ENOUGH...
...THEN EVEN IF YOU DO MORPH...
...IT WON'T BE A PROBLEM.
BUT THAT'S...
TAKAKURA, YOU'D GO TO ALL THAT EFFORT FOR HIM?!
YOU'D NEVER BE ABLE TO SLEEP PEACEFULLY AGAIN!
YOUR LIFE WOULD BE IN DANGER!

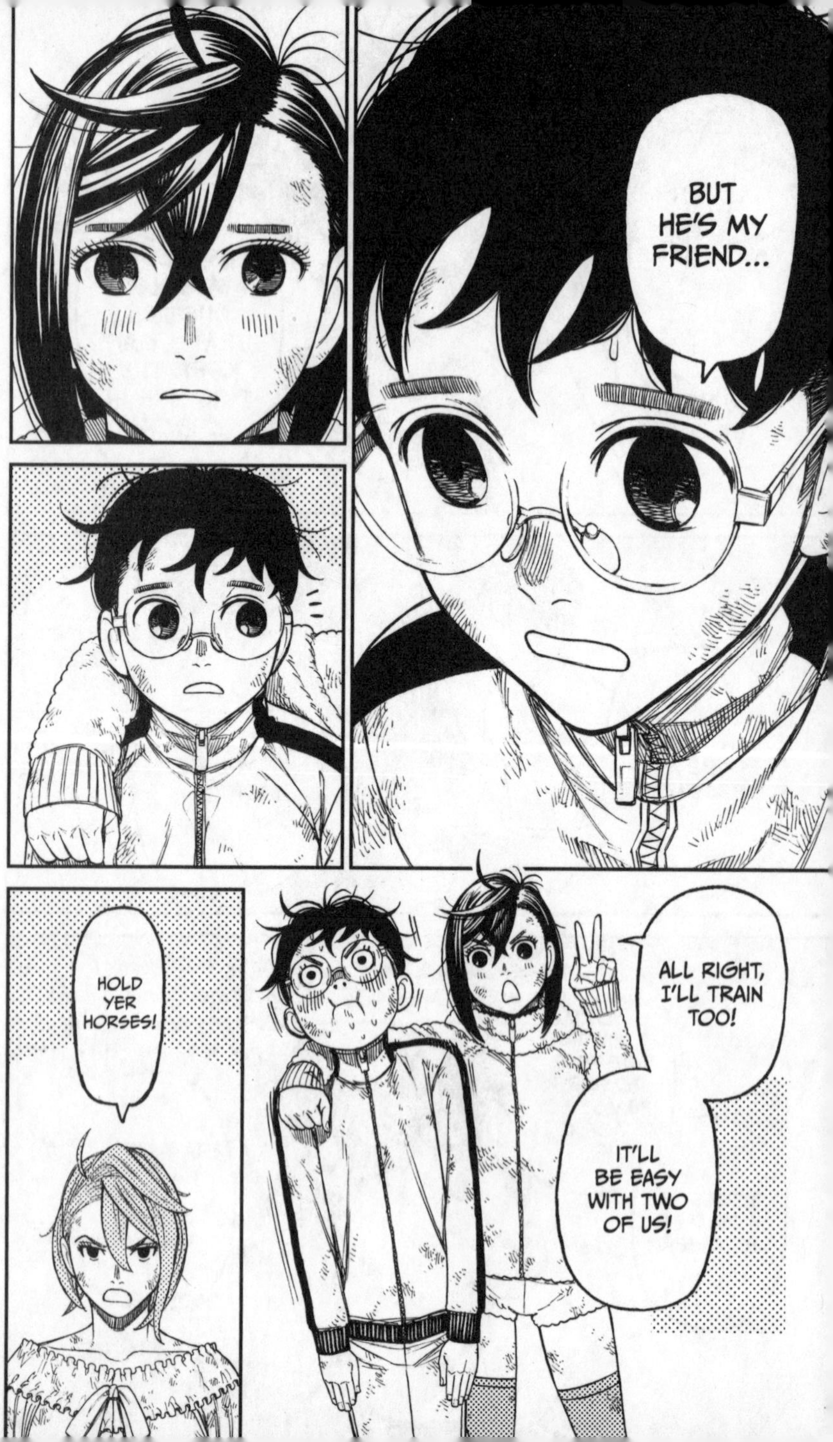
BUT HE'S MY FRIEND...
ALL RIGHT, I'LL TRAIN TOO!
IT'LL BE EASY WITH TWO OF US!
HOLD YER HORSES!

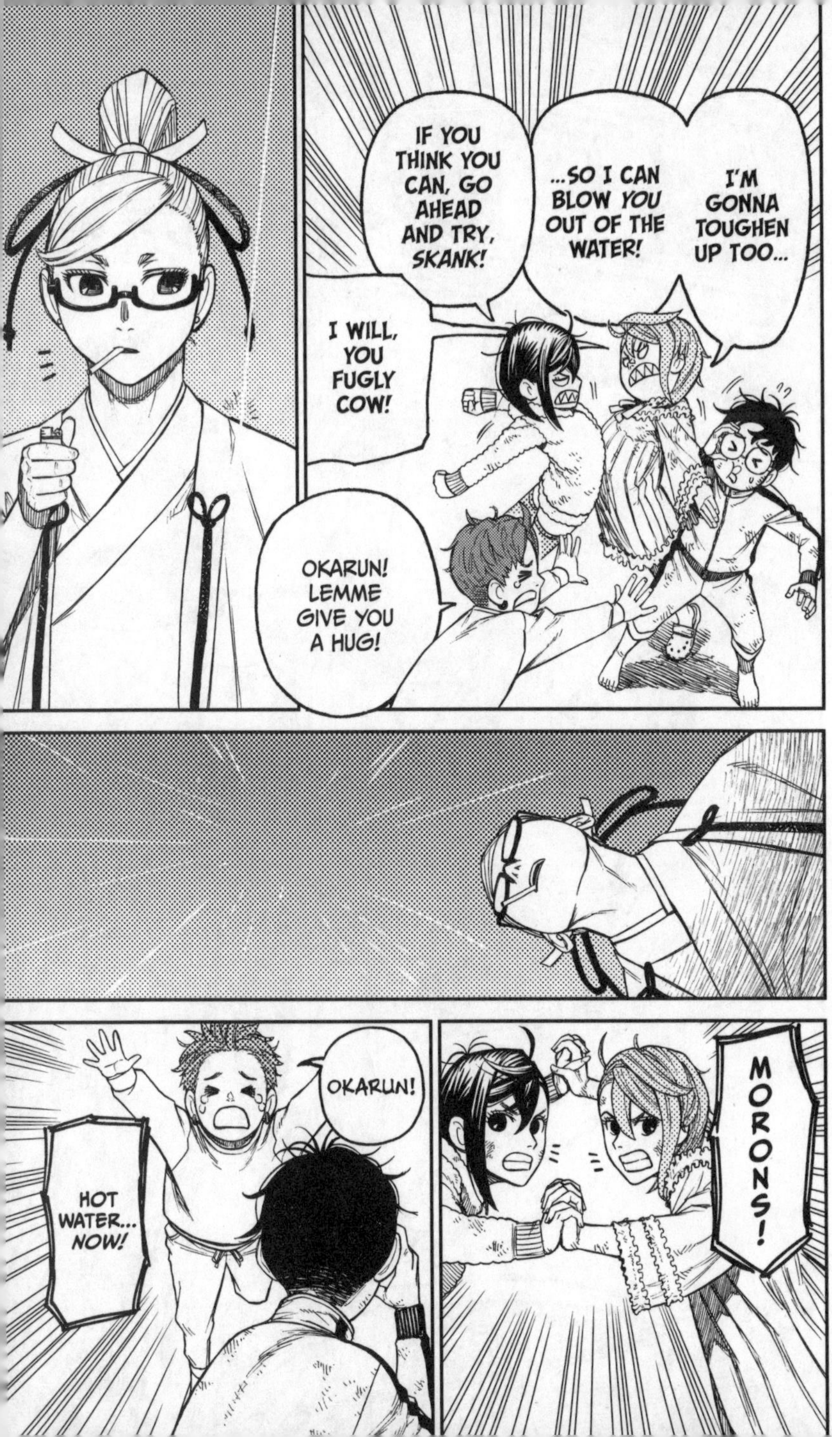
I'M GONNA TOUGHEN UP TOO...
...SO I CAN BLOW *YOU* OUT OF THE WATER!
IF YOU THINK YOU CAN, GO AHEAD AND TRY, *SKANK!*
I WILL, YOU FUGLY COW!
OKARUN! LEMME GIVE YOU A HUG!
MORONS!
OKARUN!
HOT WATER... *NOW!*

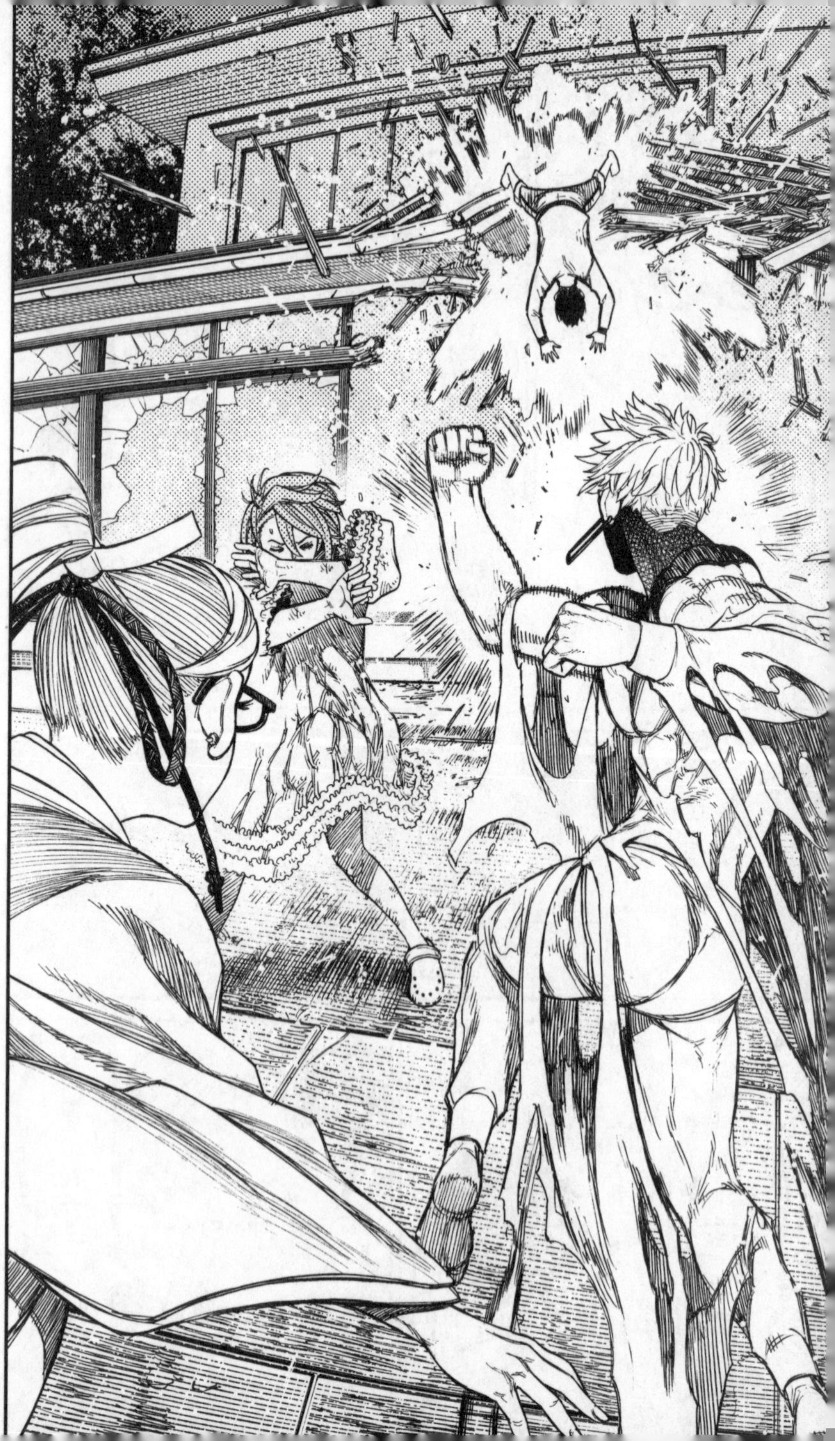

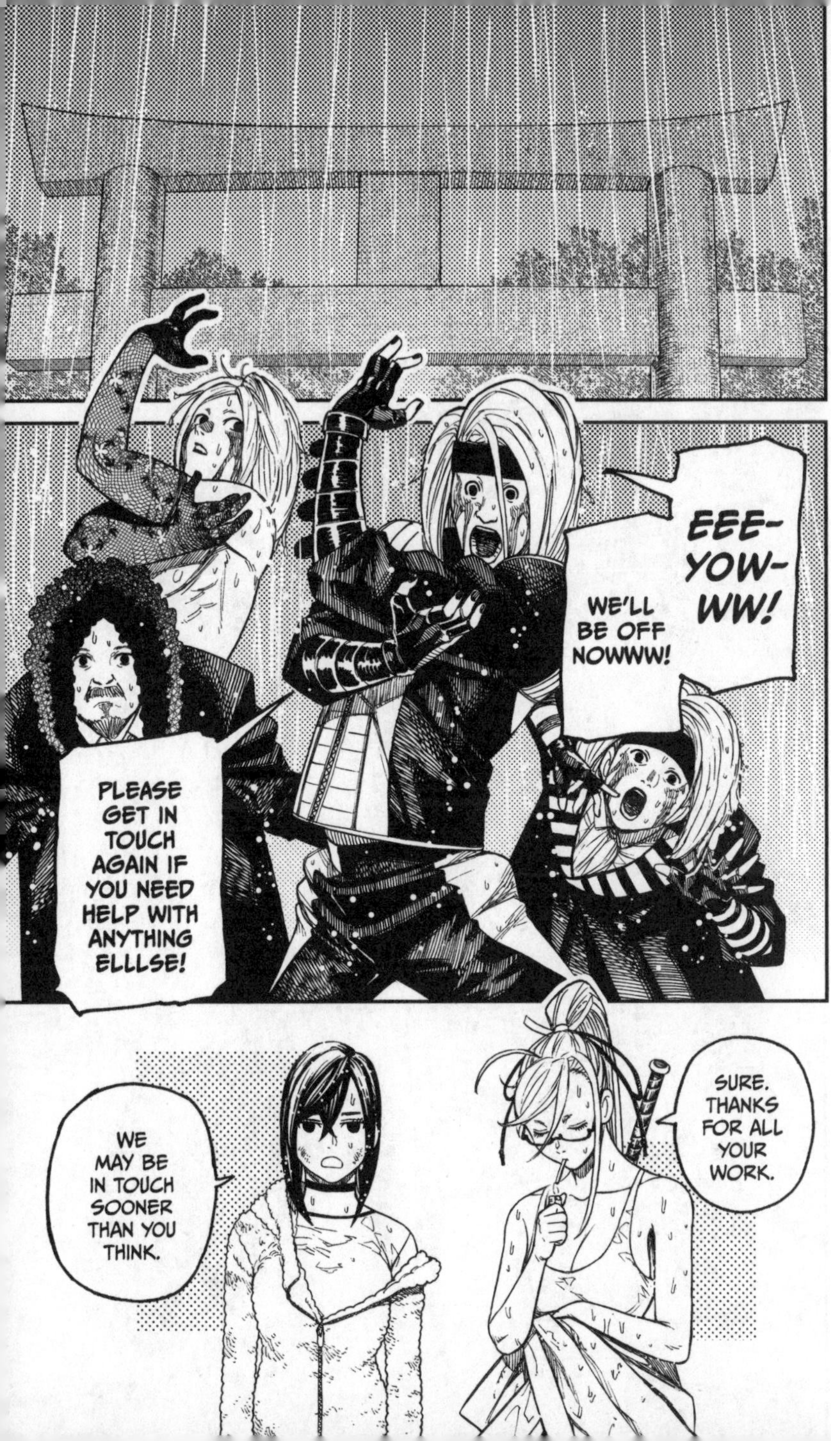
EEE-YOW-WW!
WE'LL BE OFF NOWWW!
PLEASE GET IN TOUCH AGAIN IF YOU NEED HELP WITH ANYTHING ELLLSE!
SURE. THANKS FOR ALL YOUR WORK.
WE MAY BE IN TOUCH SOONER THAN YOU THINK.

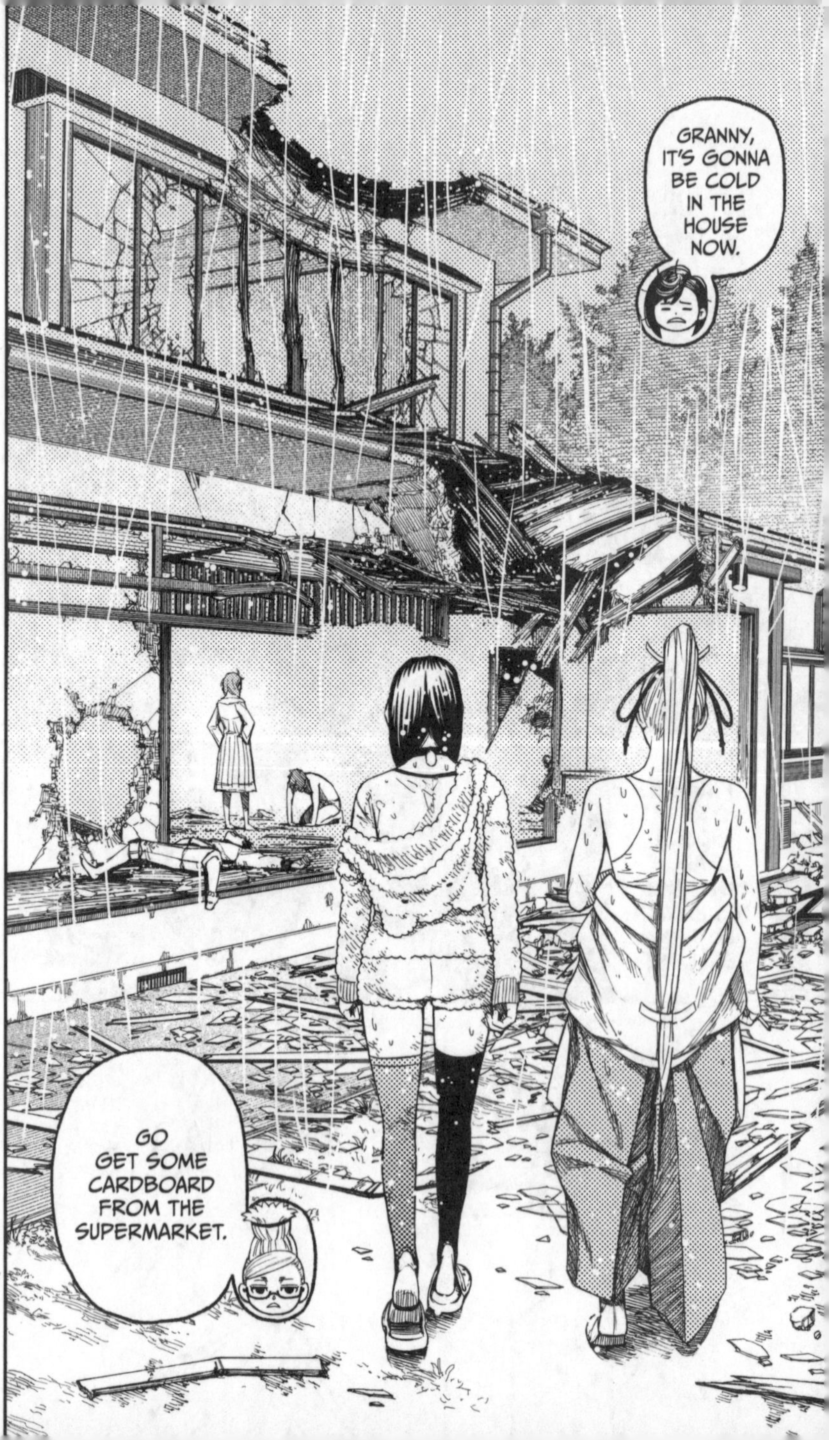
GRANNY, IT'S GONNA BE COLD IN THE HOUSE NOW.
GO GET SOME CARDBOARD FROM THE SUPERMARKET.

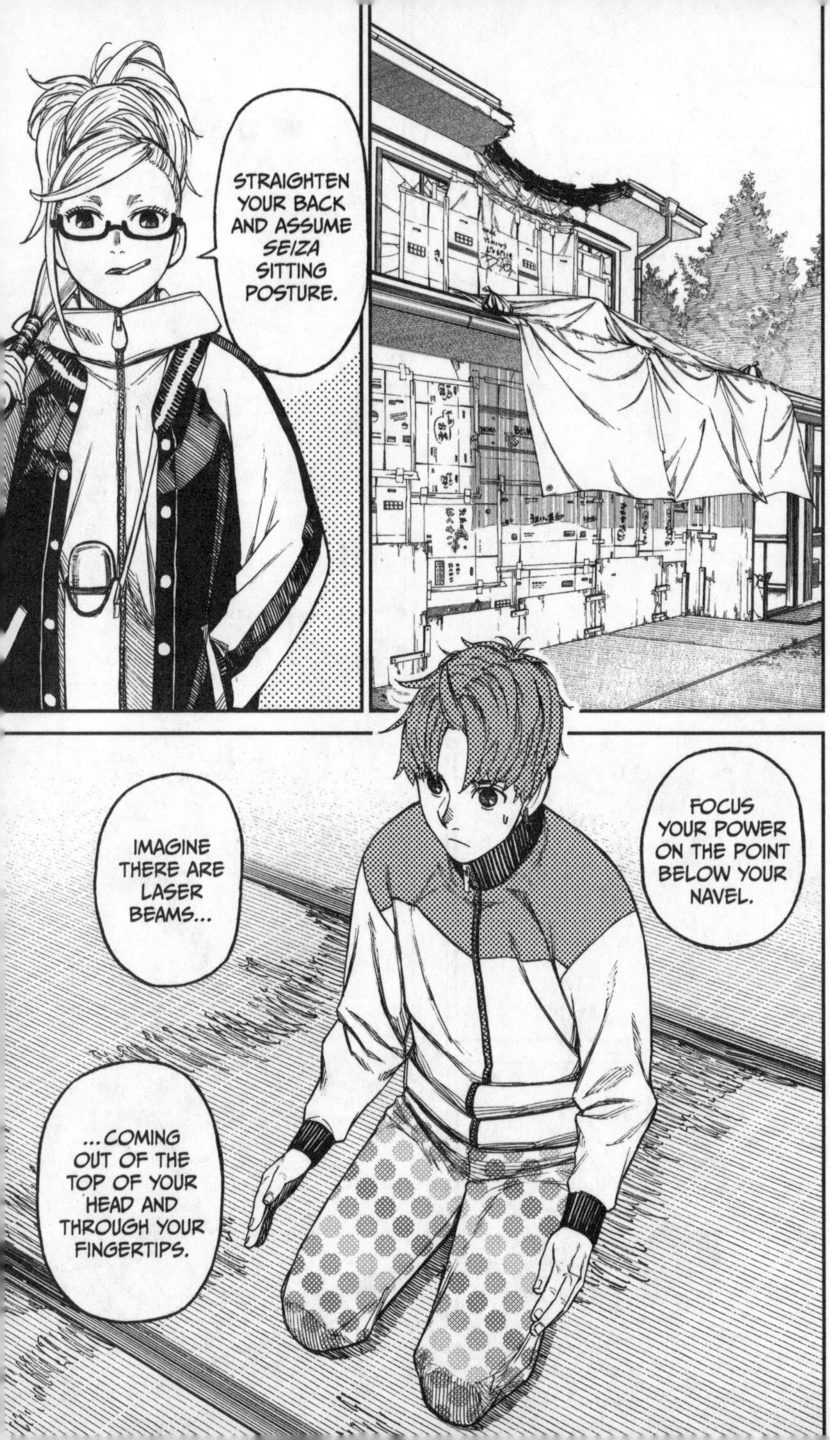
STRAIGHTEN YOUR BACK AND ASSUME SEIZA SITTING POSTURE.
FOCUS YOUR POWER ON THE POINT BELOW YOUR NAVEL.
IMAGINE THERE ARE LASER BEAMS...
...COMING OUT OF THE TOP OF YOUR HEAD AND THROUGH YOUR FINGERTIPS.

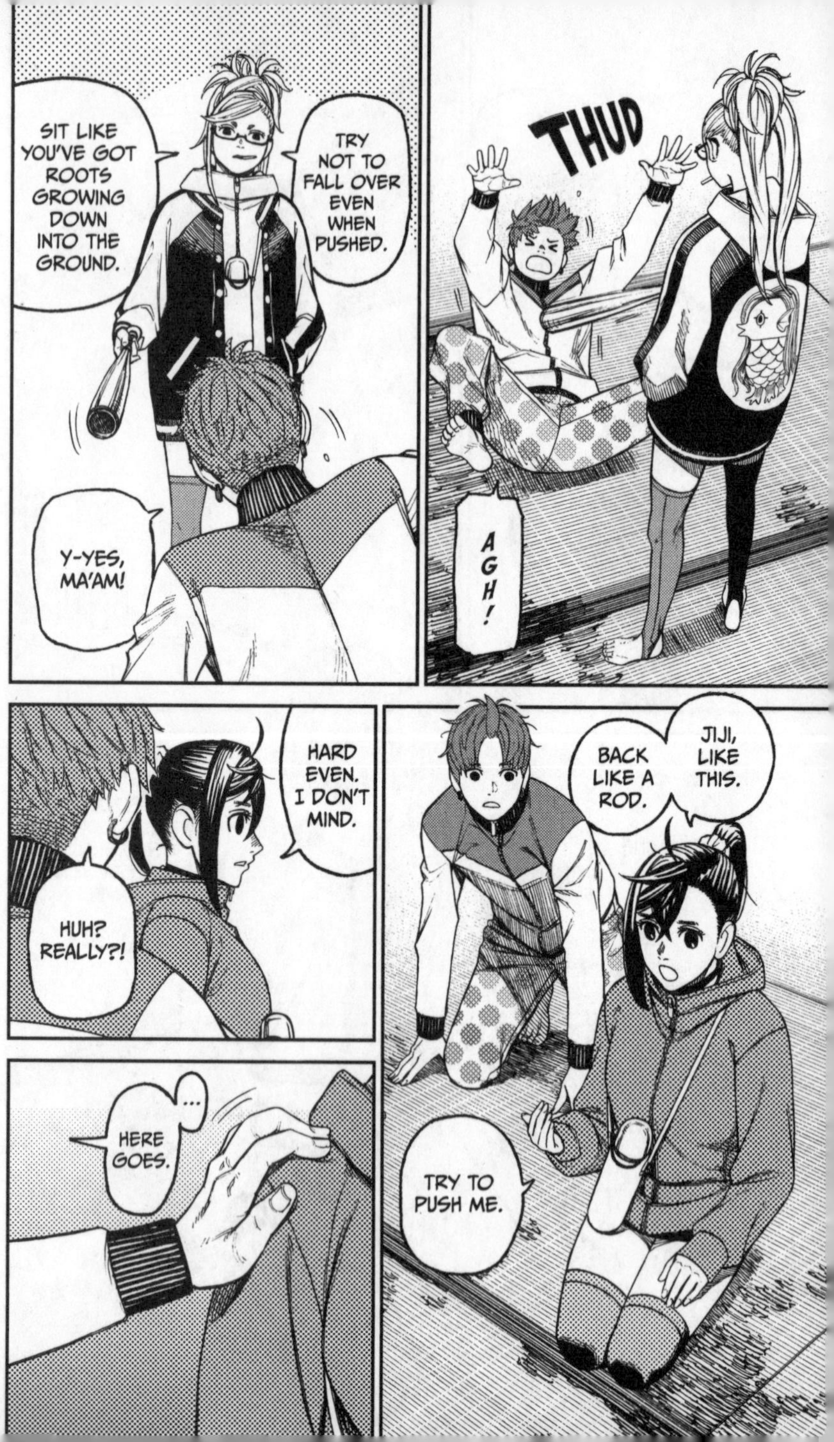
THUD
AGH!
TRY NOT TO FALL OVER EVEN WHEN PUSHED.
SIT LIKE YOU'VE GOT ROOTS GROWING DOWN INTO THE GROUND.
Y-YES, MA'AM!
JIJI, LIKE THIS.
BACK LIKE A ROD.
TRY TO PUSH ME.
HARD EVEN. I DON'T MIND.
HUH? REALLY?!
...
HERE GOES.

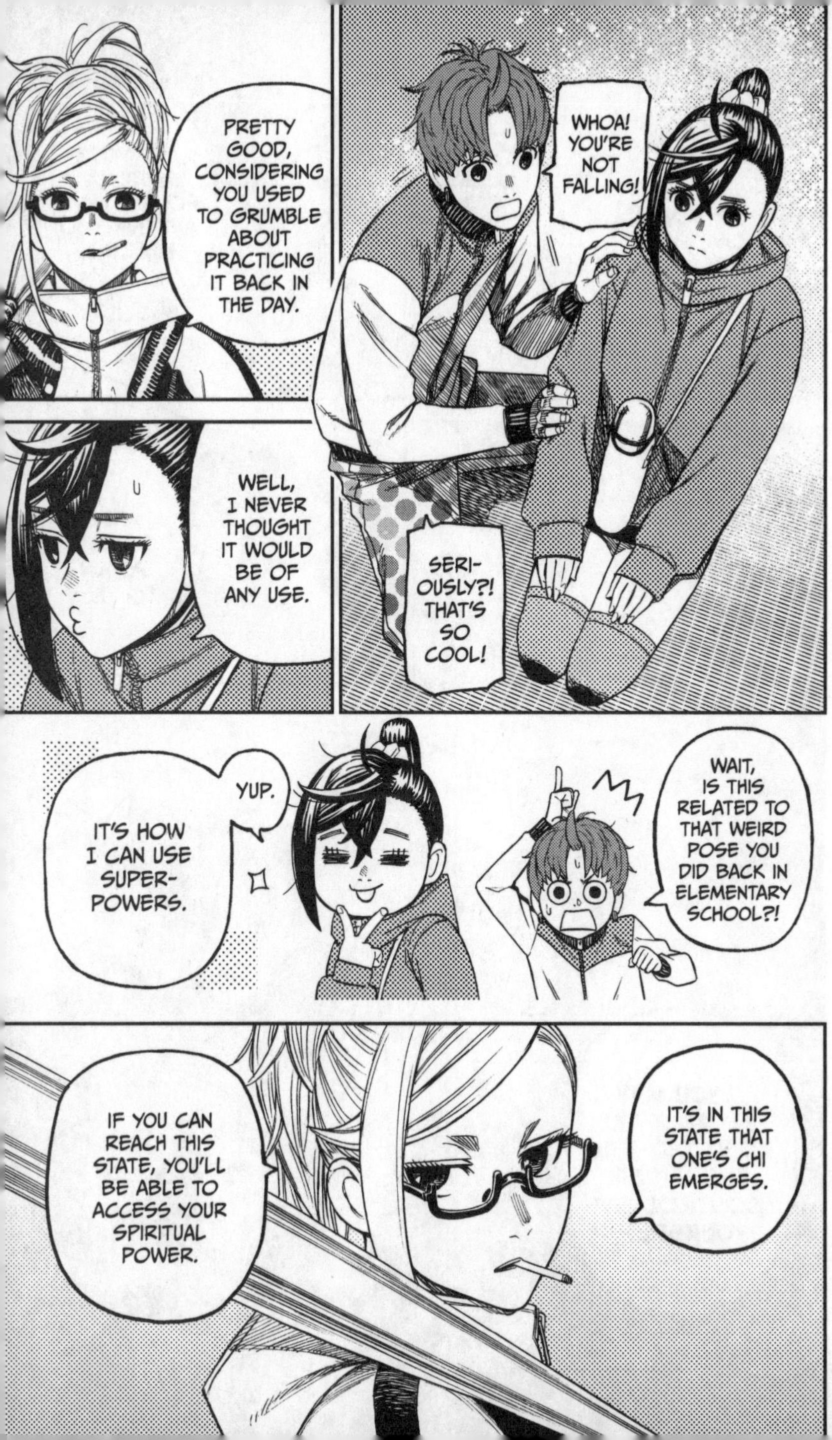
WHOA! YOU'RE NOT FALLING!
SERI-OUSLY?! THAT'S SO COOL!
PRETTY GOOD, CONSIDERING YOU USED TO GRUMBLE ABOUT PRACTICING IT BACK IN THE DAY.
WELL, I NEVER THOUGHT IT WOULD BE OF ANY USE.
WAIT, IS THIS RELATED TO THAT WEIRD POSE YOU DID BACK IN ELEMENTARY SCHOOL?!
YUP.
IT'S HOW I CAN USE SUPER-POWERS.
IT'S IN THIS STATE THAT ONE'S CHI EMERGES.
IF YOU CAN REACH THIS STATE, YOU'LL BE ABLE TO ACCESS YOUR SPIRITUAL POWER.

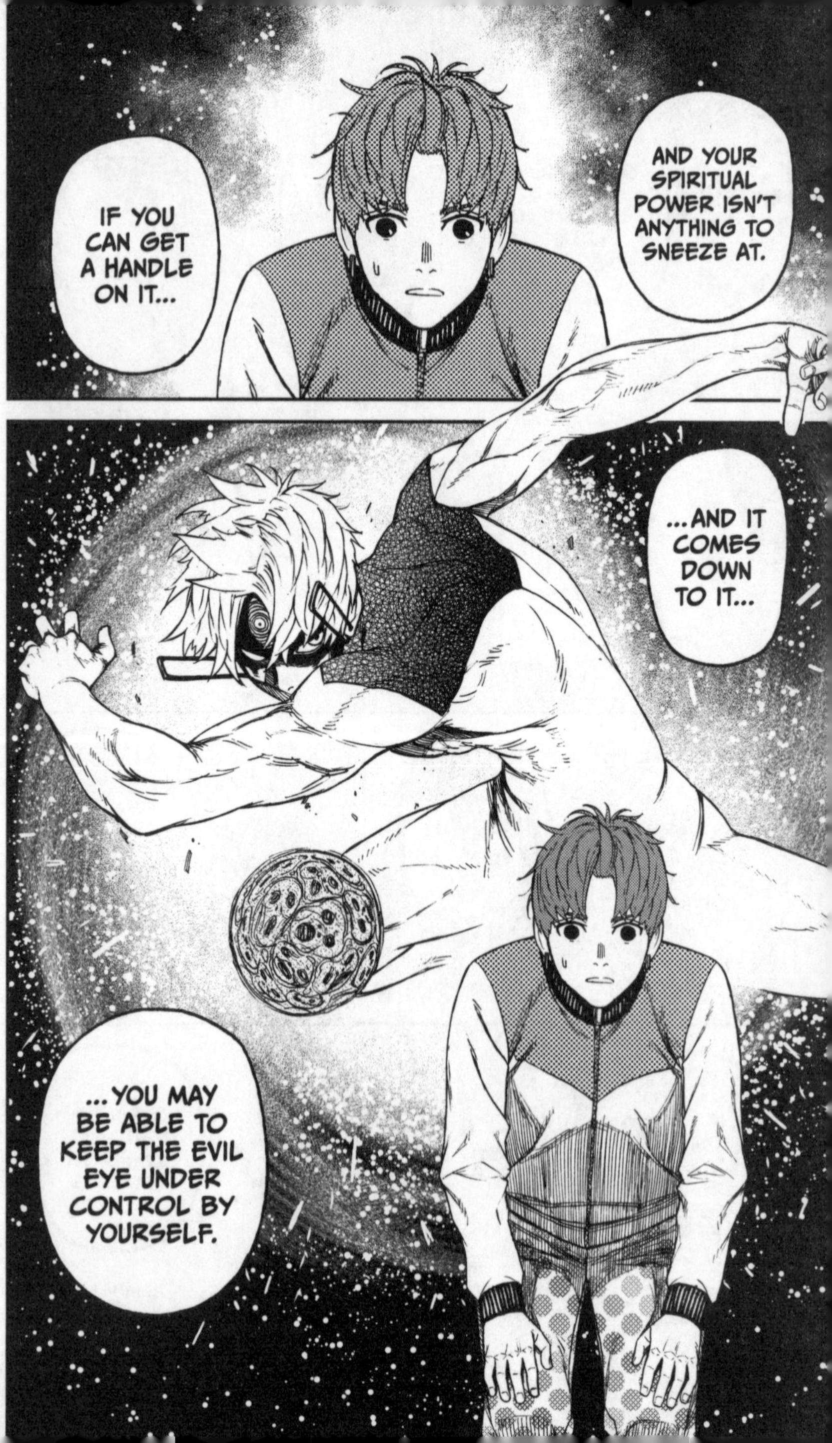
AND YOUR SPIRITUAL POWER ISN'T ANYTHING TO SNEEZE AT.
IF YOU CAN GET A HANDLE ON IT...
...AND IT COMES DOWN TO IT...
...YOU MAY BE ABLE TO KEEP THE EVIL EYE UNDER CONTROL BY YOURSELF.

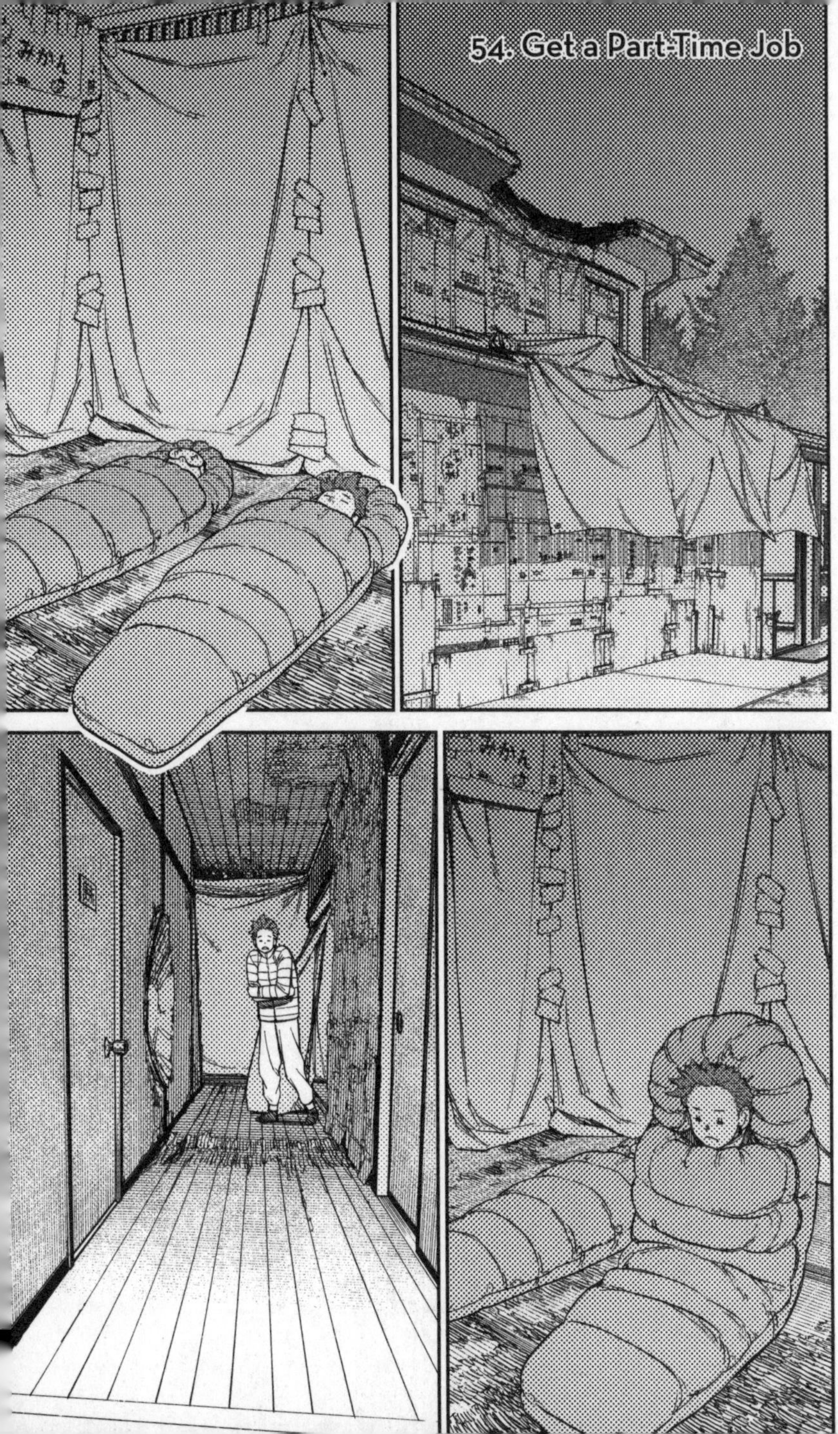
54. Get a Part-Time Job

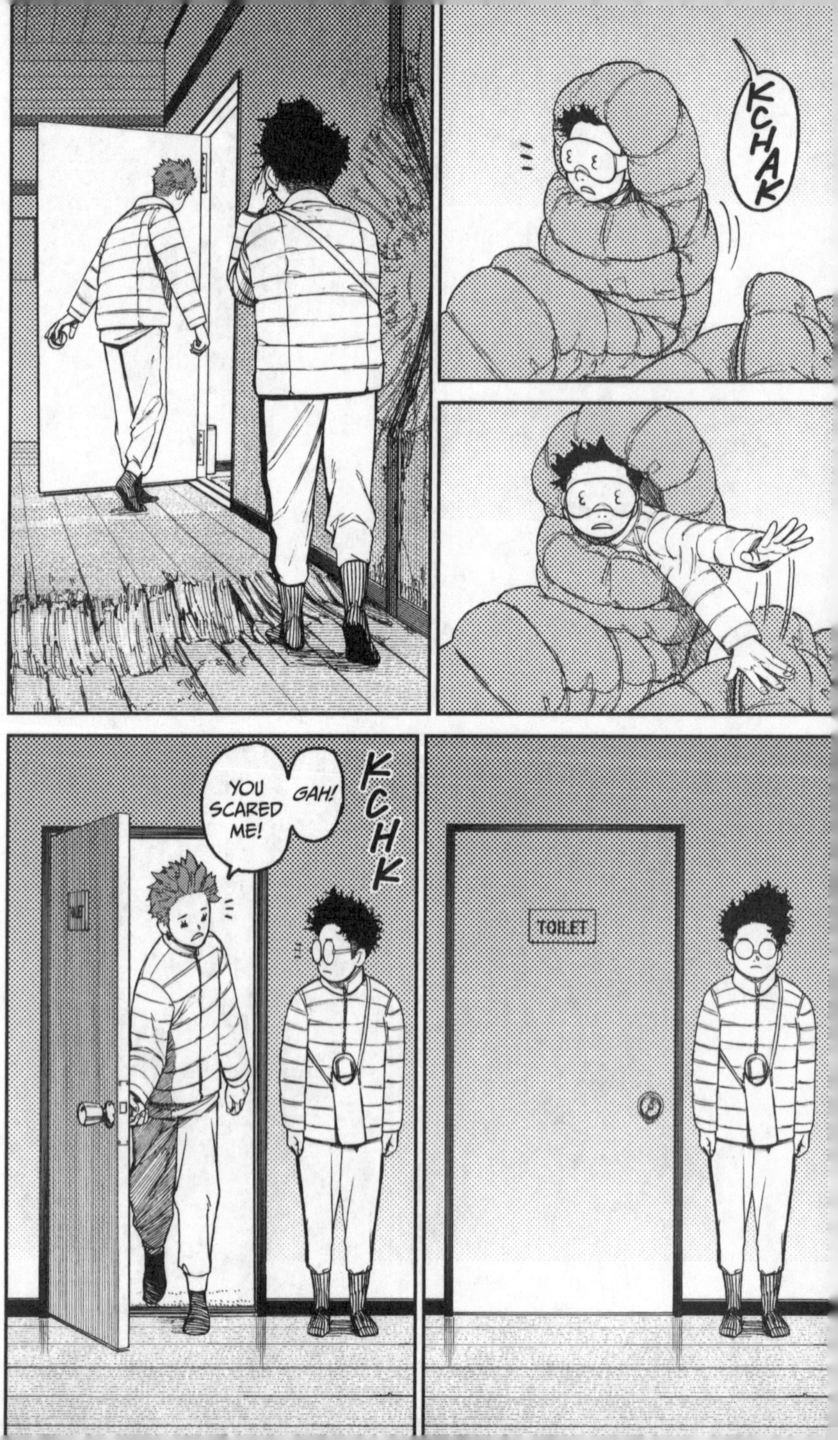
KCHAK
TOILET
KCHK
GAH!
YOU SCARED ME!

THE CARD-BOARD'S COME OFF HERE.

HEY.

SURE.

THANKS, OKARUN.

THERE'S EVENING DEW.

STAY AWAY FROM IT, JIJI.

...I CAUSED A LOT OF TROUBLE FOR MISS AYASE AND THE OTHERS.

WHEN I WAS CURSED BY TURBO GRANNY...

BUT THEY WENT OUT OF THEIR WAY TO SEE I WAS TAKEN CARE OF.

THIS IS ALL MY FAULT. I'M SORRY.

PLEASE DON'T APOLO-GIZE.

WE'RE ALL IN THIS TOGETHER.

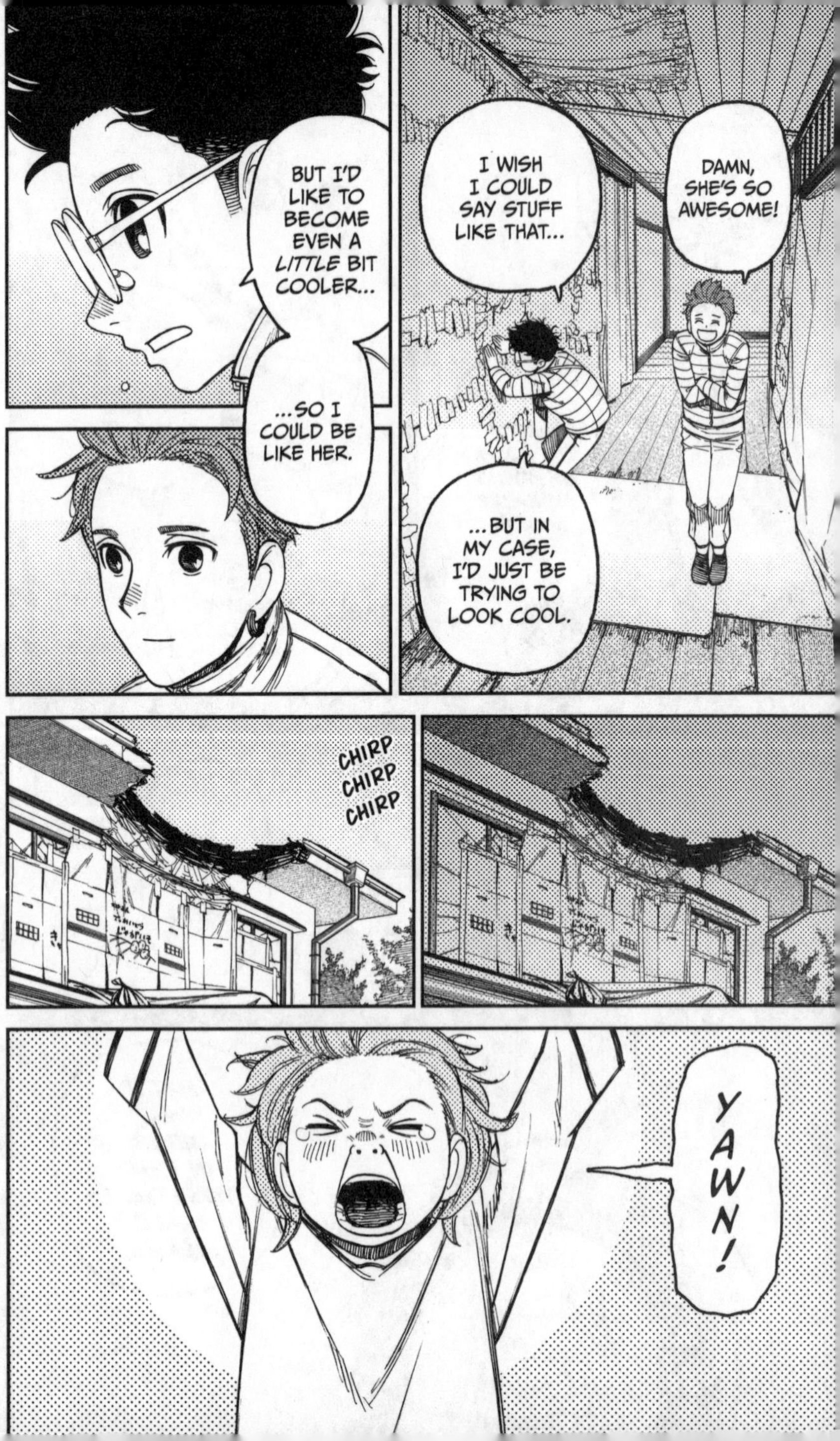
DAMN, SHE'S SO AWESOME!
I WISH I COULD SAY STUFF LIKE THAT...
...BUT IN MY CASE, I'D JUST BE TRYING TO LOOK COOL.
BUT I'D LIKE TO BECOME EVEN A *LITTLE* BIT COOLER...
...SO I COULD BE LIKE HER.
CHIRP CHIRP CHIRP
YAWN!

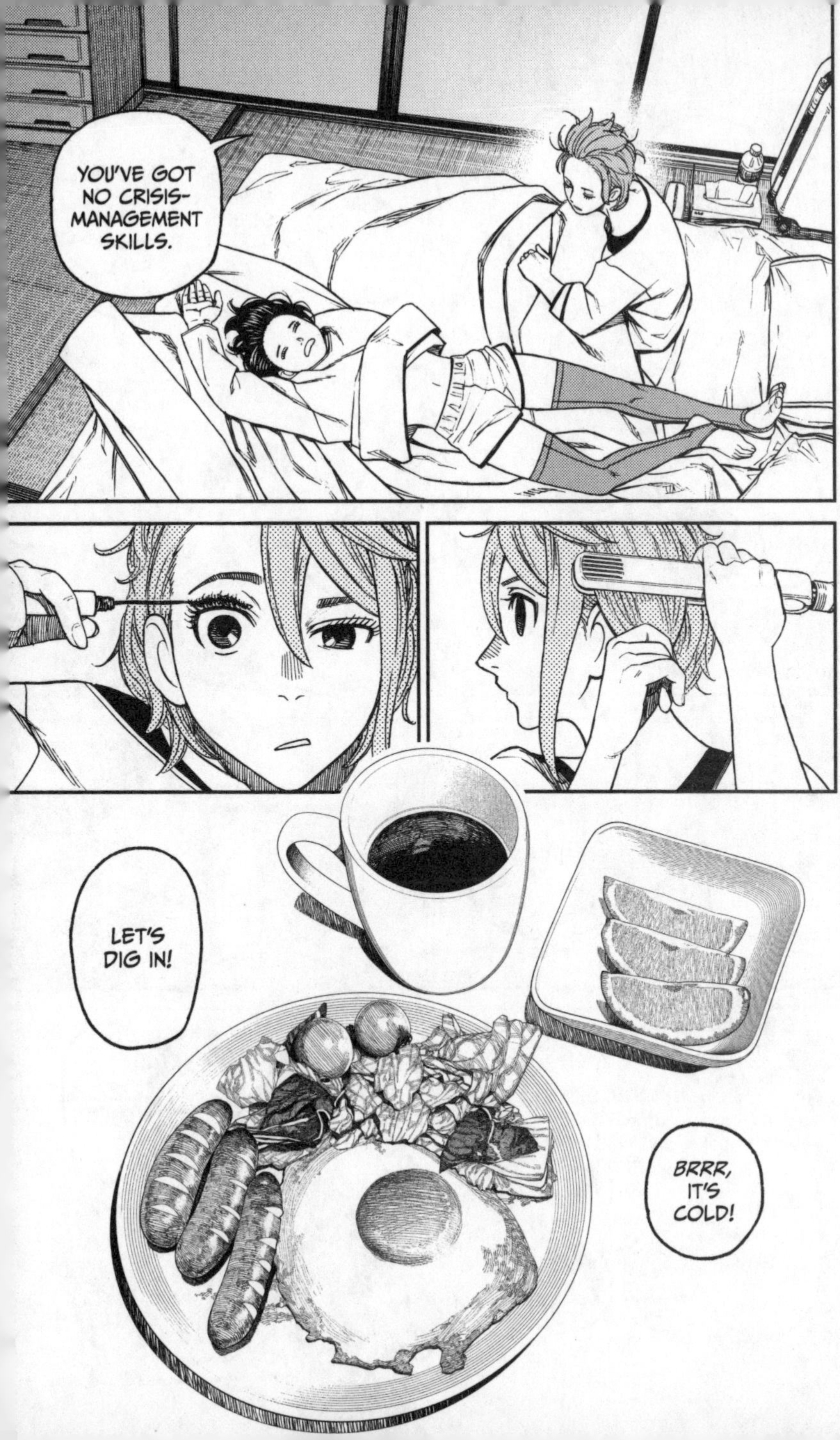
YOU'VE GOT NO CRISIS-MANAGEMENT SKILLS.
BRRR, IT'S COLD!
LET'S DIG IN!

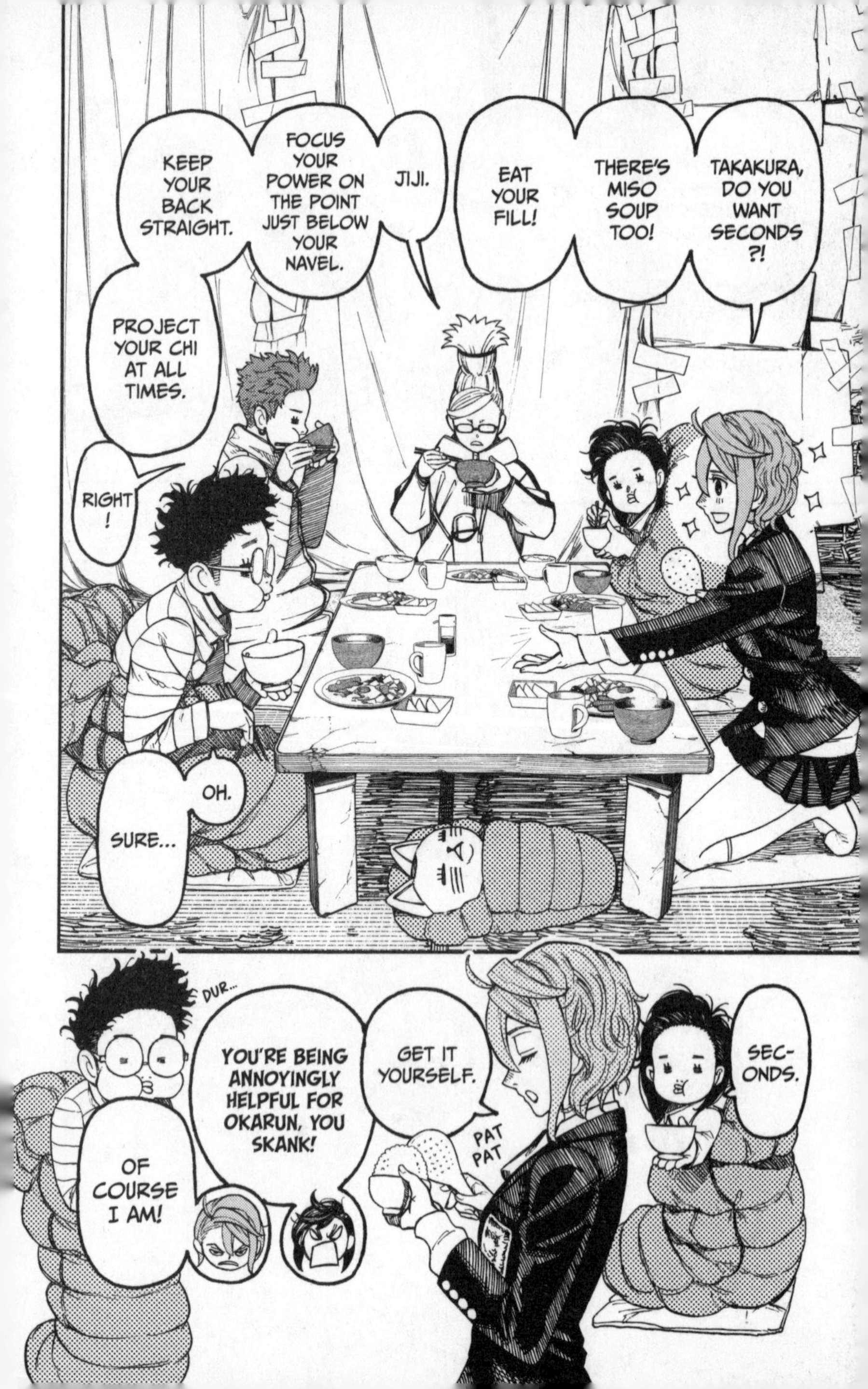
TAKAKURA, DO YOU WANT SECONDS?!
THERE'S MISO SOUP TOO!
EAT YOUR FILL!
JIJI.
FOCUS YOUR POWER ON THE POINT JUST BELOW YOUR NAVEL.
KEEP YOUR BACK STRAIGHT.
PROJECT YOUR CHI AT ALL TIMES.
RIGHT!
OH.
SURE...
SEC-ONDS.
GET IT YOURSELF.
PAT PAT
YOU'RE BEING ANNOYINGLY HELPFUL FOR OKARUN, YOU SKANK!
OF COURSE I AM!
DUR...

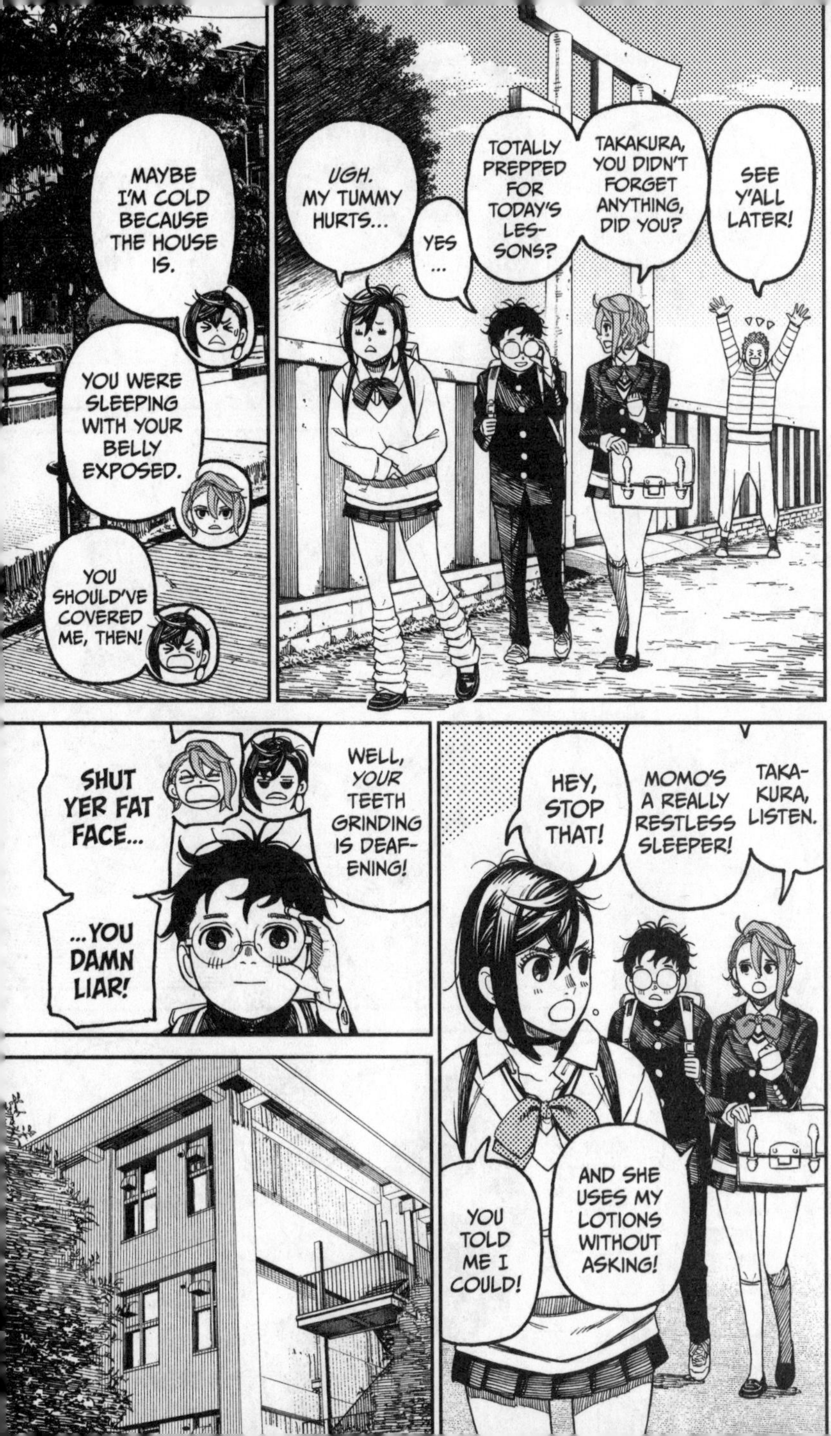
SEE Y'ALL LATER!
TAKAKURA, YOU DIDN'T FORGET ANYTHING, DID YOU?
TOTALLY PREPPED FOR TODAY'S LES-SONS?
YES ...
UGH. MY TUMMY HURTS...
MAYBE I'M COLD BECAUSE THE HOUSE IS.
YOU WERE SLEEPING WITH YOUR BELLY EXPOSED.
YOU SHOULD'VE COVERED ME, THEN!
TAKA-KURA, LISTEN.
MOMO'S A REALLY RESTLESS SLEEPER!
HEY, STOP THAT!
AND SHE USES MY LOTIONS WITHOUT ASKING!
YOU TOLD ME I COULD!
WELL, YOUR TEETH GRINDING IS DEAF-ENING!
SHUT YER FAT FACE...
...YOU DAMN LIAR!

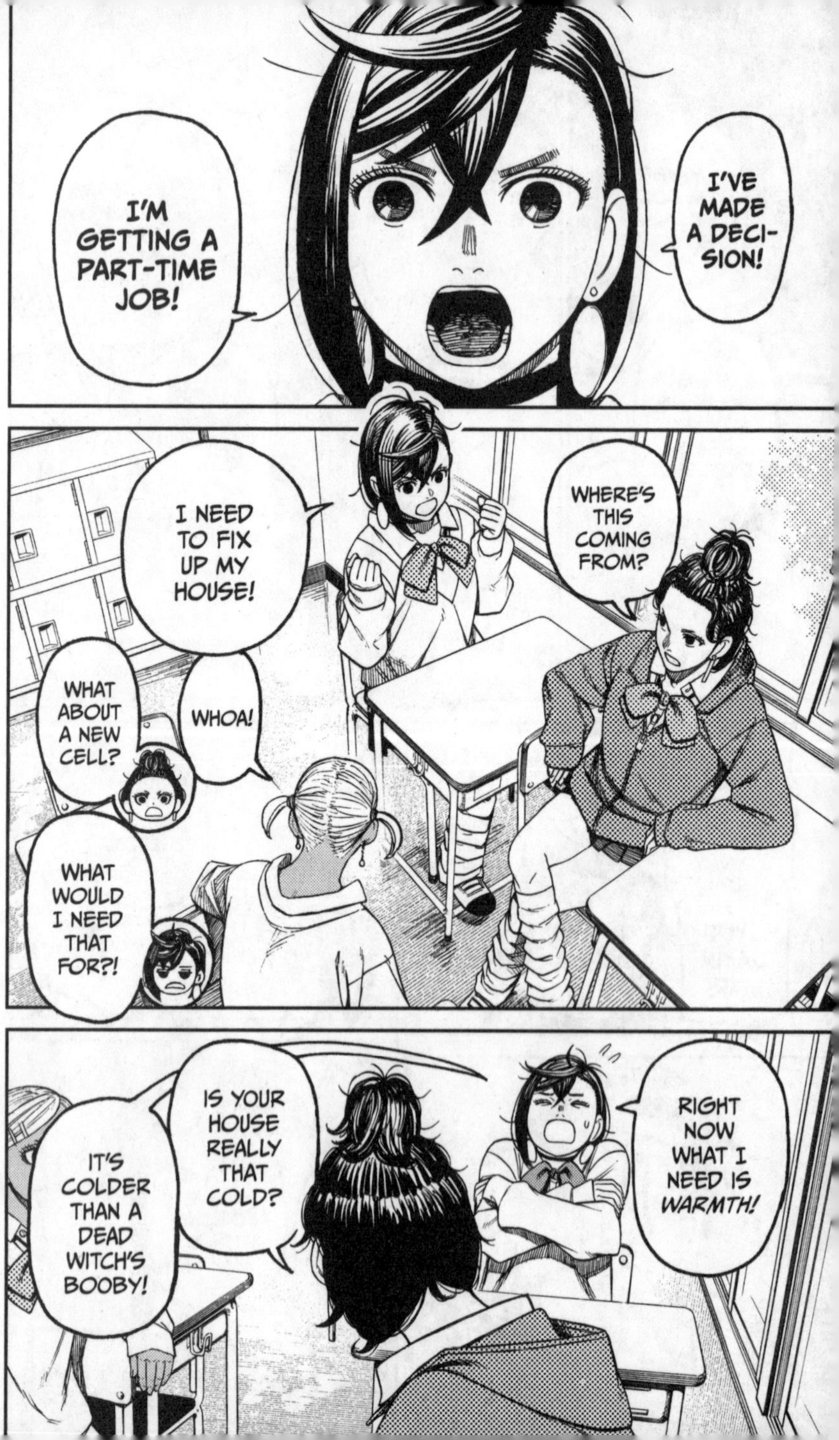
I'VE MADE A DECI-SION!
I'M GETTING A PART-TIME JOB!
WHERE'S THIS COMING FROM?
I NEED TO FIX UP MY HOUSE!
WHOA!
WHAT ABOUT A NEW CELL?
WHAT WOULD I NEED THAT FOR?!
RIGHT NOW WHAT I NEED IS *WARMTH!*
IS YOUR HOUSE REALLY THAT COLD?
IT'S COLDER THAN A DEAD WITCH'S BOOBY!

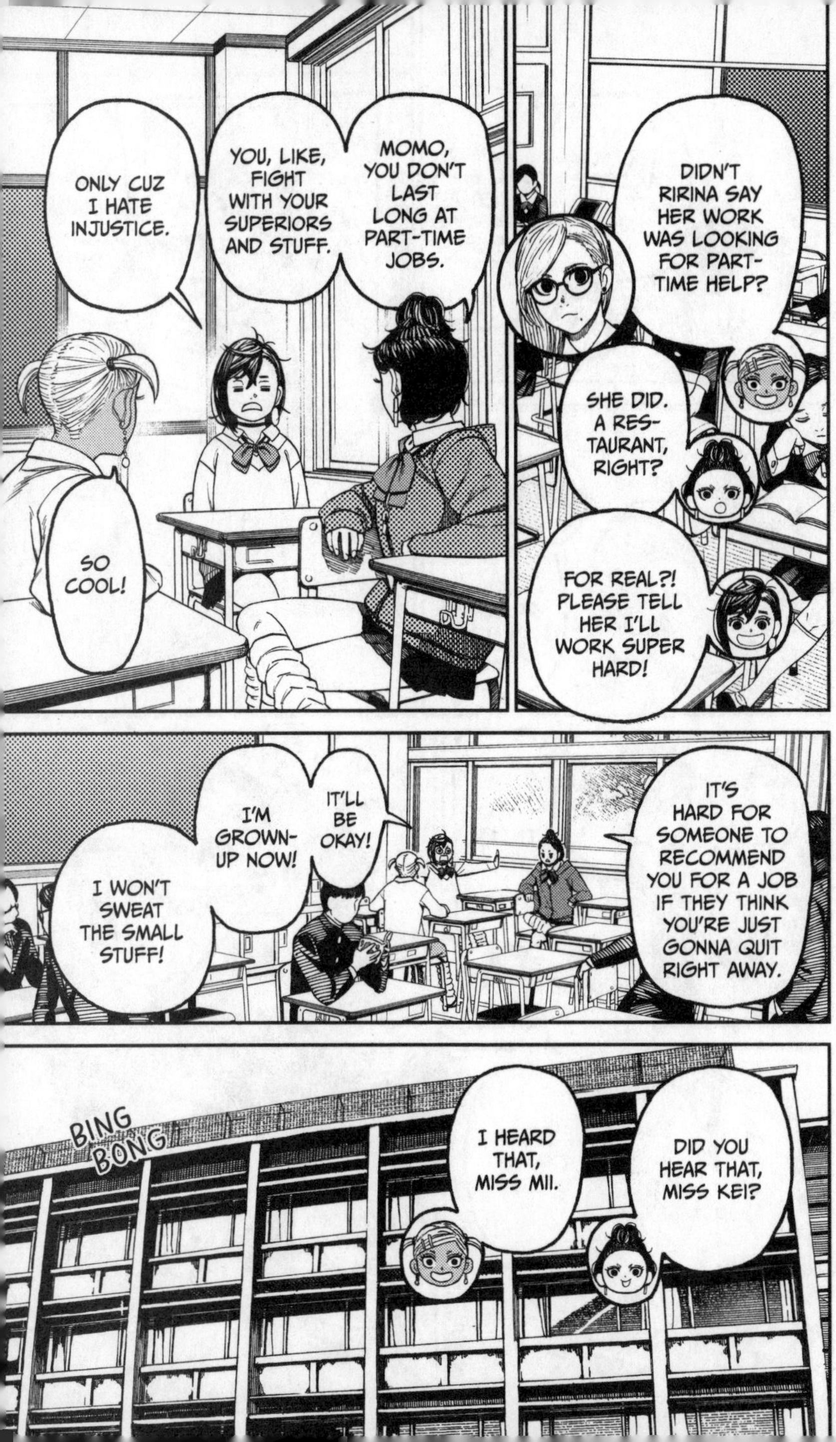
DIDN'T RIRINA SAY HER WORK WAS LOOKING FOR PART-TIME HELP?
SHE DID. A RES-TAURANT, RIGHT?
FOR REAL?! PLEASE TELL HER I'LL WORK SUPER HARD!
MOMO, YOU DON'T LAST LONG AT PART-TIME JOBS.
YOU, LIKE, FIGHT WITH YOUR SUPERIORS AND STUFF.
ONLY CUZ I HATE INJUSTICE.
SO COOL!
IT'S HARD FOR SOMEONE TO RECOMMEND YOU FOR A JOB IF THEY THINK YOU'RE JUST GONNA QUIT RIGHT AWAY.
IT'LL BE OKAY!
I'M GROWN-UP NOW!
I WON'T SWEAT THE SMALL STUFF!
DID YOU HEAR THAT, MISS KEI?
I HEARD THAT, MISS MII.
BING BONG

NO, IT WOULD NOT.

SO IF MOMO AND JIJI HAD TEA TOGETHER, WOULD *THAT* BE A DATE?

WOULDN'T YOU CALL THAT A DATE?!

WE'RE JUST GOING TO HAVE SOME TEA!

I DON'T GO ON DATES!

THEN WHAT'S THE DIFF, YOU PIECE O'...?!

MRF MRF MRF!

FINE! DON'T HAVE A SINGLE DROP THEN!

I WON'T!

YOU'LL GET THIRSTY.

I WON'T DRINK A SINGLE DROP OF TEA!

OKARUN! RIGHT HERE, RIGHT HERE!

I WILL NOT!

MAID CAFE Moe! Moe! Tri-Beam! MOE! MOE! TRI-BEAM!

5F 6F 7

WHUT THE...

OKA-RUN!

AAH!

MISS AYASE!

THREE!

HOW MANY IN YOUR PARTY?

WELCOME BACK, MASTER!

HEY, MAID LADY!

SERVE THIS CUS-TOMER!

....!

EXCUSE ME. THAT MAID'S GOT A BAD ATTITUDE.

FINE. WELC'M.

THIS WAY.

MISS AYASE! BE MORE COURTE-OUS!

AND SPEAK CLEARLY!

YES, MA'AM ...

WELCOME TO OUR ESTAB-LISHMENT, YOU SACK OF SHIT.

SORRY! IT SLIPPED OUT!

YOU'RE SUPPOSED TO SAY, "WELCOME BACK"!

MISS AYASE! HOW COULD YOU?!

I THINK I'LL HAVE THE TEA.

HMM. LET'S SEE...

PURE APPLE JUICE.

MAY WE TAKE YOUR ORDER?

MISS AYASE'S MAKING ALL THIS EFFORT...

BUT I DO! I WANT SOMETHING!

HUH ?!

YOU DIDN'T NEED ANYTHING TO DRINK, RIGHT, OKARUN?

BUT YOU SAID BEFORE YOU DIDN'T NEED ANYTHING TO DRINK, TURD!

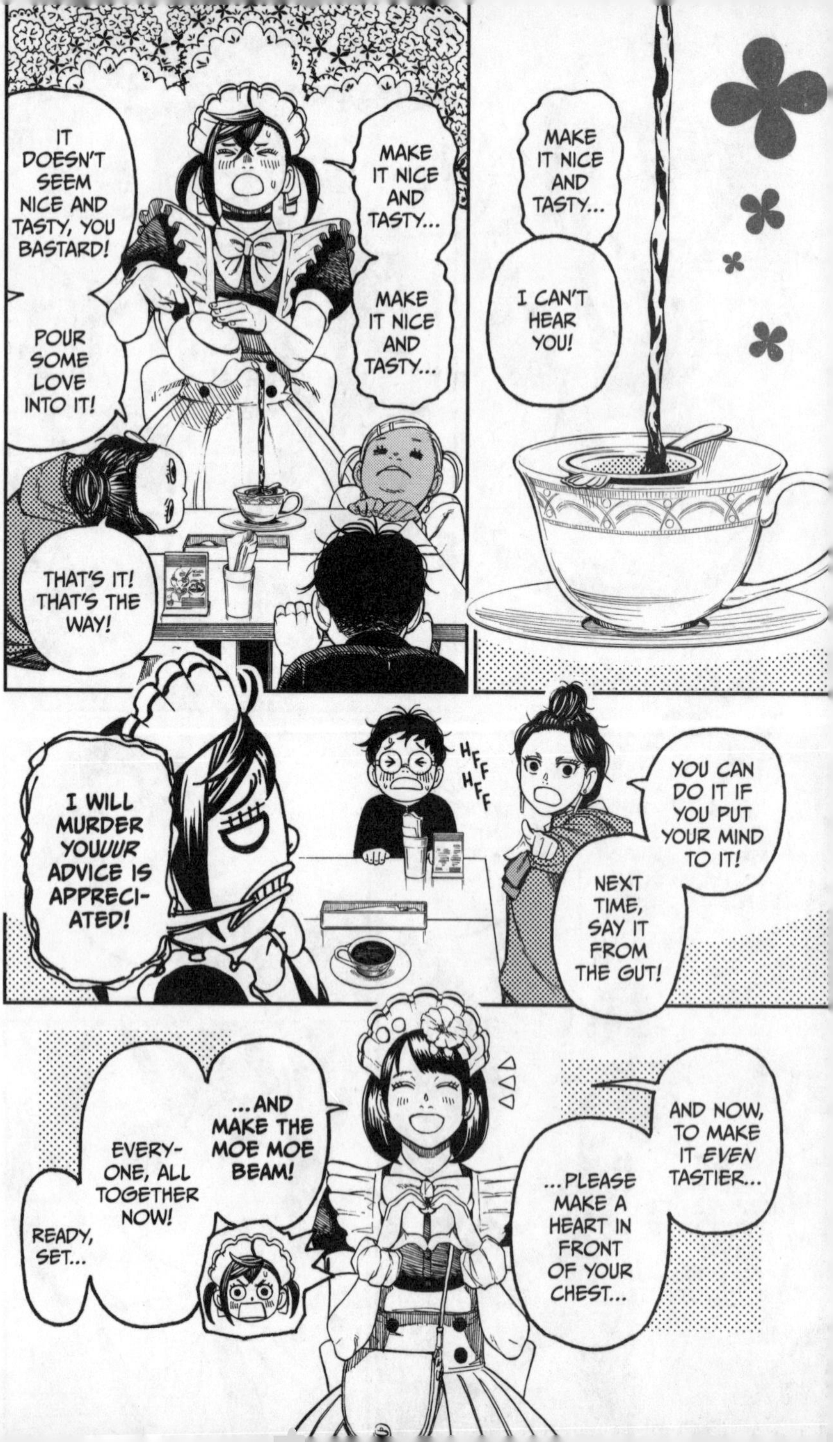
MAKE IT NICE AND TASTY...
I CAN'T HEAR YOU!
MAKE IT NICE AND TASTY...
MAKE IT NICE AND TASTY...
IT DOESN'T SEEM NICE AND TASTY, YOU BASTARD!
POUR SOME LOVE INTO IT!
THAT'S IT! THAT'S THE WAY!
YOU CAN DO IT IF YOU PUT YOUR MIND TO IT!
NEXT TIME, SAY IT FROM THE GUT!
HFF HFF
I WILL MURDER YOUUUR ADVICE IS APPRECIATED!
AND NOW, TO MAKE IT *EVEN* TASTIER...
...PLEASE MAKE A HEART IN FRONT OF YOUR CHEST...
...AND MAKE THE MOE MOE BEAM!
EVERYONE, ALL TOGETHER NOW!
READY, SET...

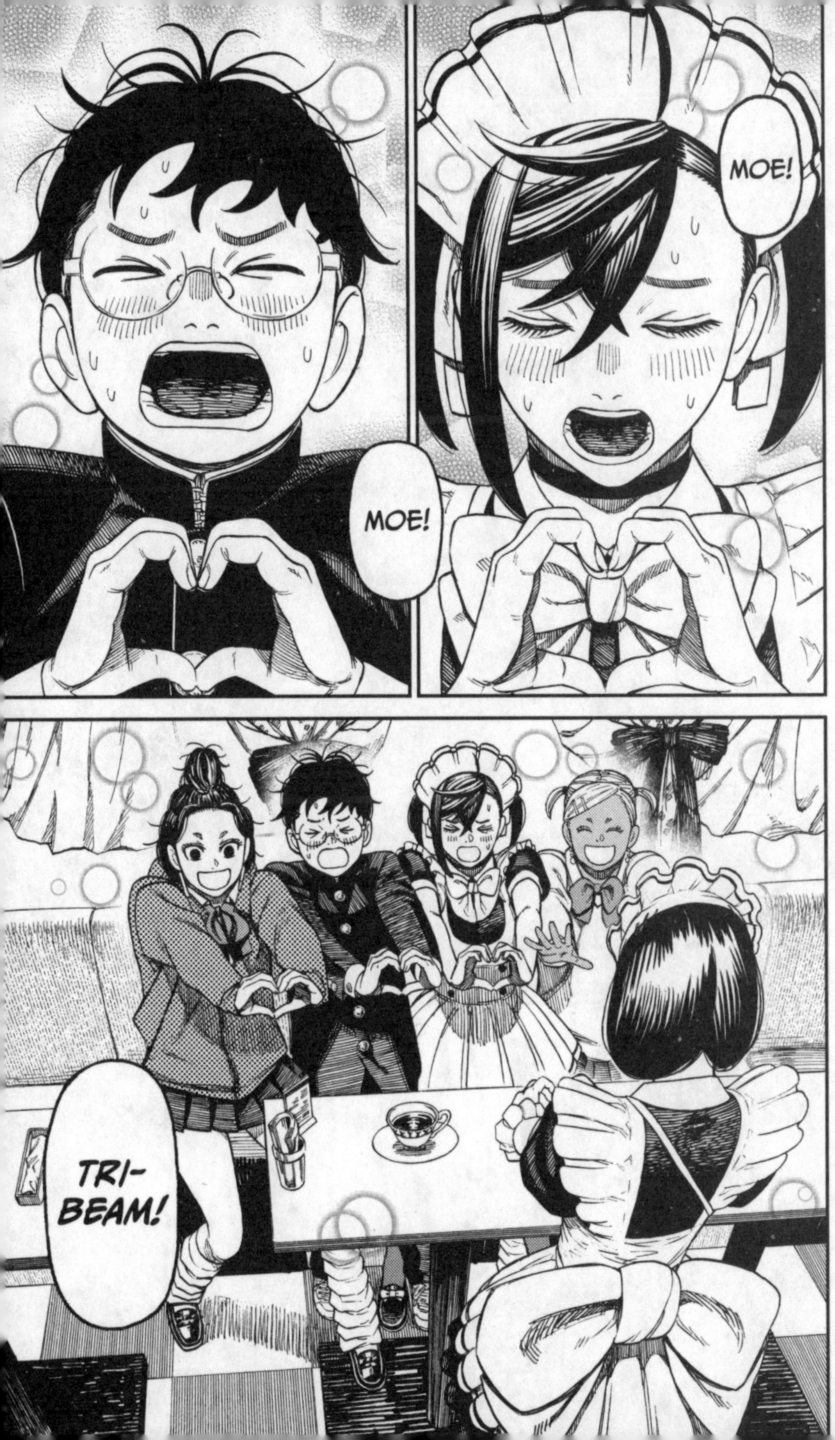
MOE!
MOE!
TRI-BEAM!

DAN DA DAN

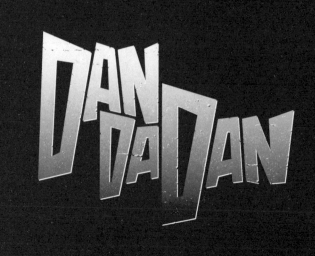

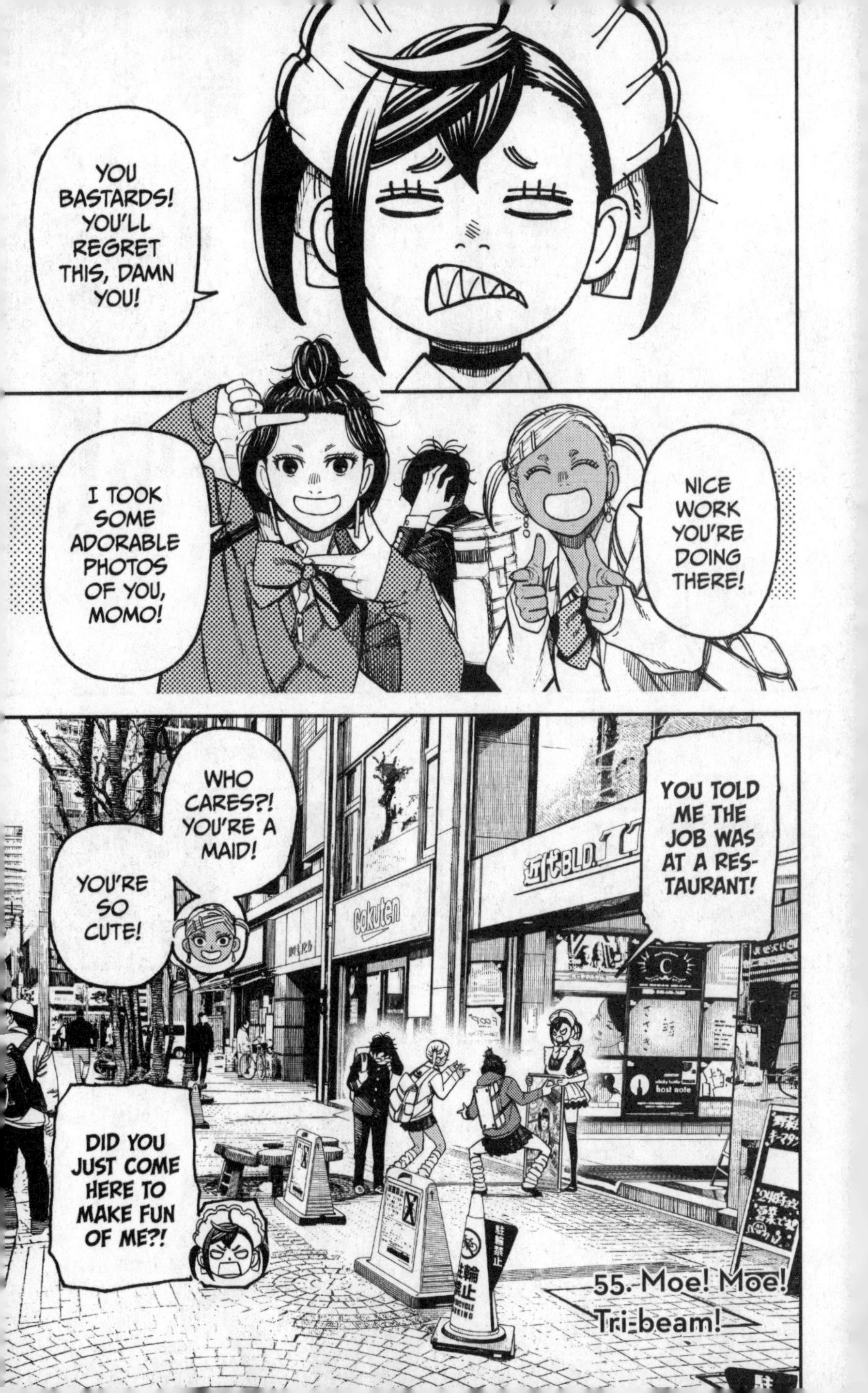
YOU BASTARDS! YOU'LL REGRET THIS, DAMN YOU!
NICE WORK YOU'RE DOING THERE!
I TOOK SOME ADORABLE PHOTOS OF YOU, MOMO!
YOU TOLD ME THE JOB WAS AT A RES-TAURANT!
近代BLD.
Gokuten
WHO CARES?! YOU'RE A MAID!
YOU'RE SO CUTE!
DID YOU JUST COME HERE TO MAKE FUN OF ME?!
55. Moe! Moe! Tri-beam!

WHAT'S UP?

OKARUN, LET'S GO.

ACTUALLY, I'M GOING TO STAY...

GIVE IT YOUR ALL!

SEE YA. THANKS FOR YOUR SERVICE.

SHOO! SHOO!

LEAVE! GO!

YOU'RE ON THE ROAD TO RENOVATING!

JIJI WILL BE WAITING FOR YOU.

OKARUN, YOU GOTTA GET OUTTA HERE ASAP.

Moe! Moe! Tri-Beam!

HMMM?

HAVE FUN!

MISS AYASE, WHAT TIME ARE YOU HERE TILL?

GEEZ, IT'S COLD!

UH...

TEN.

SORRY FOR BARGING INTO YOUR PLACE OF WORK.

YOU SHOULD BE!

DON'T EVER COME HERE AGAIN!

HUH?!

ALL RIGHT.

THEN I'LL STAY HERE UNTIL YOU'RE DONE.

IT'S DANGEROUS FOR A GIRL TO GO HOME...

AND IT'S FREEZING. YOU'LL CATCH A COLD!

NO. I TOLD YOU TO LEAVE.

...ALONE AT NIGHT.

TAKE CARE.

OKAY, THEN...

NUH-UH!

I'M TOUGH.

I'LL BE FINE.

I... SEE...

REALLY?!

MOMO, YOU WERE REALLY GREAT TODAY!

SEE YOU AGAIN SOON, OKAY?!

THANK YOU FOR EVERYTHING!

I'M SORRY FOR ALL THE HEADACHES I CAUSED YOU!

YUP!

I'LL BE OFF, THEN!

TAKE CARE!

HUH. GUESS I'LL HEAD HOME, THEN.

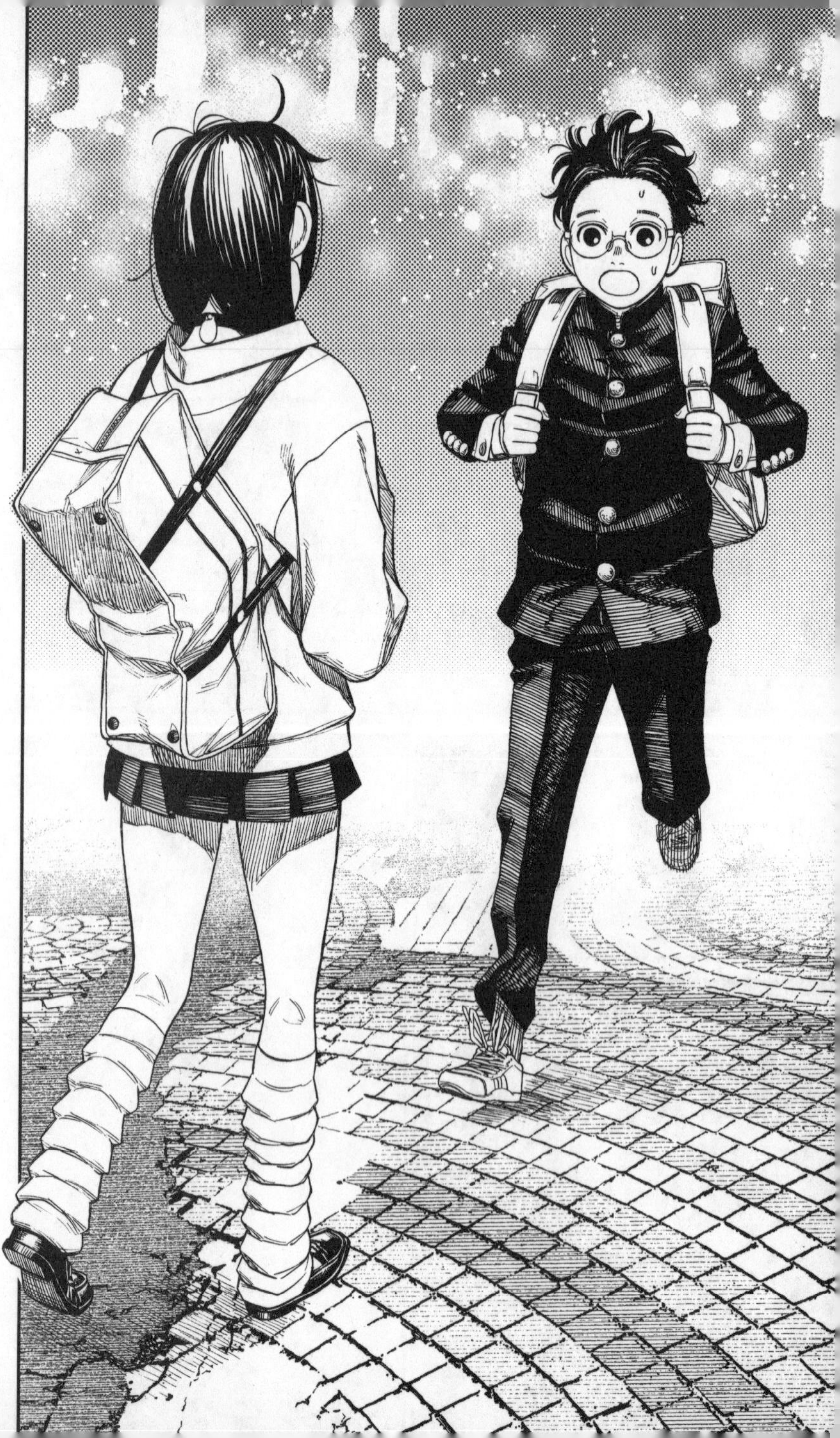

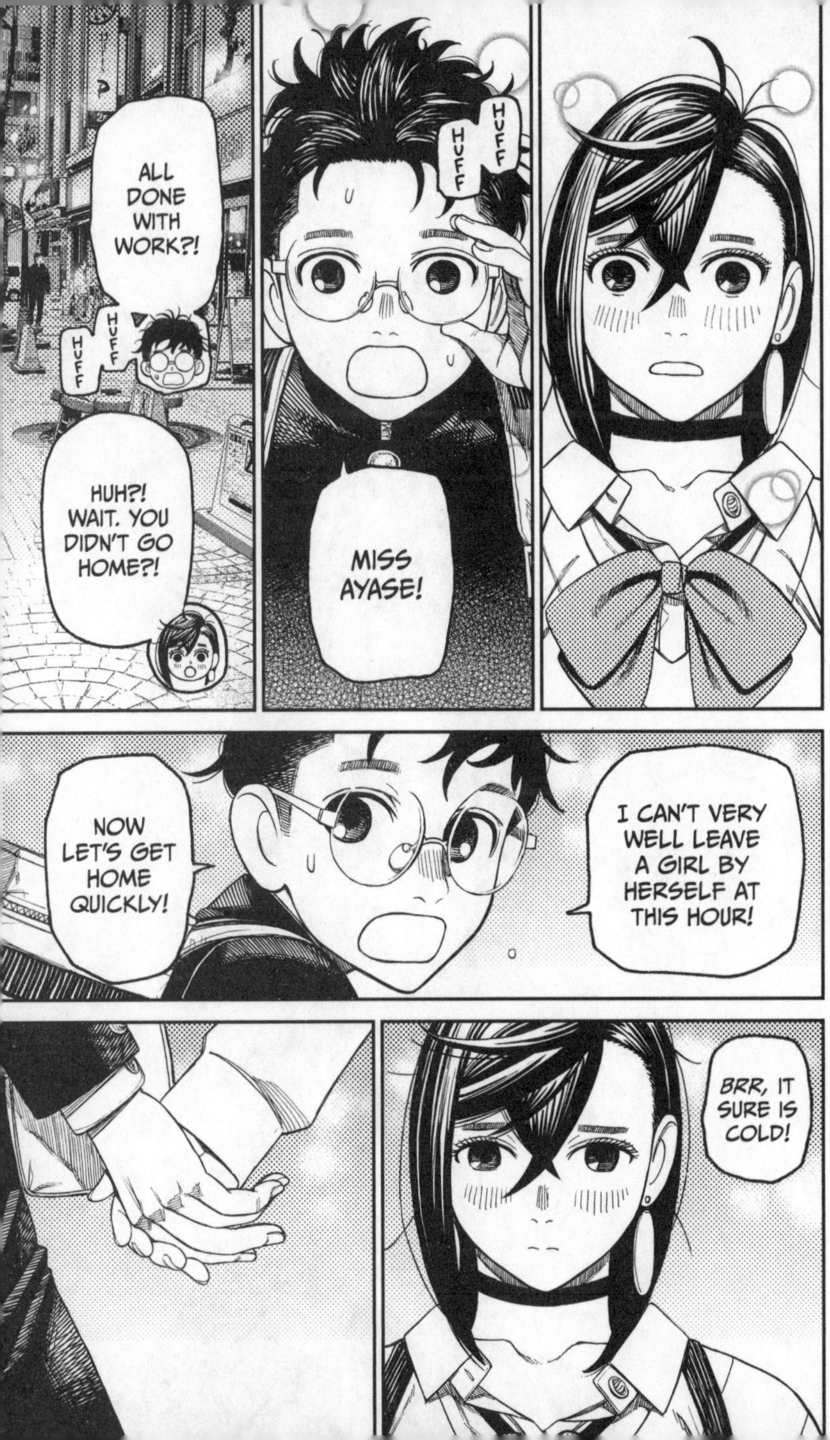
HUFF HUFF
MISS AYASE!
ALL DONE WITH WORK?!
HUFF HUFF
HUH?! WAIT. YOU DIDN'T GO HOME?!
I CAN'T VERY WELL LEAVE A GIRL BY HERSELF AT THIS HOUR!
NOW LET'S GET HOME QUICKLY!
BRR, IT SURE IS COLD!

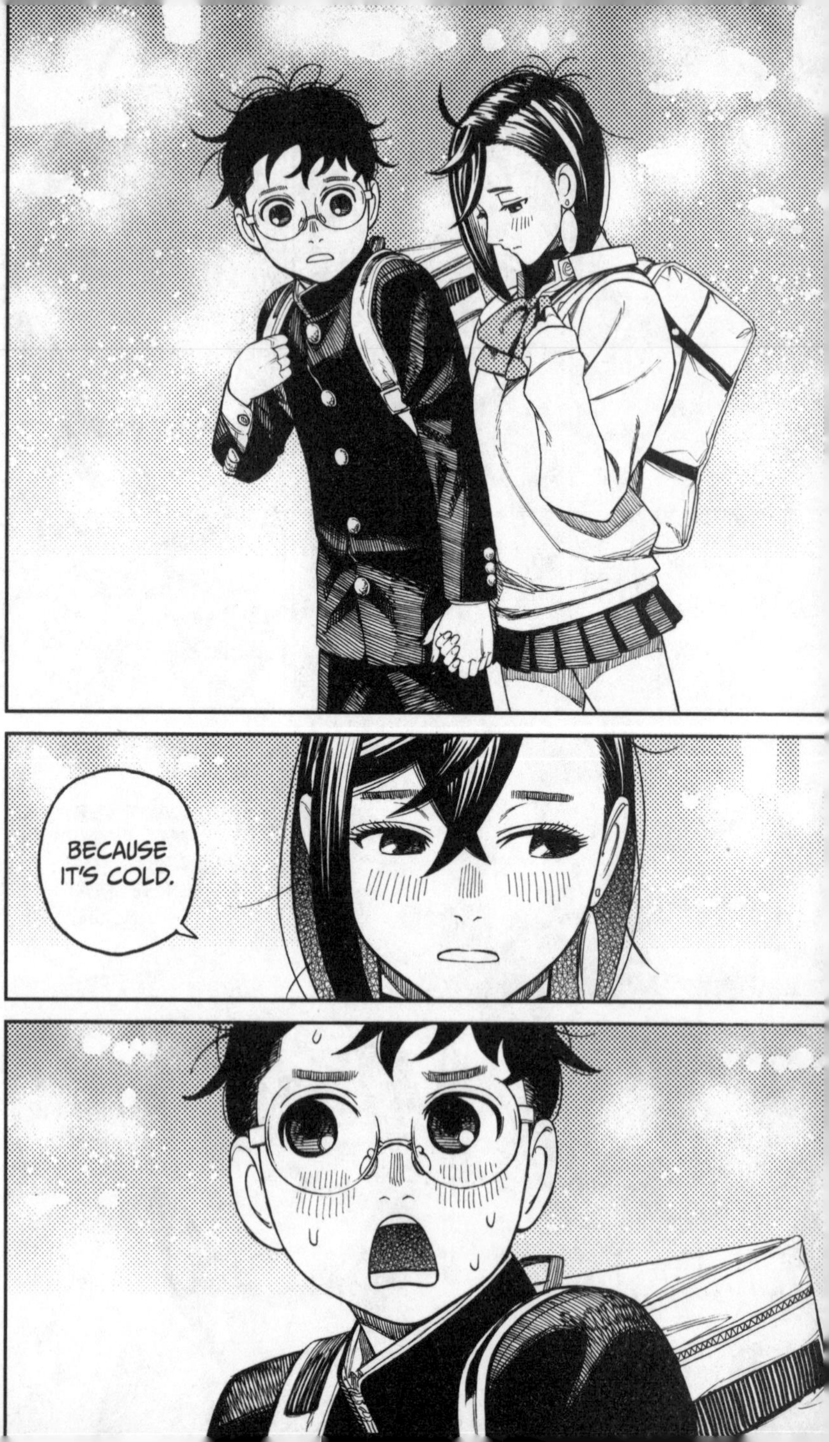
BECAUSE IT'S COLD.

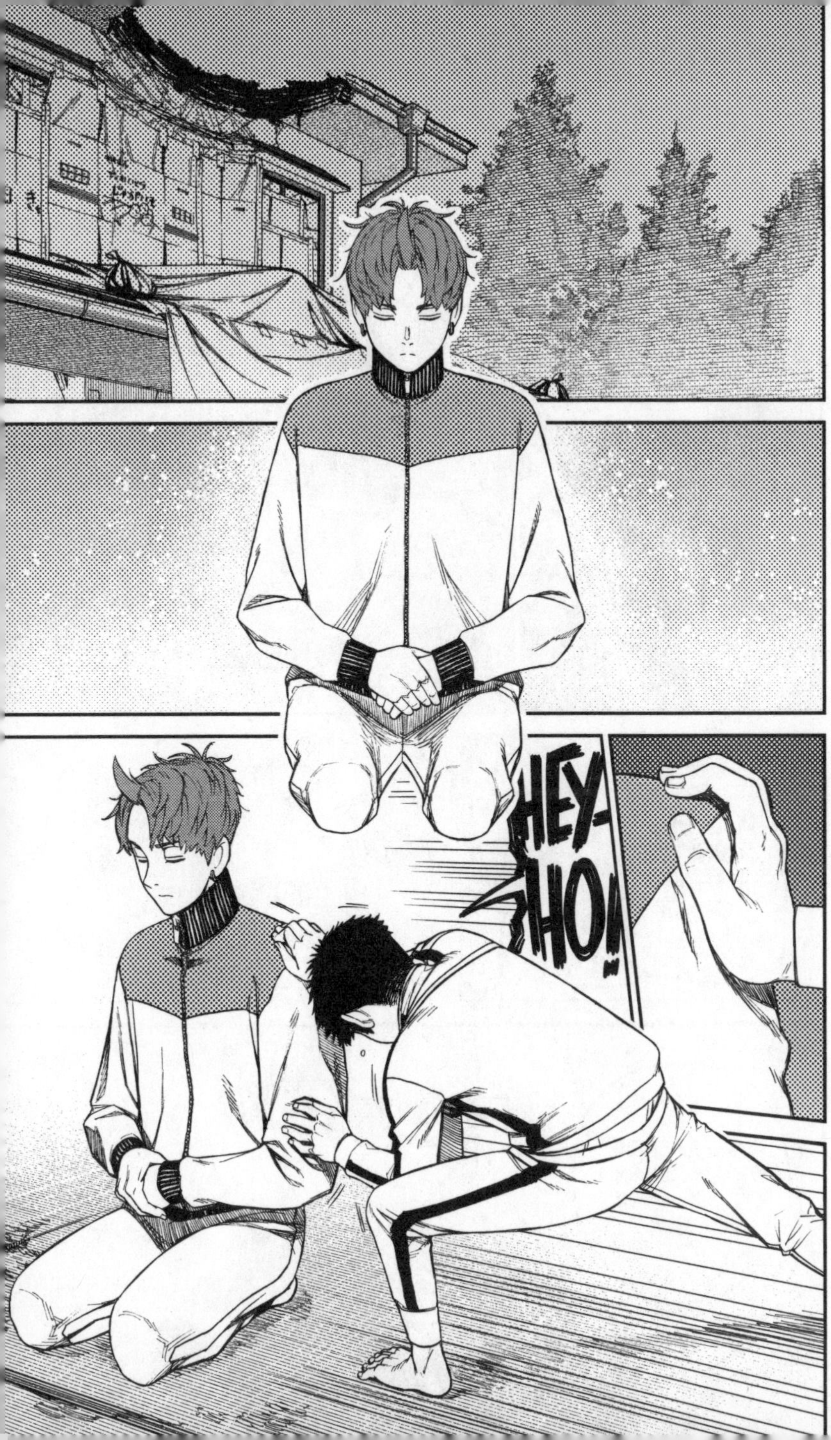
HEY-SHO!!

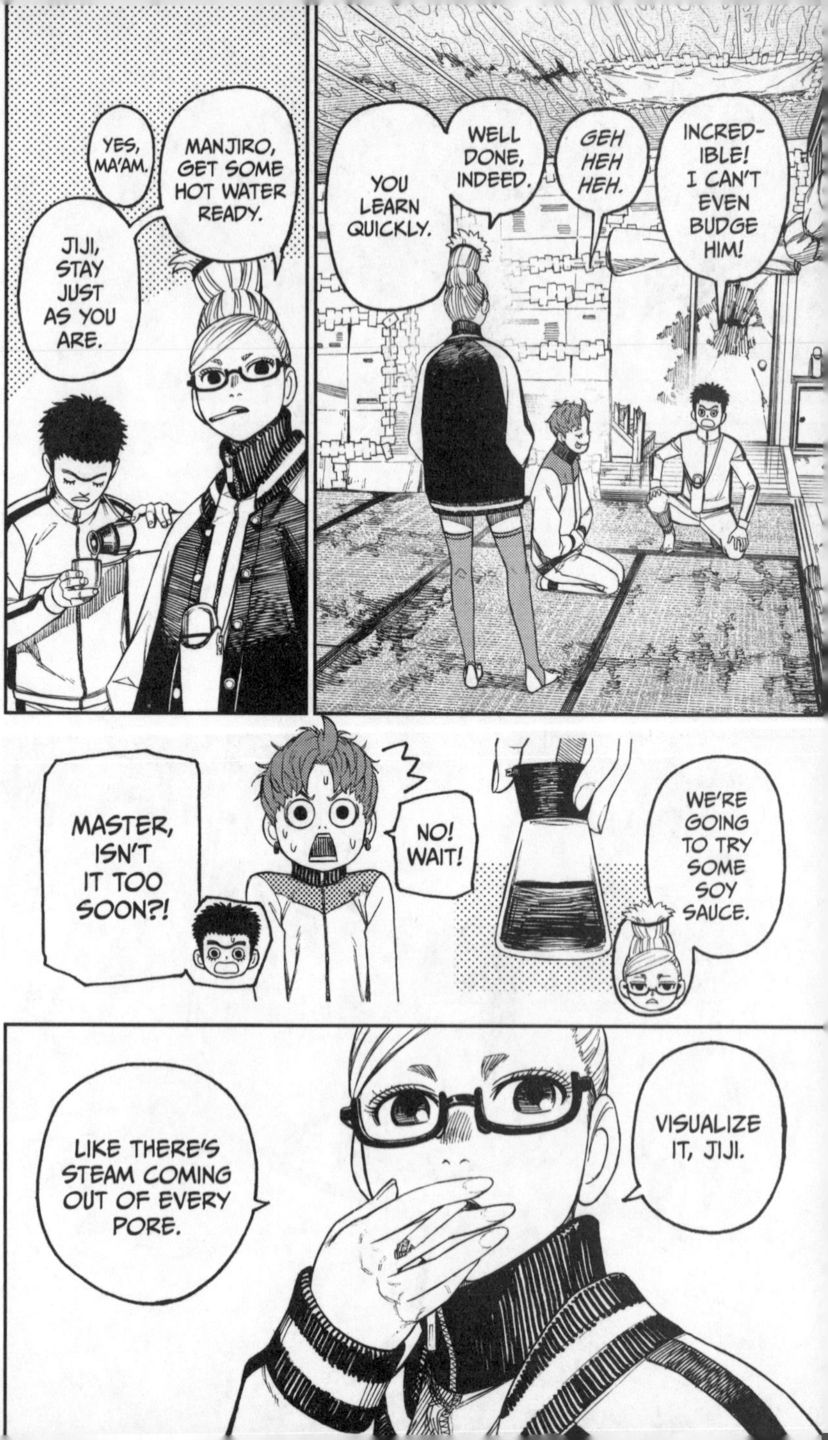
INCREDIBLE! I CAN'T EVEN BUDGE HIM!
GEH HEH HEH.
WELL DONE, INDEED.
YOU LEARN QUICKLY.
MANJIRO, GET SOME HOT WATER READY.
YES, MA'AM.
JIJI, STAY JUST AS YOU ARE.
WE'RE GOING TO TRY SOME SOY SAUCE.
NO! WAIT!
MASTER, ISN'T IT TOO SOON?!
VISUALIZE IT, JIJI.
LIKE THERE'S STEAM COMING OUT OF EVERY PORE.

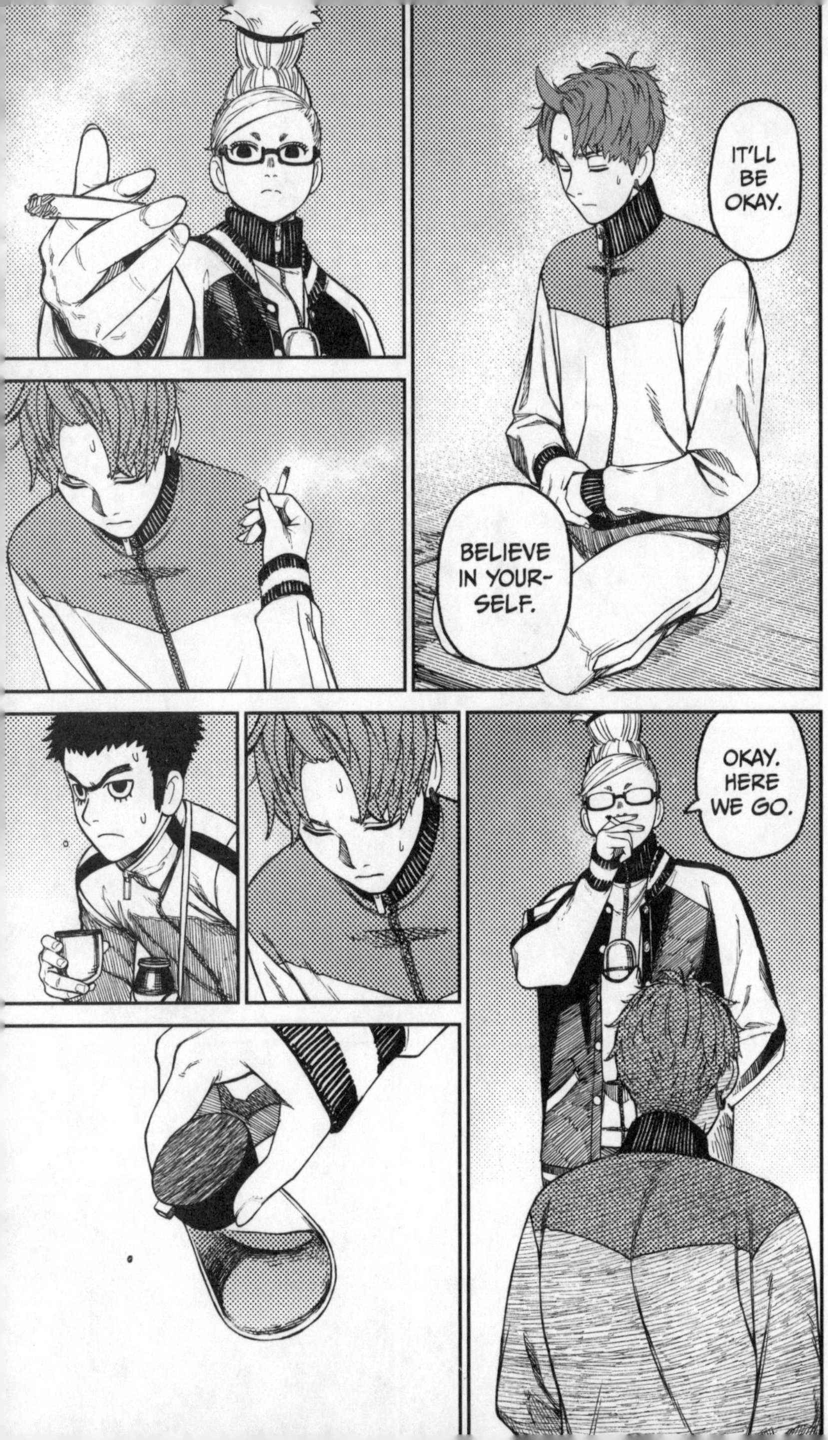
IT'LL BE OKAY.
BELIEVE IN YOUR-SELF.
OKAY. HERE WE GO.

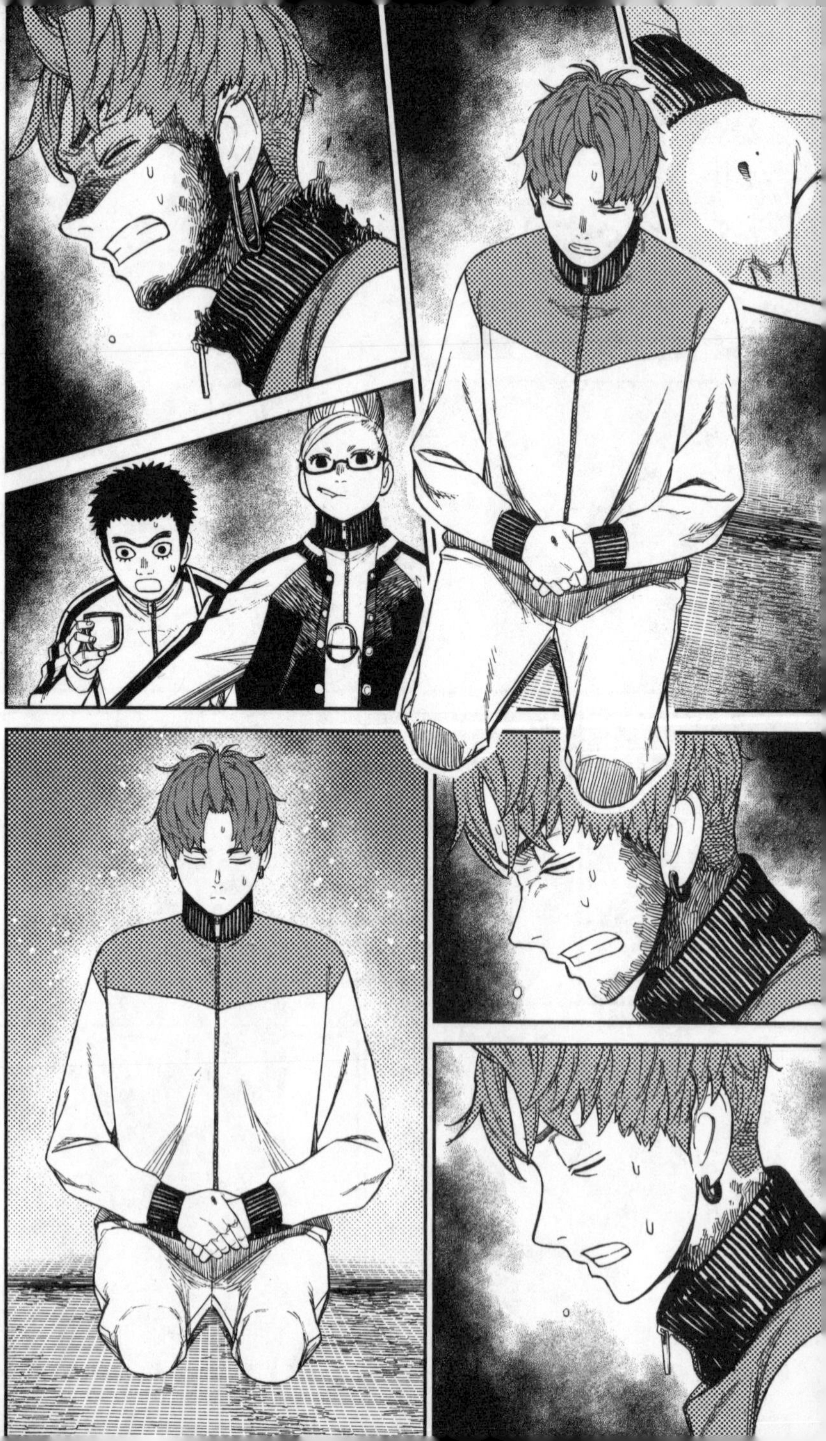

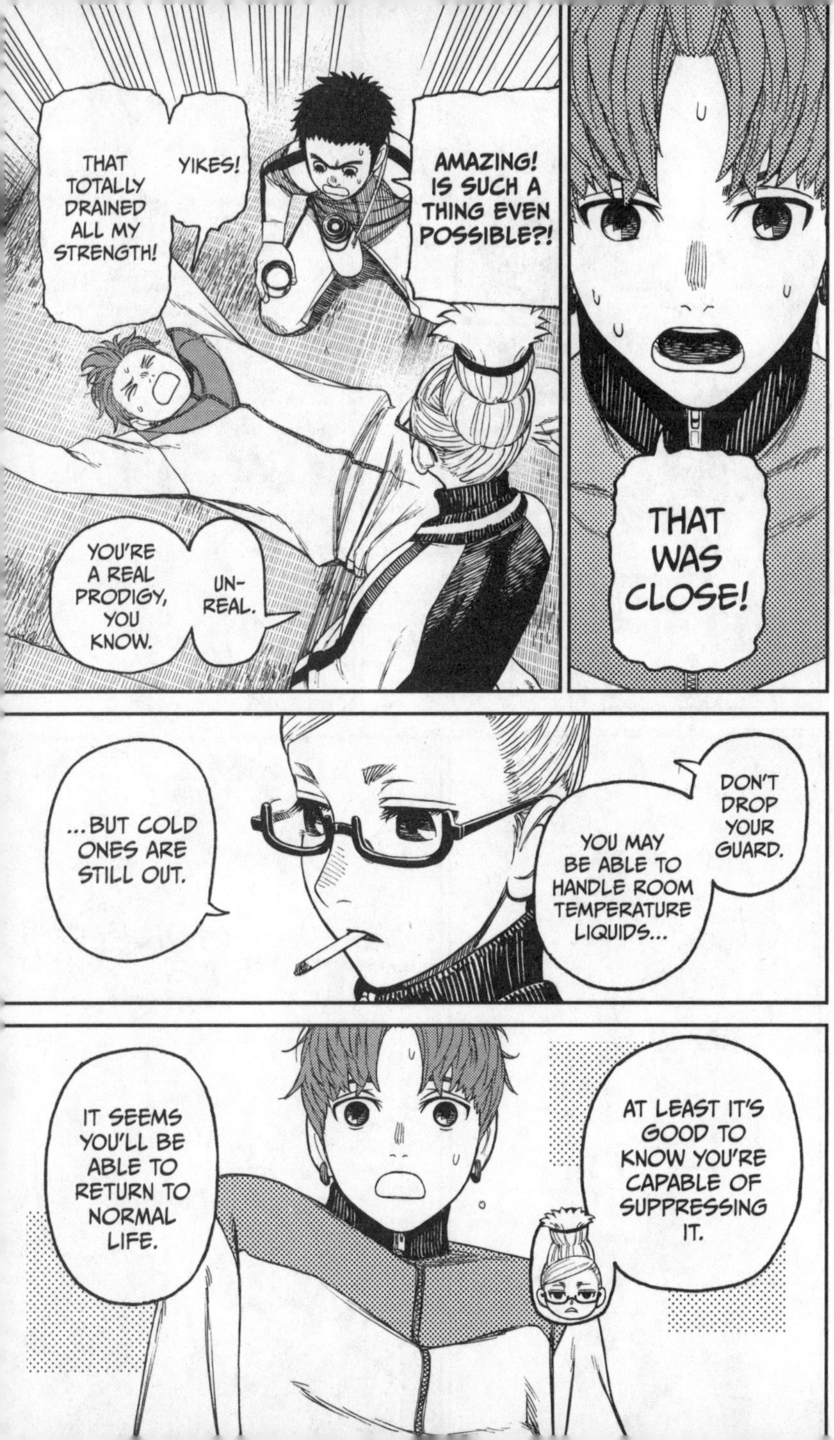
THAT WAS CLOSE!
AMAZING! IS SUCH A THING EVEN POSSIBLE?!
YIKES!
THAT TOTALLY DRAINED ALL MY STRENGTH!
UN-REAL.
YOU'RE A REAL PRODIGY, YOU KNOW.
DON'T DROP YOUR GUARD.
YOU MAY BE ABLE TO HANDLE ROOM TEMPERATURE LIQUIDS...
...BUT COLD ONES ARE STILL OUT.
AT LEAST IT'S GOOD TO KNOW YOU'RE CAPABLE OF SUPPRESSING IT.
IT SEEMS YOU'LL BE ABLE TO RETURN TO NORMAL LIFE.

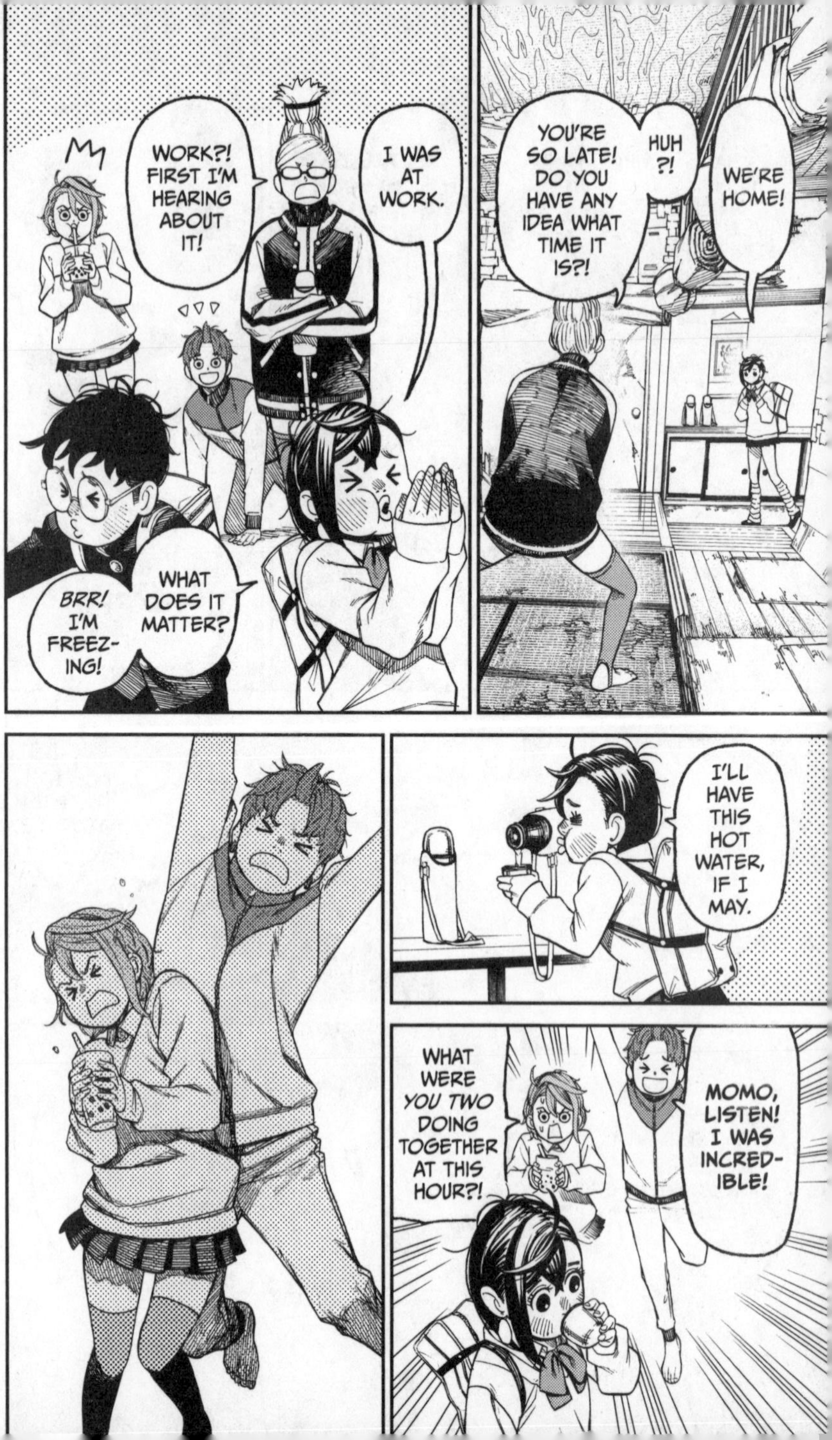
WE'RE HOME!
HUH?!
YOU'RE SO LATE! DO YOU HAVE ANY IDEA WHAT TIME IT IS?!
I WAS AT WORK.
WORK?! FIRST I'M HEARING ABOUT IT!
WHAT DOES IT MATTER?
BRR! I'M FREEZ-ING!
I'LL HAVE THIS HOT WATER, IF I MAY.
MOMO, LISTEN! I WAS INCRED-IBLE!
WHAT WERE *YOU TWO* DOING TOGETHER AT THIS HOUR?!

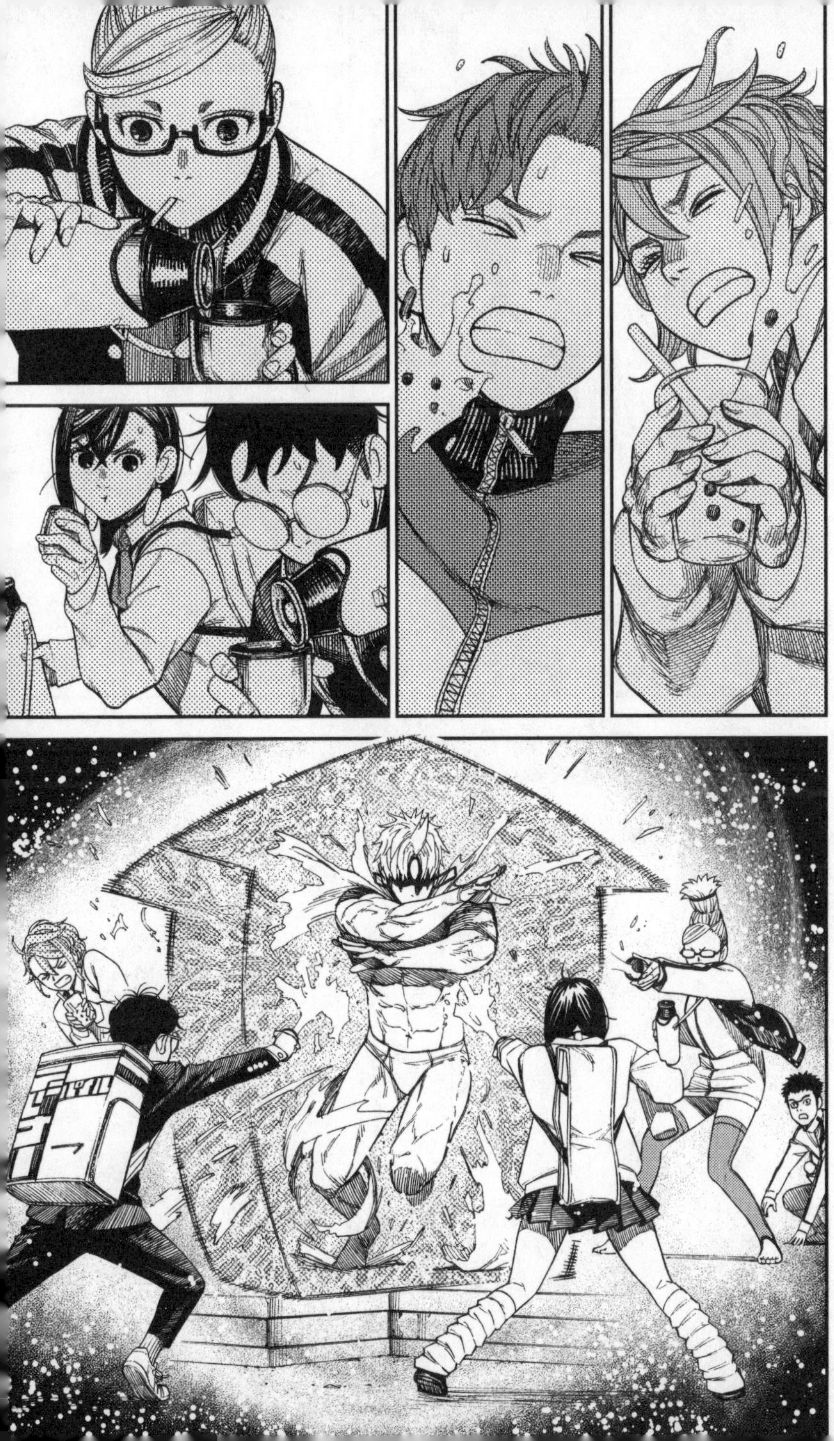

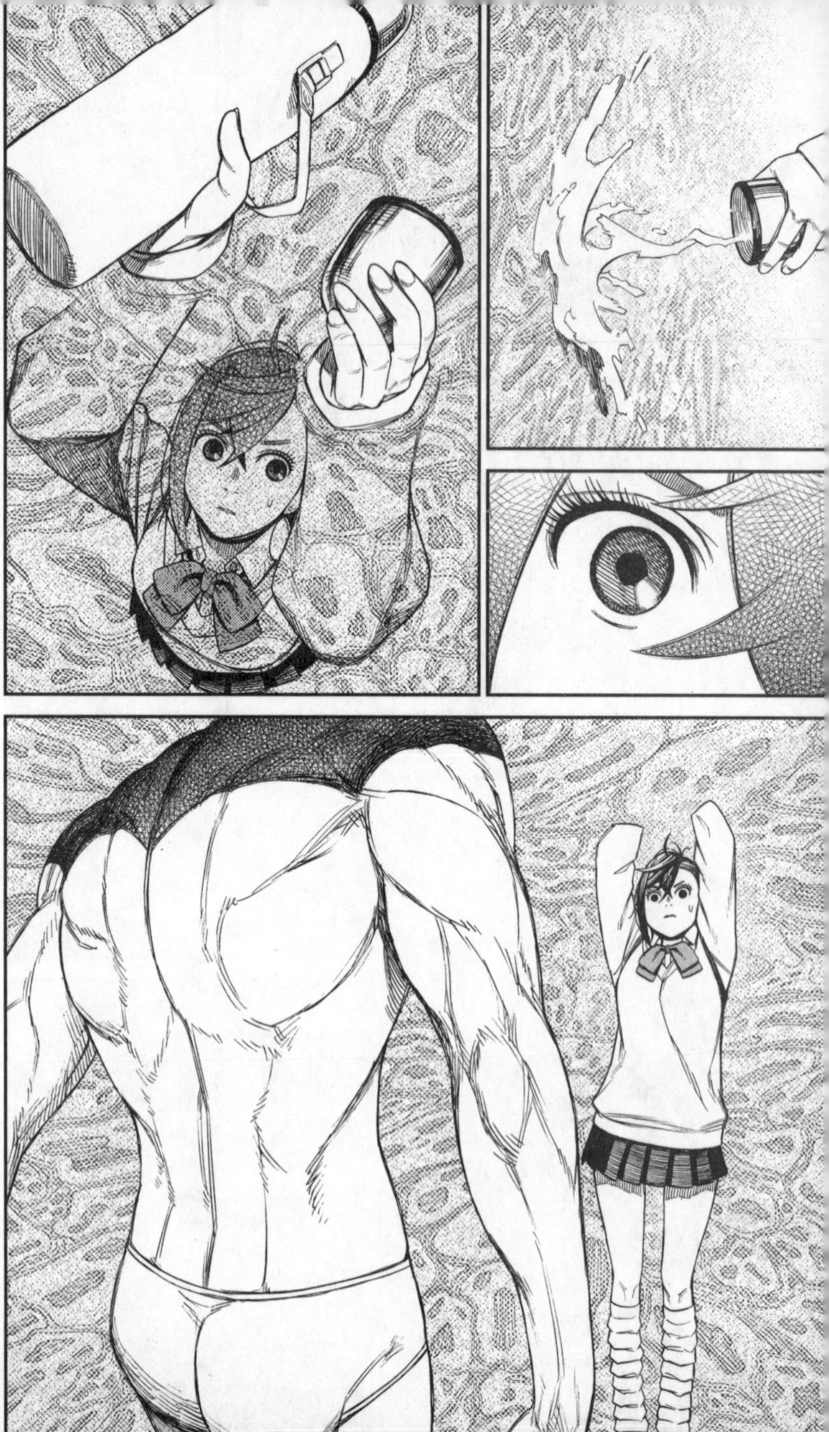

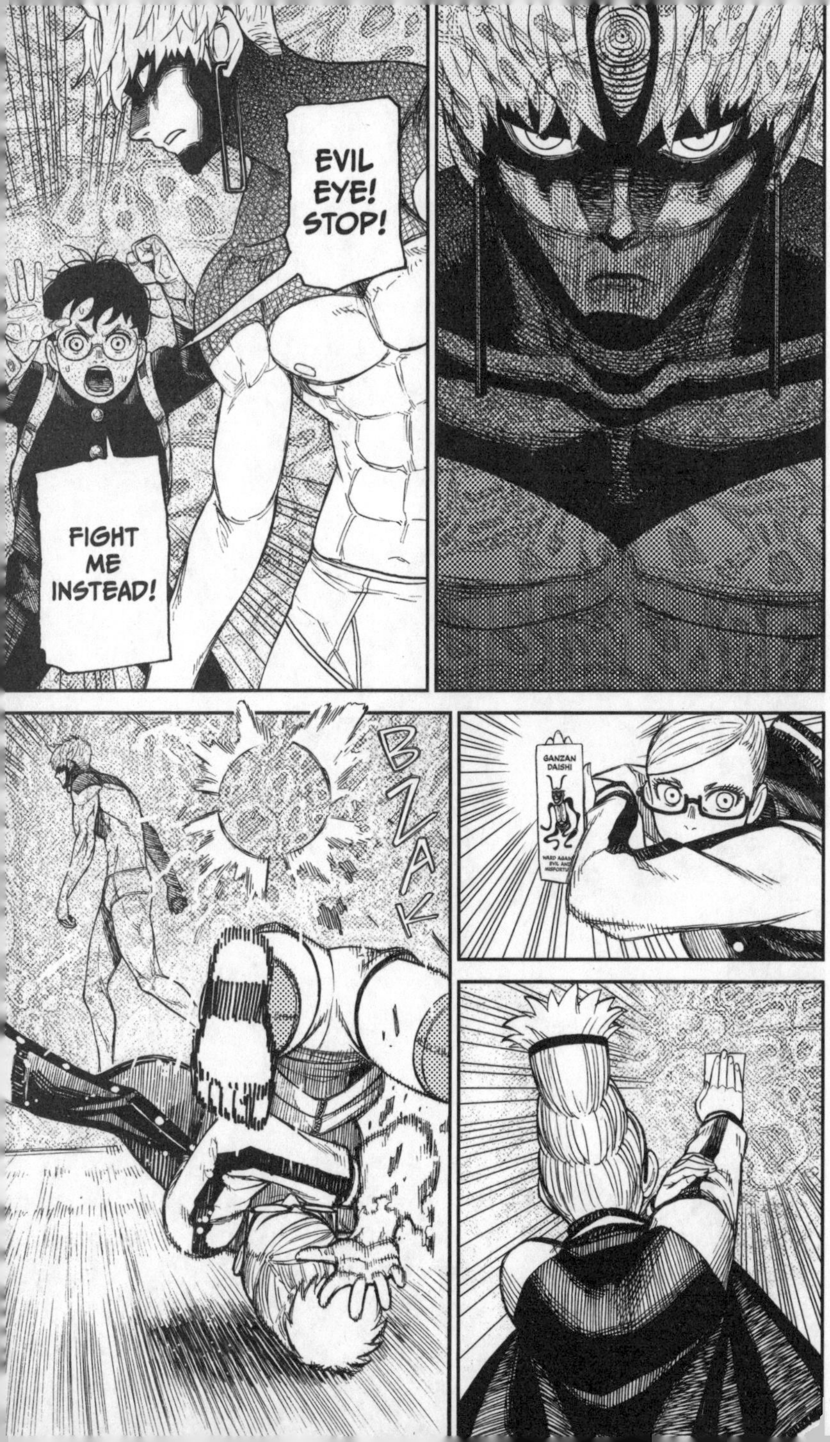
EVIL EYE! STOP!
FIGHT ME INSTEAD!
GANZAN DAISHI
BZAK

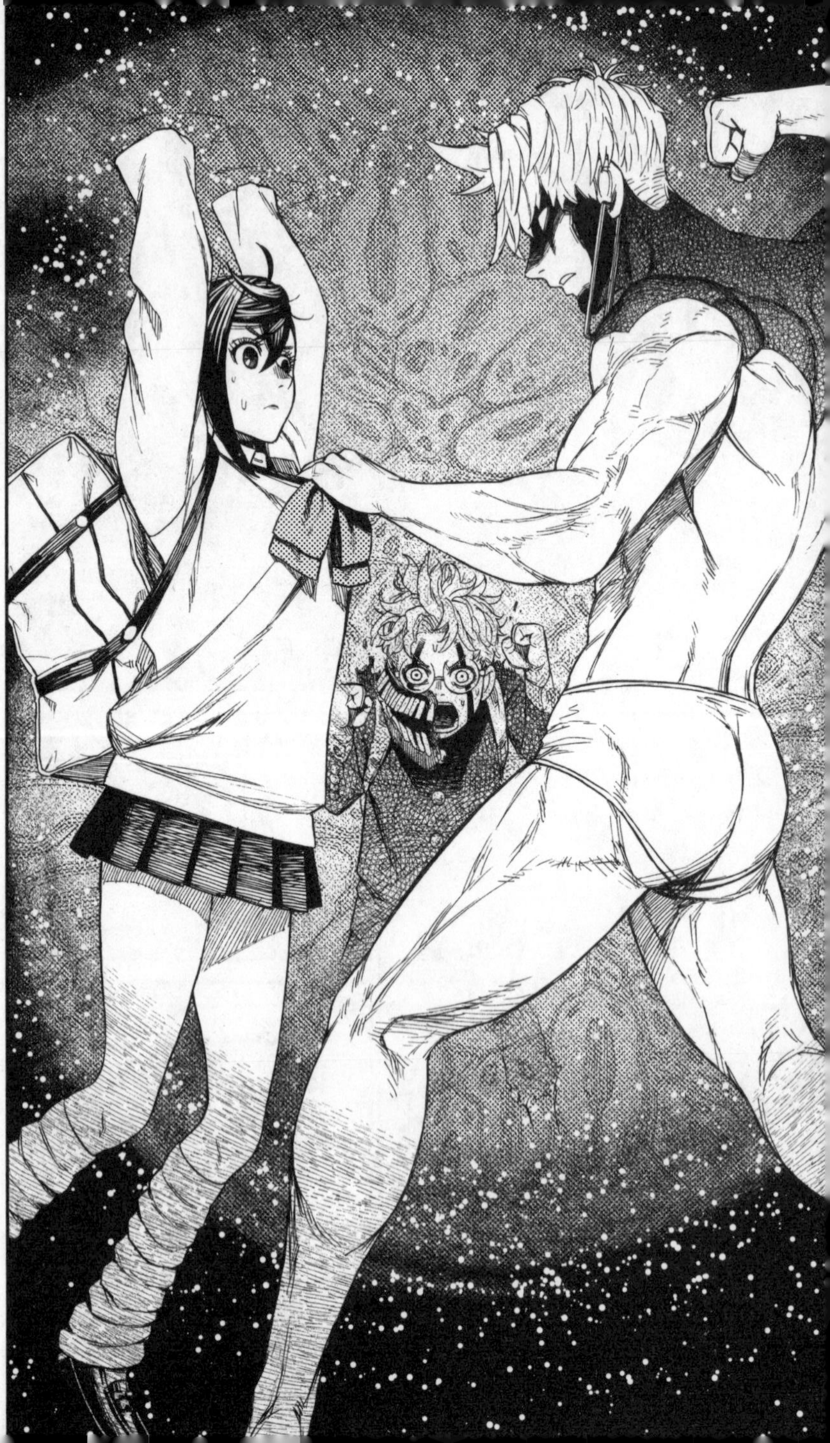

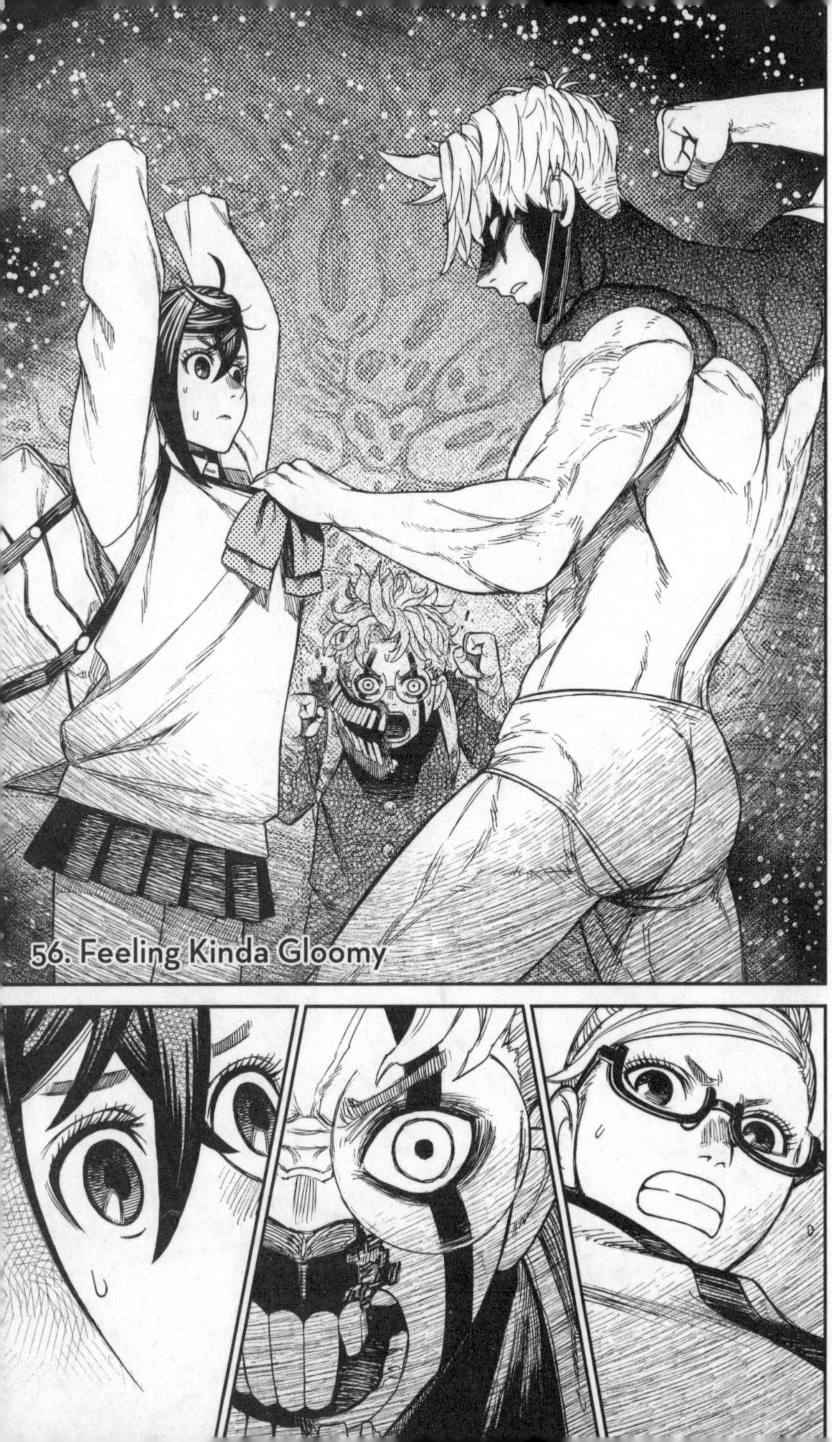
56. Feeling Kinda Gloomy

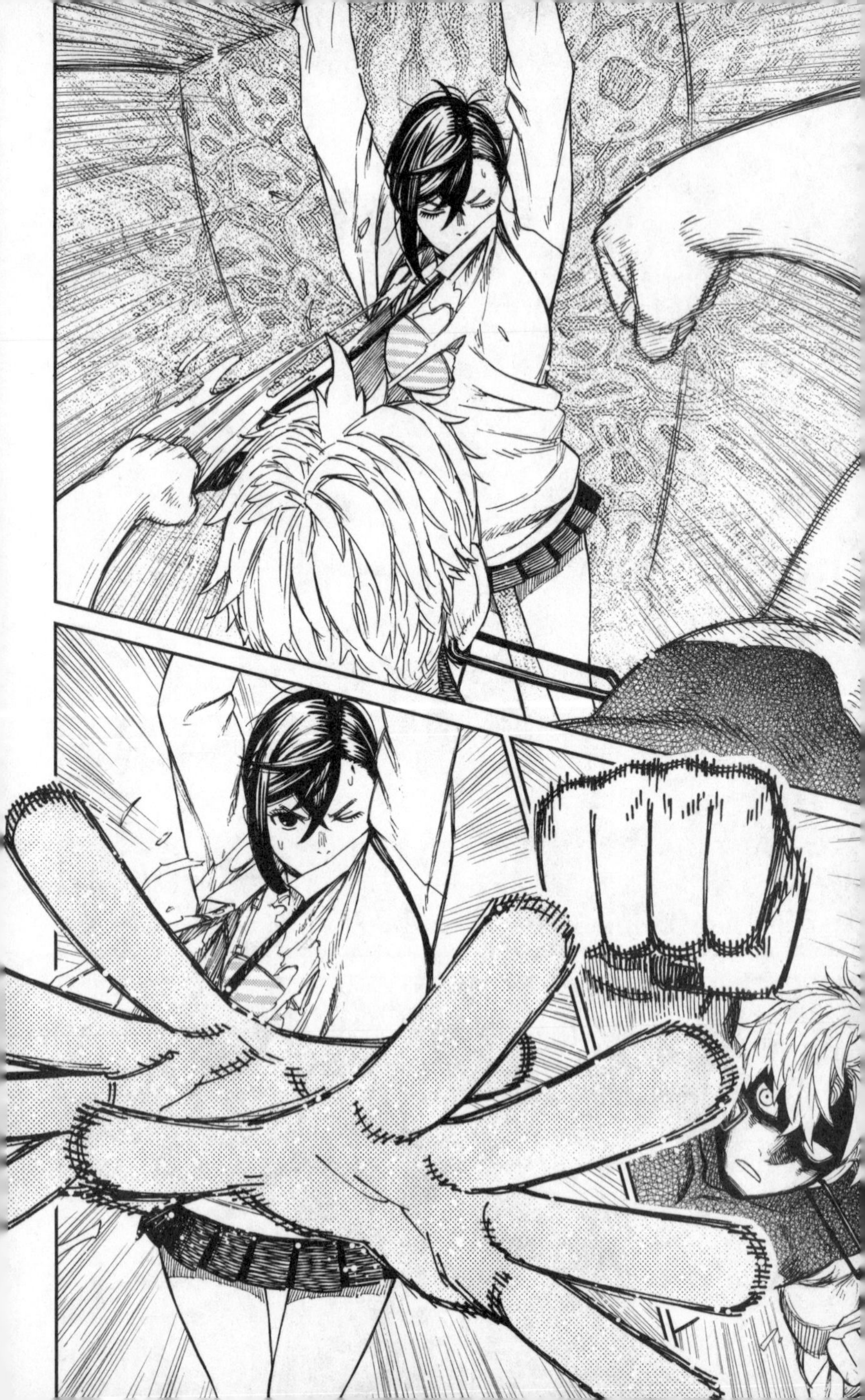

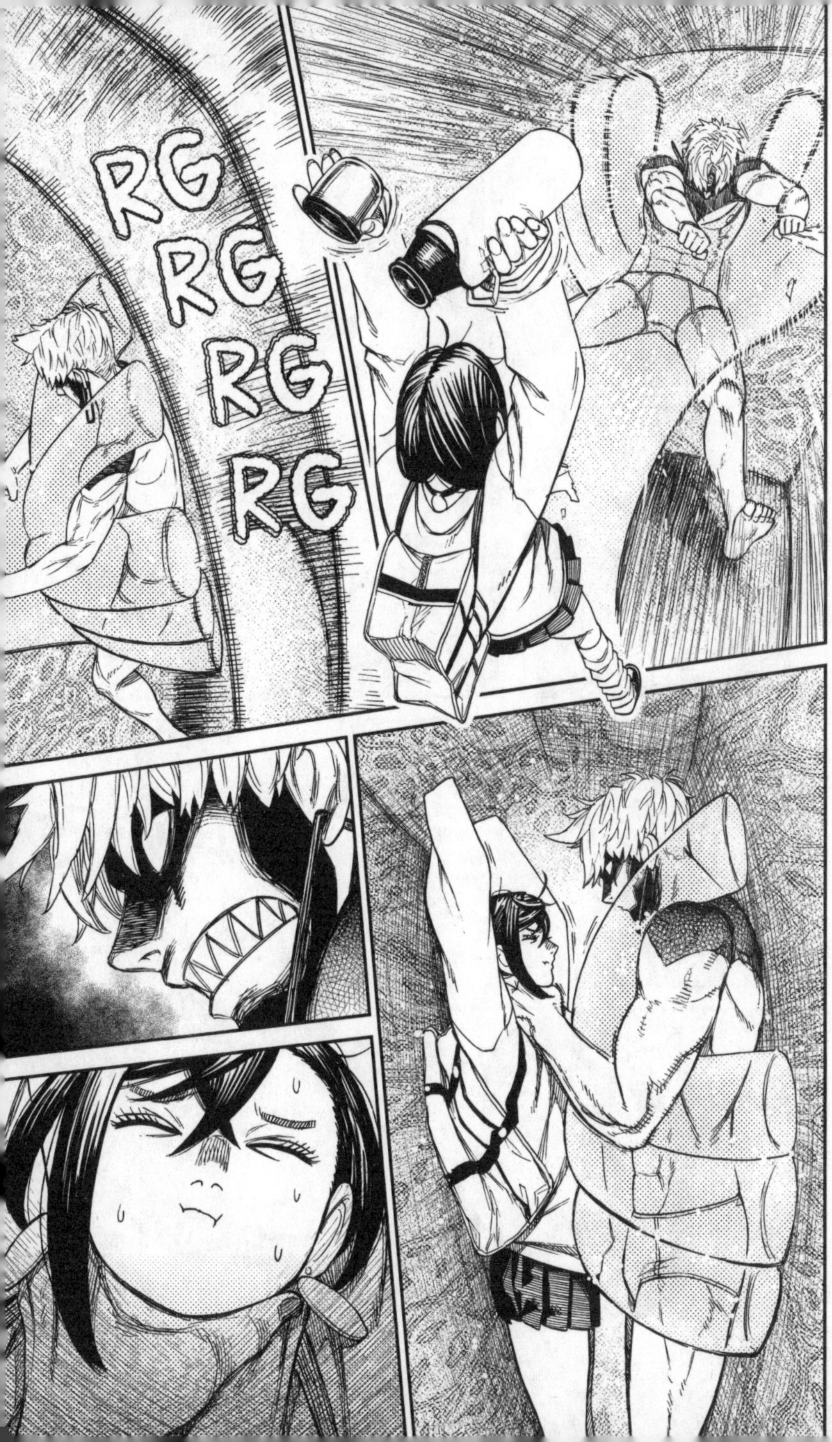
RG
RG
RG
RG

I'LL HAVE SOME OF THIS HOT WATER, IF I MAY.

THAT WAS CLOSE!

THANK GOD I DIDN'T SWALLOW IT!

I... CAN'T BELIEVE I DID THAT!

MOMO! I'M SO SORRY!

IT'S OKAY! IT'S OKAY!

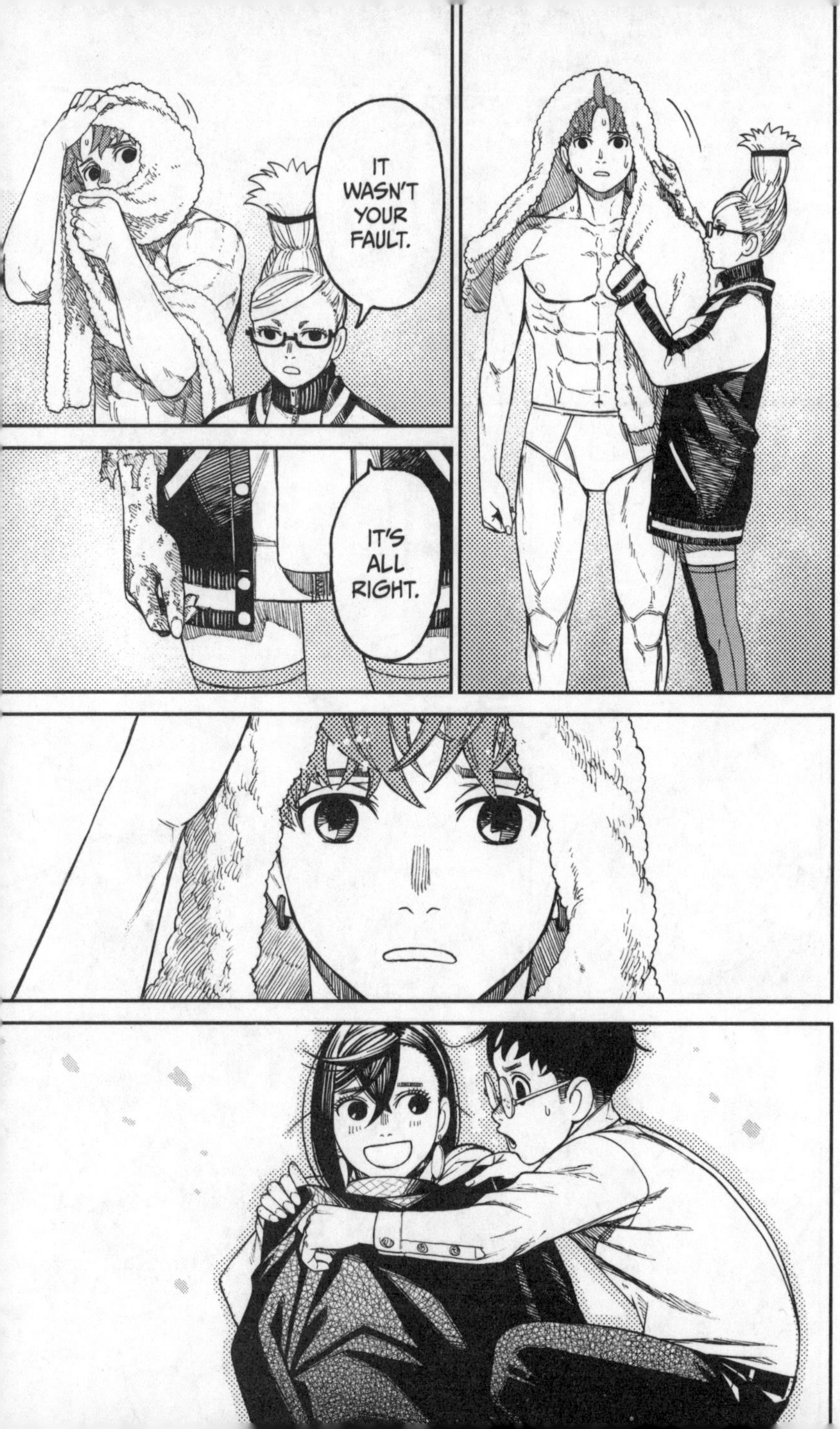
IT WASN'T YOUR FAULT.
IT'S ALL RIGHT.

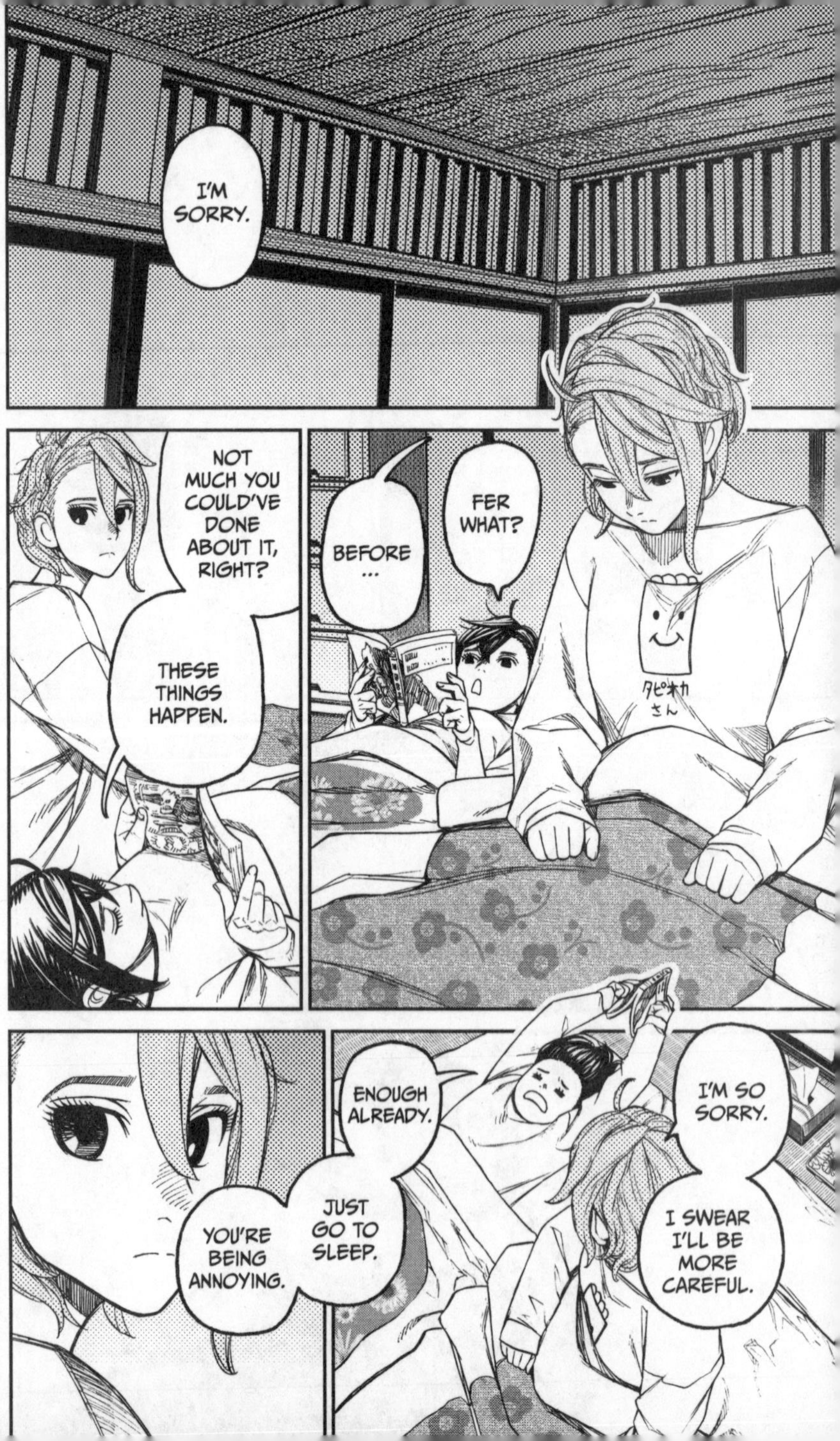
I'M SORRY.
FER WHAT?
BEFORE ...
タピオカさん
NOT MUCH YOU COULD'VE DONE ABOUT IT, RIGHT?
THESE THINGS HAPPEN.
I'M SO SORRY.
I SWEAR I'LL BE MORE CAREFUL.
ENOUGH ALREADY.
JUST GO TO SLEEP.
YOU'RE BEING ANNOYING.

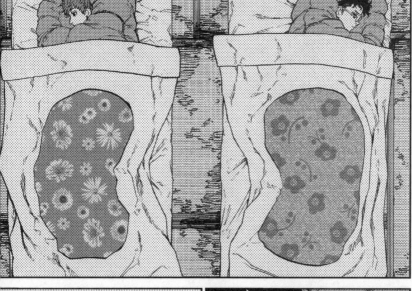

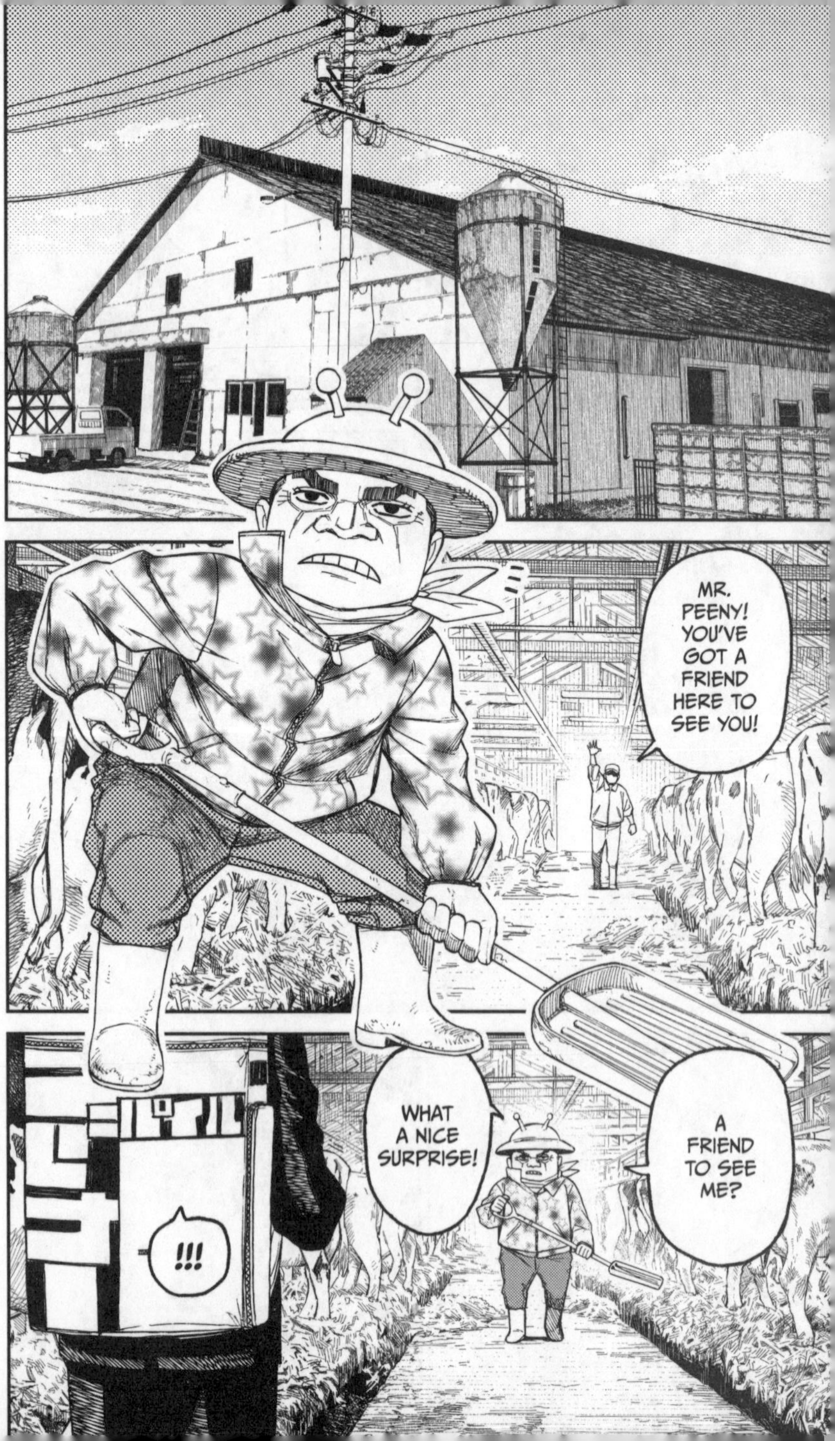
MR. PEENY! YOU'VE GOT A FRIEND HERE TO SEE YOU!
A FRIEND TO SEE ME?
WHAT A NICE SURPRISE!
!!!

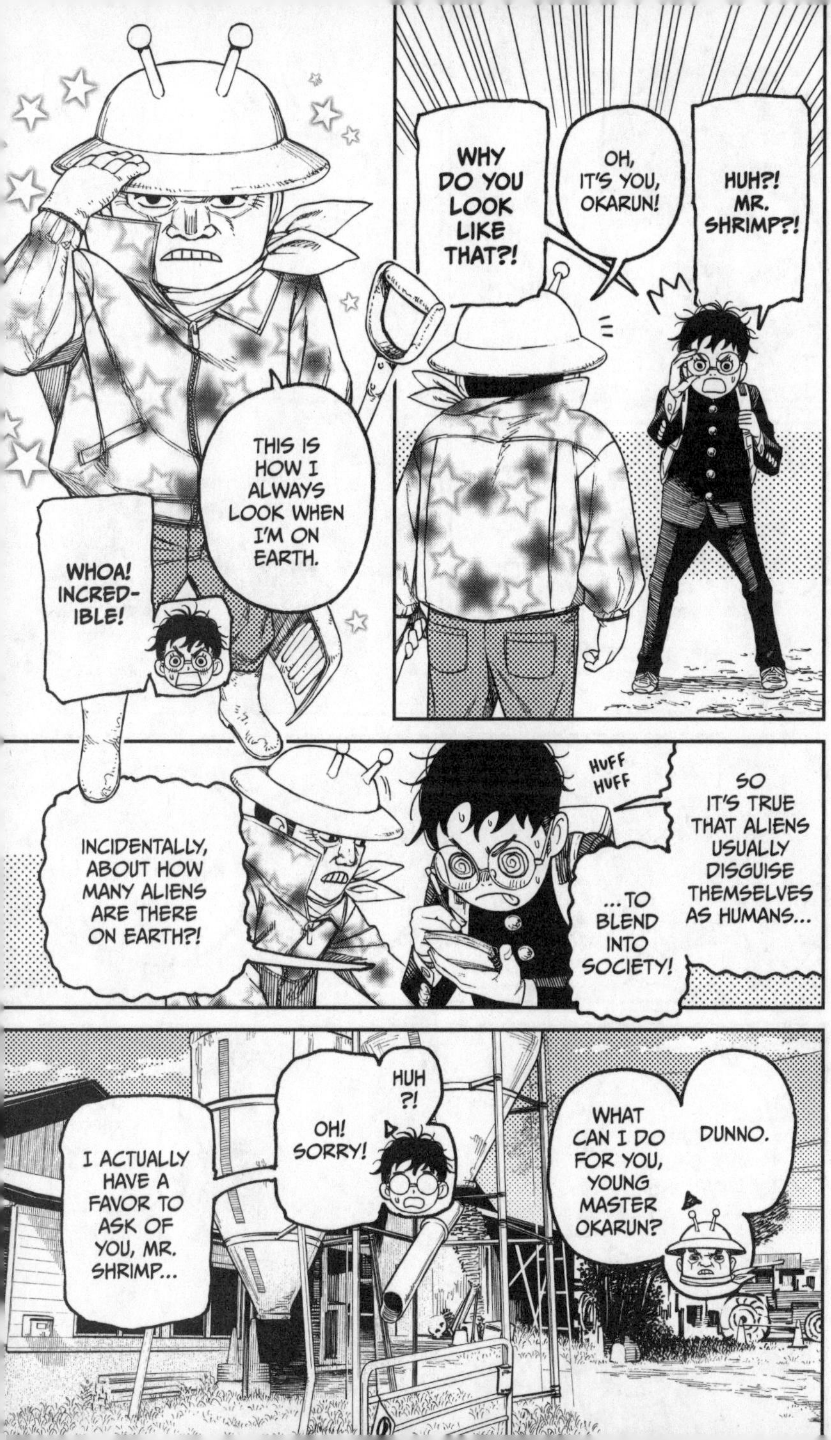
HUH?! MR. SHRIMP?!
OH, IT'S YOU, OKARUN!
WHY DO YOU LOOK LIKE THAT?!
THIS IS HOW I ALWAYS LOOK WHEN I'M ON EARTH.
WHOA! INCRED-IBLE!
SO IT'S TRUE THAT ALIENS USUALLY DISGUISE THEMSELVES AS HUMANS...
HUFF HUFF
...TO BLEND INTO SOCIETY!
INCIDENTALLY, ABOUT HOW MANY ALIENS ARE THERE ON EARTH?!
DUNNO.
WHAT CAN I DO FOR YOU, YOUNG MASTER OKARUN?
HUH?!
OH! SORRY!
I ACTUALLY HAVE A FAVOR TO ASK OF YOU, MR. SHRIMP...

UH, IF I HELP, WILL YOU MAKE ME YOUR APPRENTICE?

THERE'S NO TIME TO BE PUTTING YOUR FEET UP.

EH?!

ANYWAY, COULD YOU TAKE THESE BAGS OVER THERE?

NO WAY.

WHY NOT?!

WEEZ WEEZ

I WON'T... LOSE HEART!

NOT ME...

TOMORROW, I'LL GET HIM TO TEACH ME TO PUNCH FOR SURE...

I'M BACK!

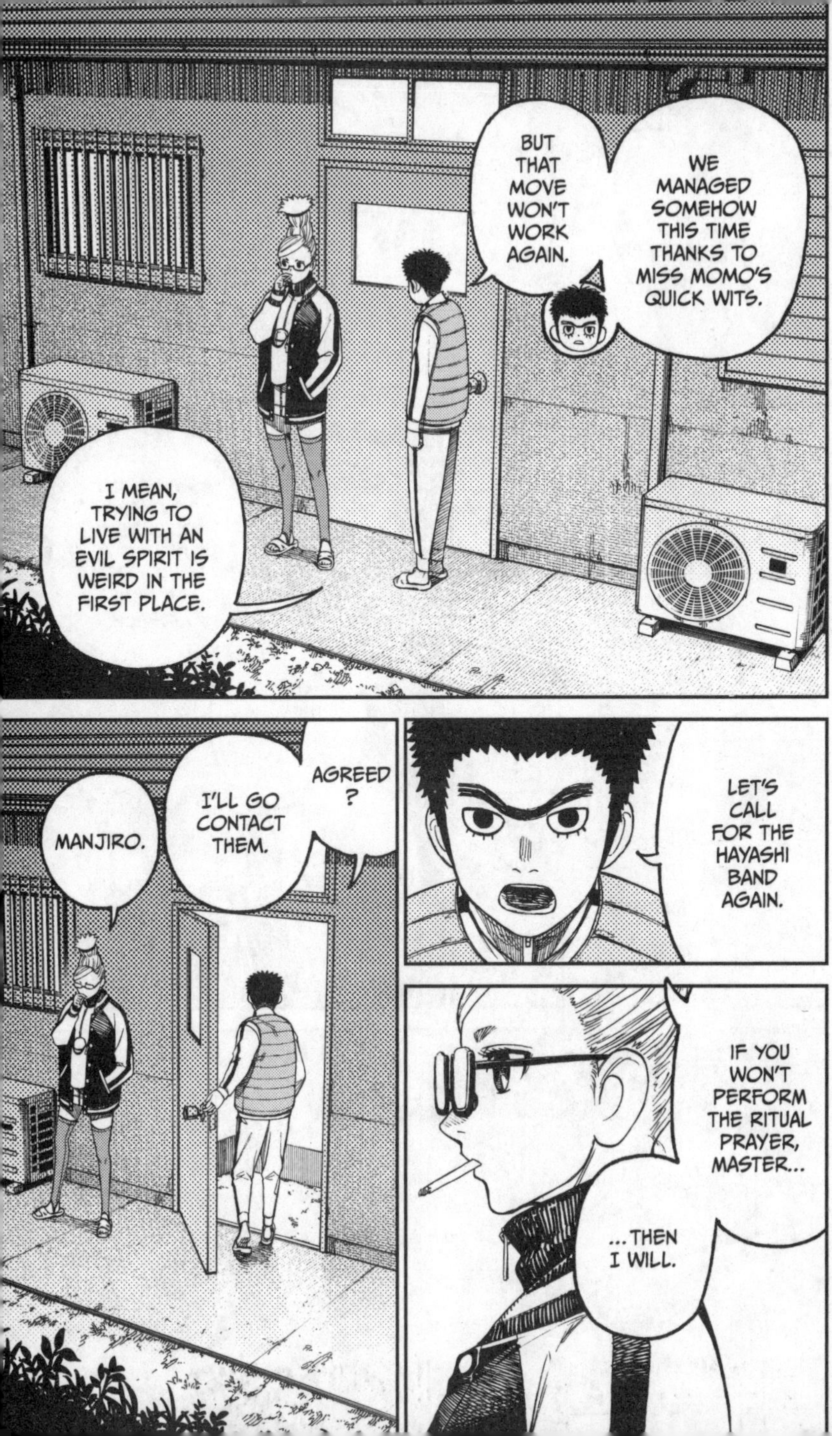
WE MANAGED SOMEHOW THIS TIME THANKS TO MISS MOMO'S QUICK WITS.
BUT THAT MOVE WON'T WORK AGAIN.
I MEAN, TRYING TO LIVE WITH AN EVIL SPIRIT IS WEIRD IN THE FIRST PLACE.
LET'S CALL FOR THE HAYASHI BAND AGAIN.
IF YOU WON'T PERFORM THE RITUAL PRAYER, MASTER...
...THEN I WILL.
AGREED?
I'LL GO CONTACT THEM.
MANJIRO.

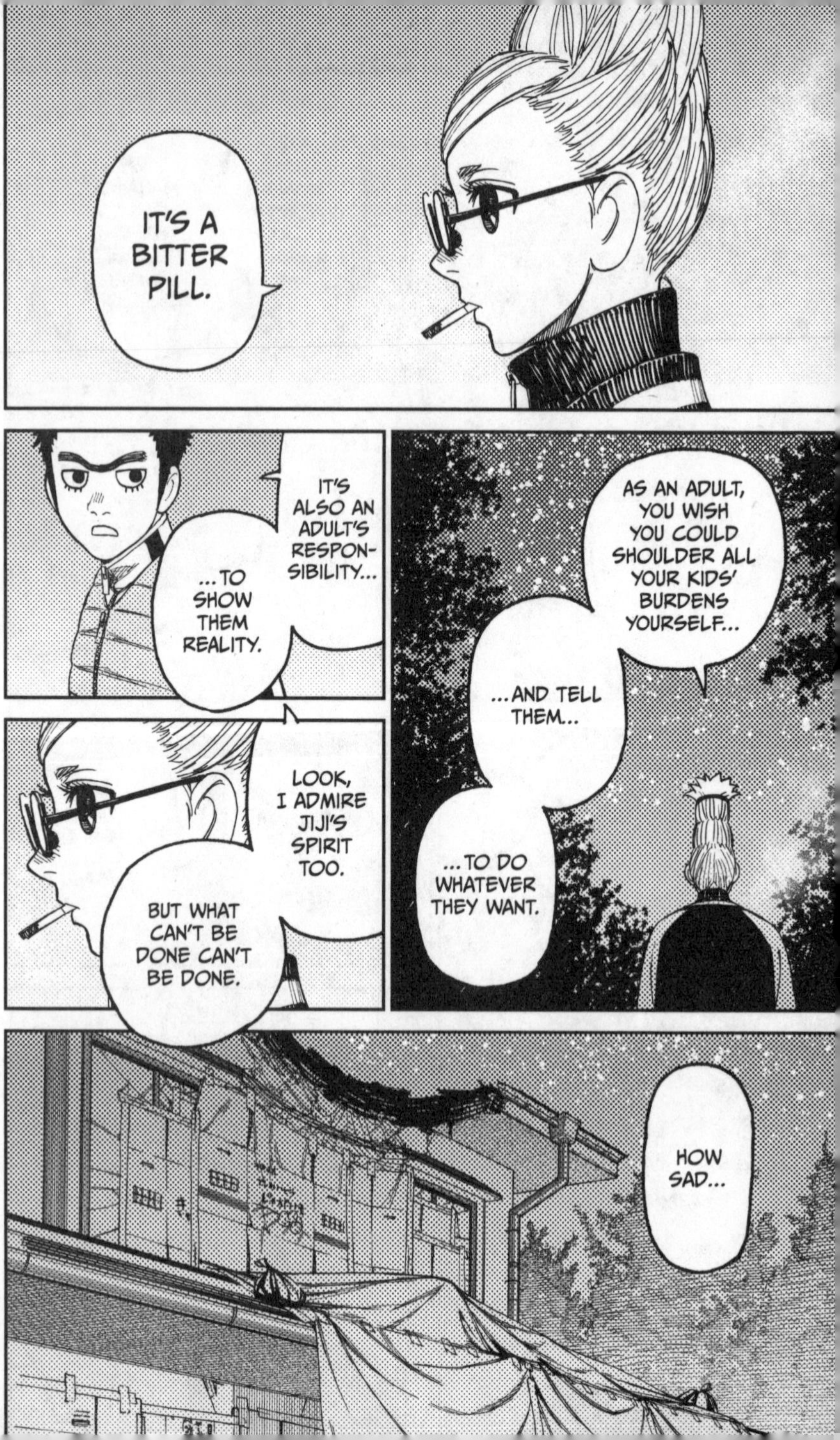
IT'S A BITTER PILL.
AS AN ADULT, YOU WISH YOU COULD SHOULDER ALL YOUR KIDS' BURDENS YOURSELF...
...AND TELL THEM...
...TO DO WHATEVER THEY WANT.
IT'S ALSO AN ADULT'S RESPON-SIBILITY...
...TO SHOW THEM REALITY.
LOOK, I ADMIRE JIJI'S SPIRIT TOO.
BUT WHAT CAN'T BE DONE CAN'T BE DONE.
HOW SAD...

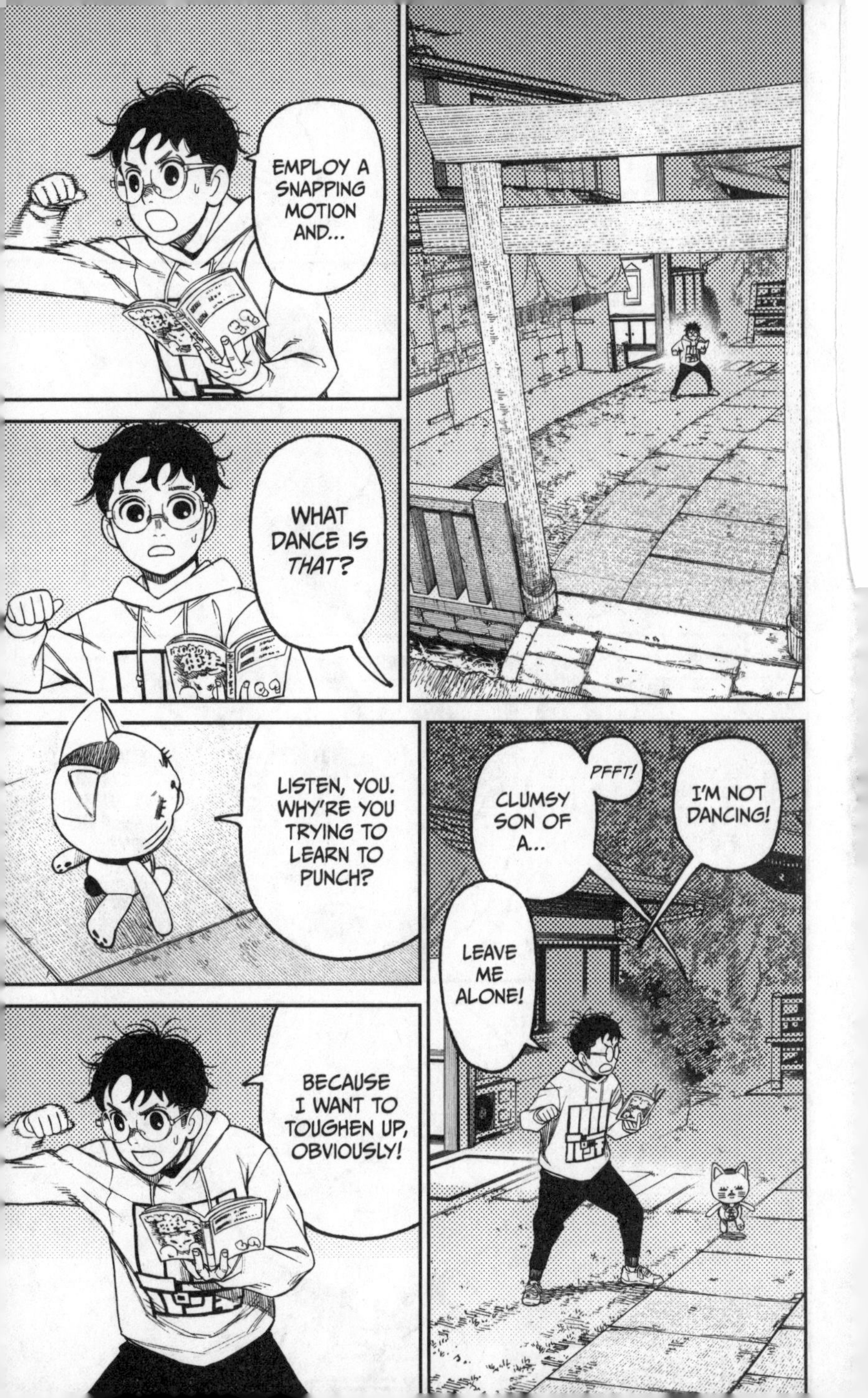
EMPLOY A SNAPPING MOTION AND...
WHAT DANCE IS *THAT*?
I'M NOT DANCING!
PFFT!
CLUMSY SON OF A...
LEAVE ME ALONE!
LISTEN, YOU. WHY'RE YOU TRYING TO LEARN TO PUNCH?
BECAUSE I WANT TO TOUGHEN UP, OBVIOUSLY!

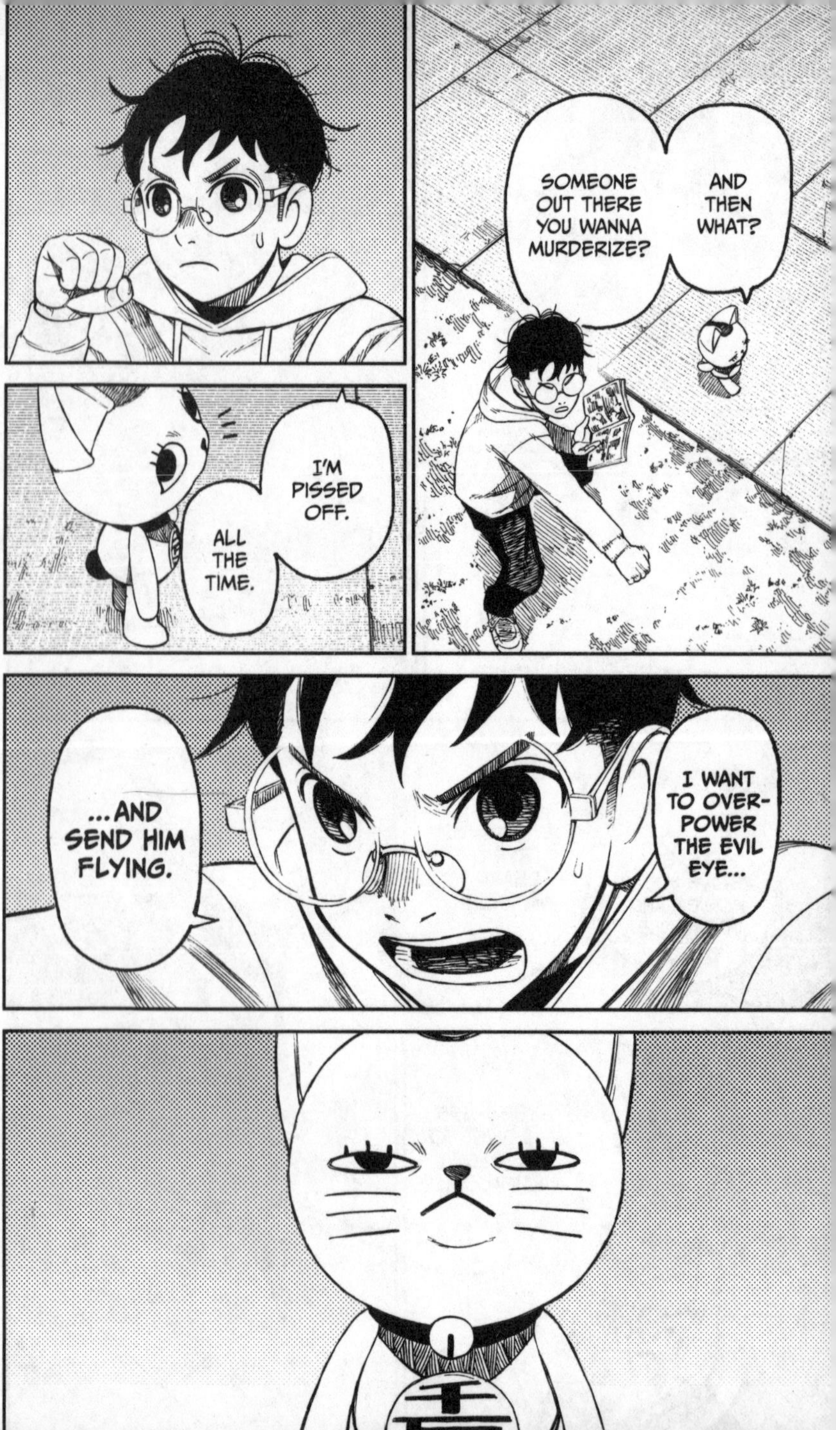
AND THEN WHAT?
SOMEONE OUT THERE YOU WANNA MURDERIZE?
I'M PISSED OFF.
ALL THE TIME.
I WANT TO OVER-POWER THE EVIL EYE...
...AND SEND HIM FLYING.

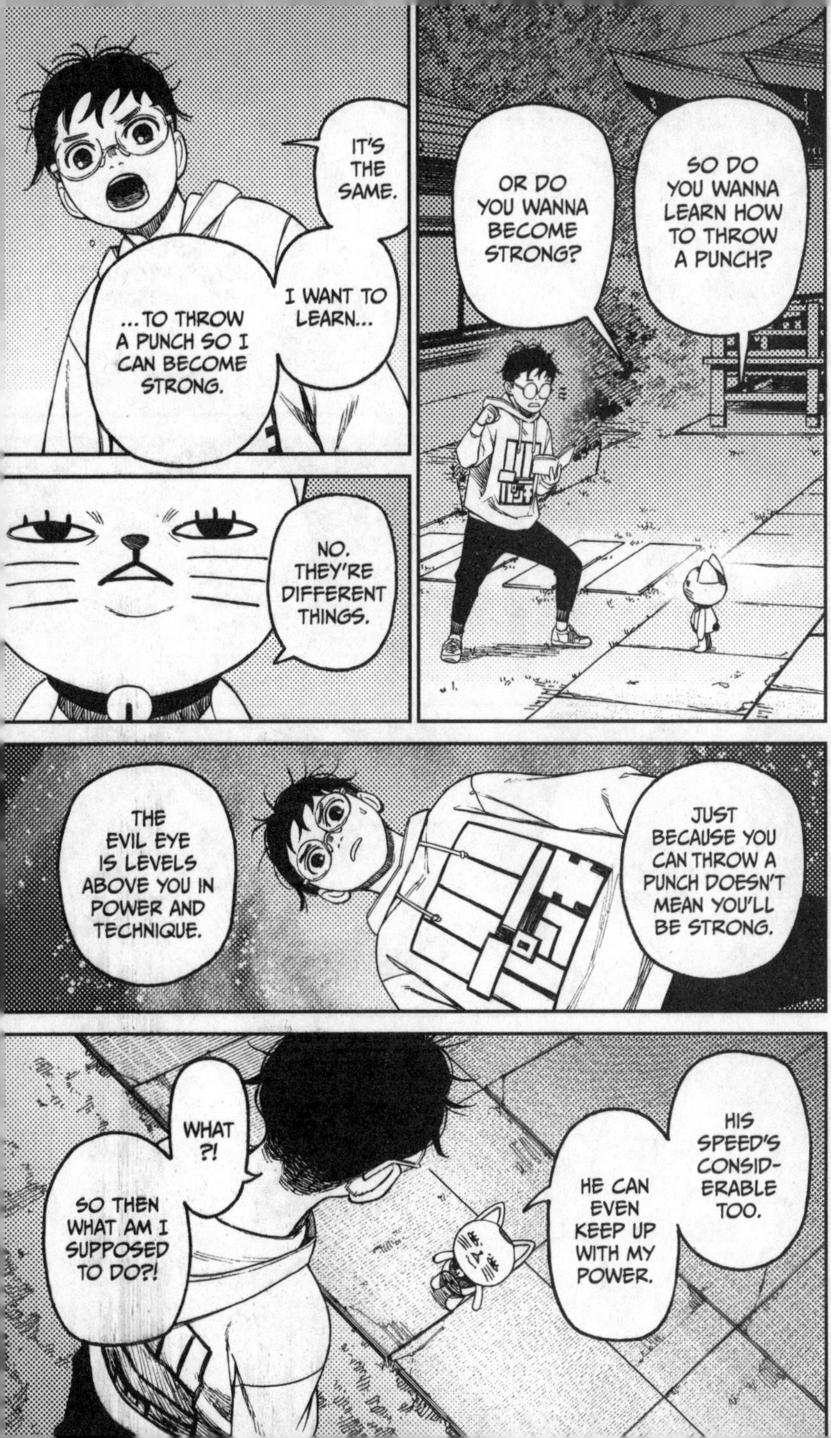
SO DO YOU WANNA LEARN HOW TO THROW A PUNCH?
OR DO YOU WANNA BECOME STRONG?
IT'S THE SAME.
I WANT TO LEARN...
...TO THROW A PUNCH SO I CAN BECOME STRONG.
NO. THEY'RE DIFFERENT THINGS.
JUST BECAUSE YOU CAN THROW A PUNCH DOESN'T MEAN YOU'LL BE STRONG.
THE EVIL EYE IS LEVELS ABOVE YOU IN POWER AND TECHNIQUE.
HIS SPEED'S CONSID-ERABLE TOO.
HE CAN EVEN KEEP UP WITH MY POWER.
WHAT?!
SO THEN WHAT AM I SUPPOSED TO DO?!

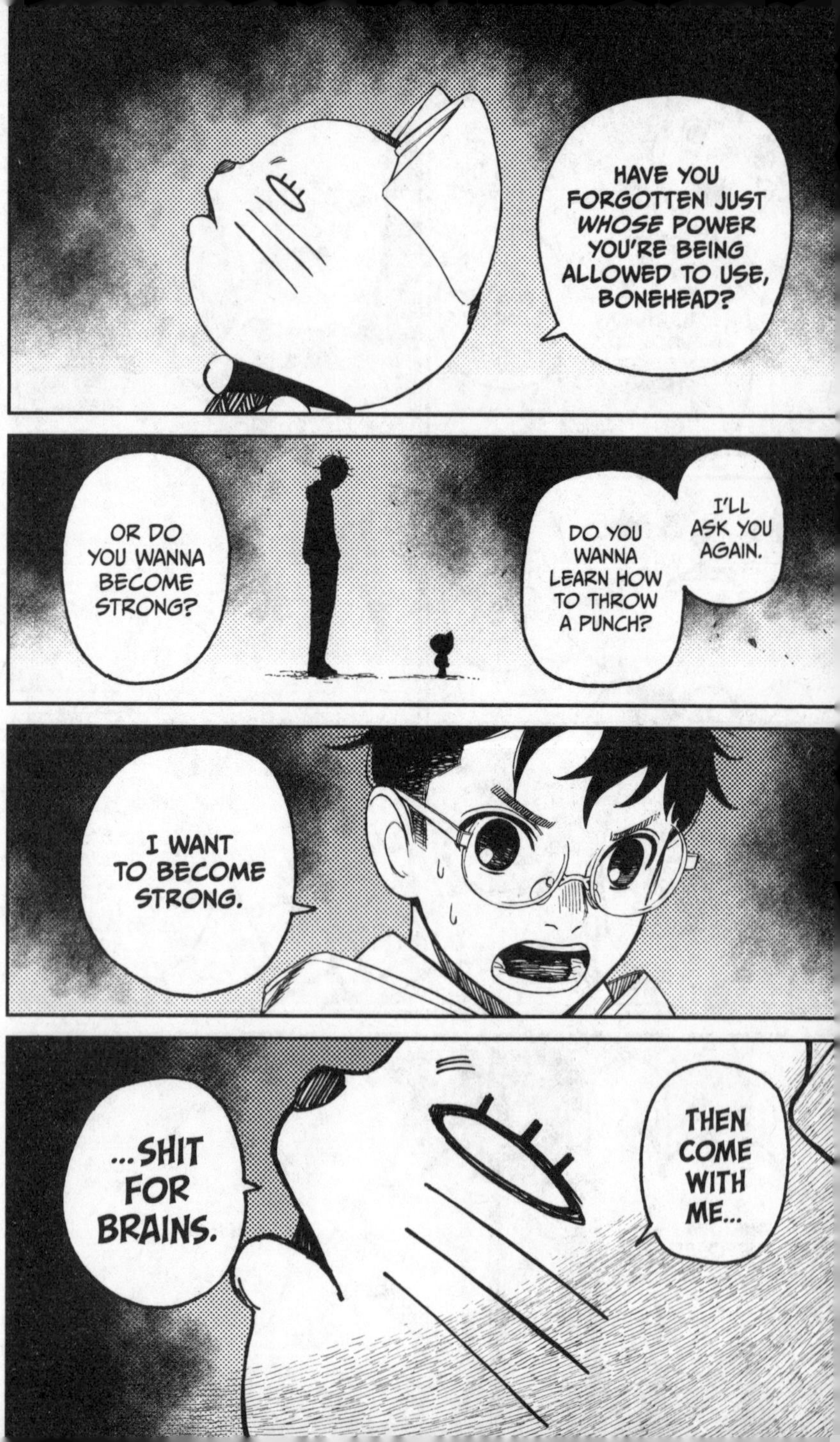
HAVE YOU FORGOTTEN JUST WHOSE POWER YOU'RE BEING ALLOWED TO USE, BONEHEAD?
I'LL ASK YOU AGAIN.
DO YOU WANNA LEARN HOW TO THROW A PUNCH?
OR DO YOU WANNA BECOME STRONG?
I WANT TO BECOME STRONG.
THEN COME WITH ME...
...SHIT FOR BRAINS.

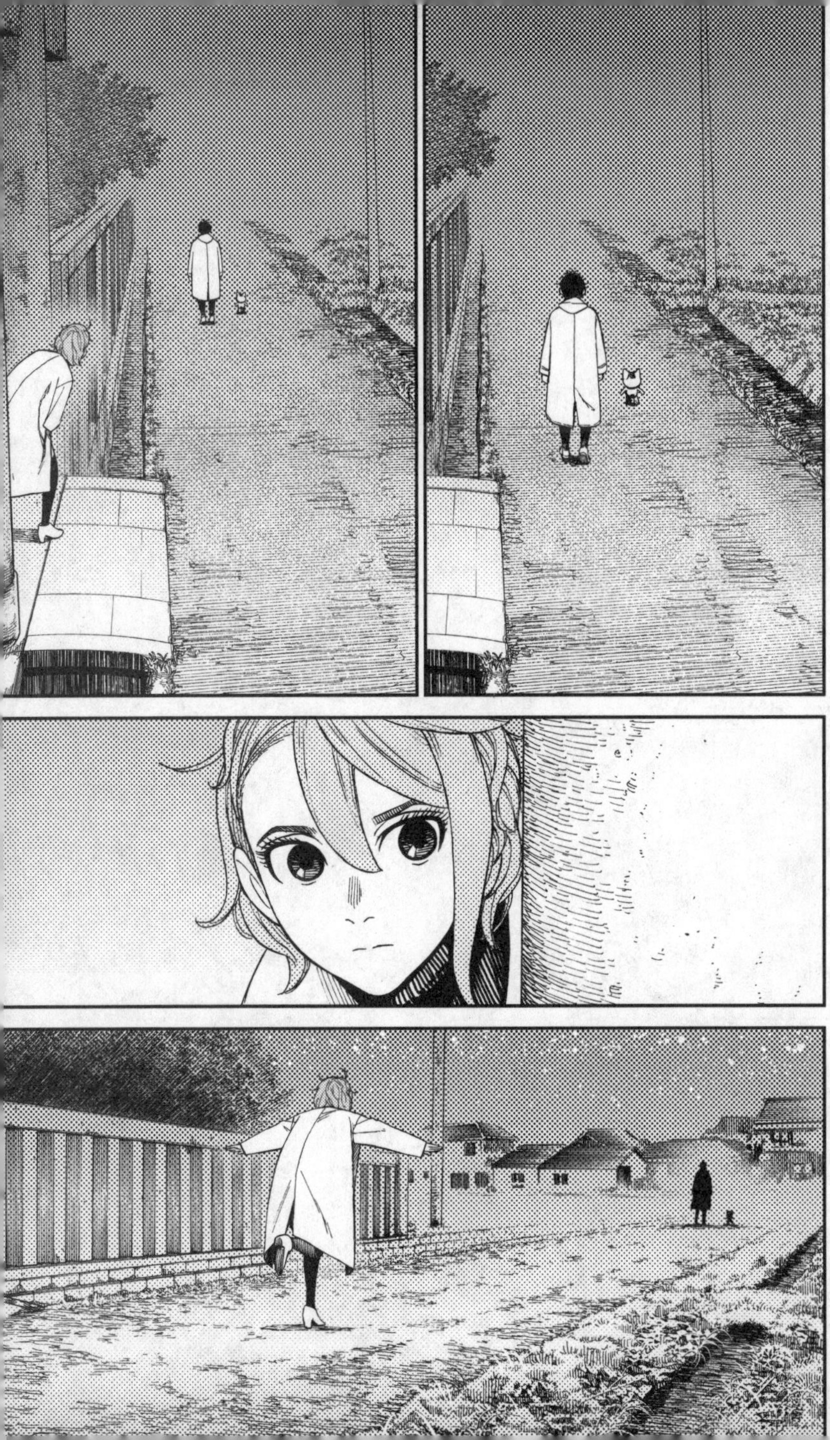

DAN DA DAN

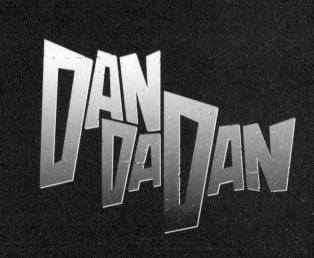

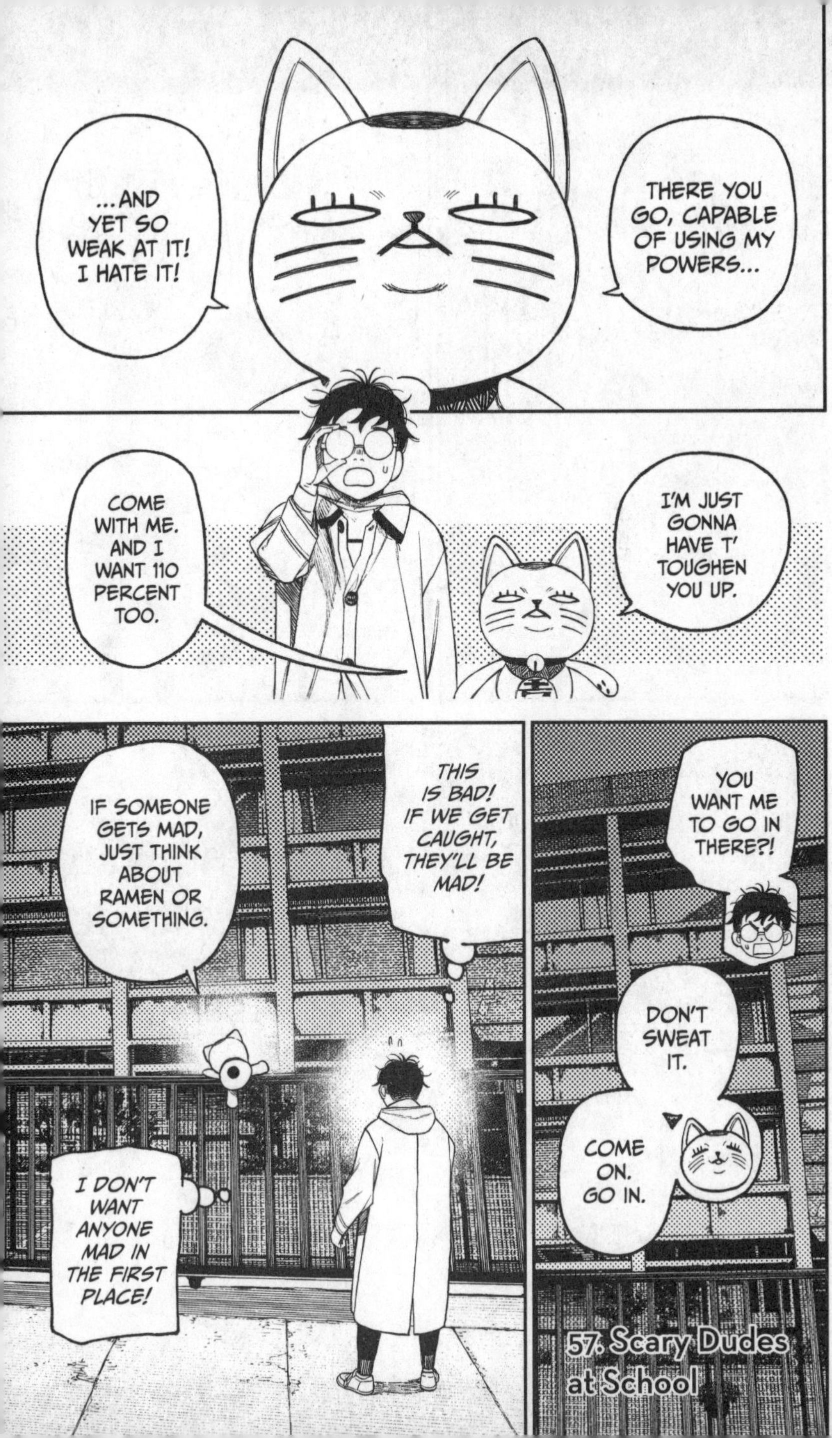
THERE YOU GO, CAPABLE OF USING MY POWERS...
...AND YET SO WEAK AT IT! I HATE IT!
I'M JUST GONNA HAVE T' TOUGHEN YOU UP.
COME WITH ME. AND I WANT 110 PERCENT TOO.
YOU WANT ME TO GO IN THERE?!
DON'T SWEAT IT.
COME ON. GO IN.
57. Scary Dudes at School
THIS IS BAD! IF WE GET CAUGHT, THEY'LL BE MAD!
IF SOMEONE GETS MAD, JUST THINK ABOUT RAMEN OR SOMETHING.
I DON'T WANT ANYONE MAD IN THE FIRST PLACE!

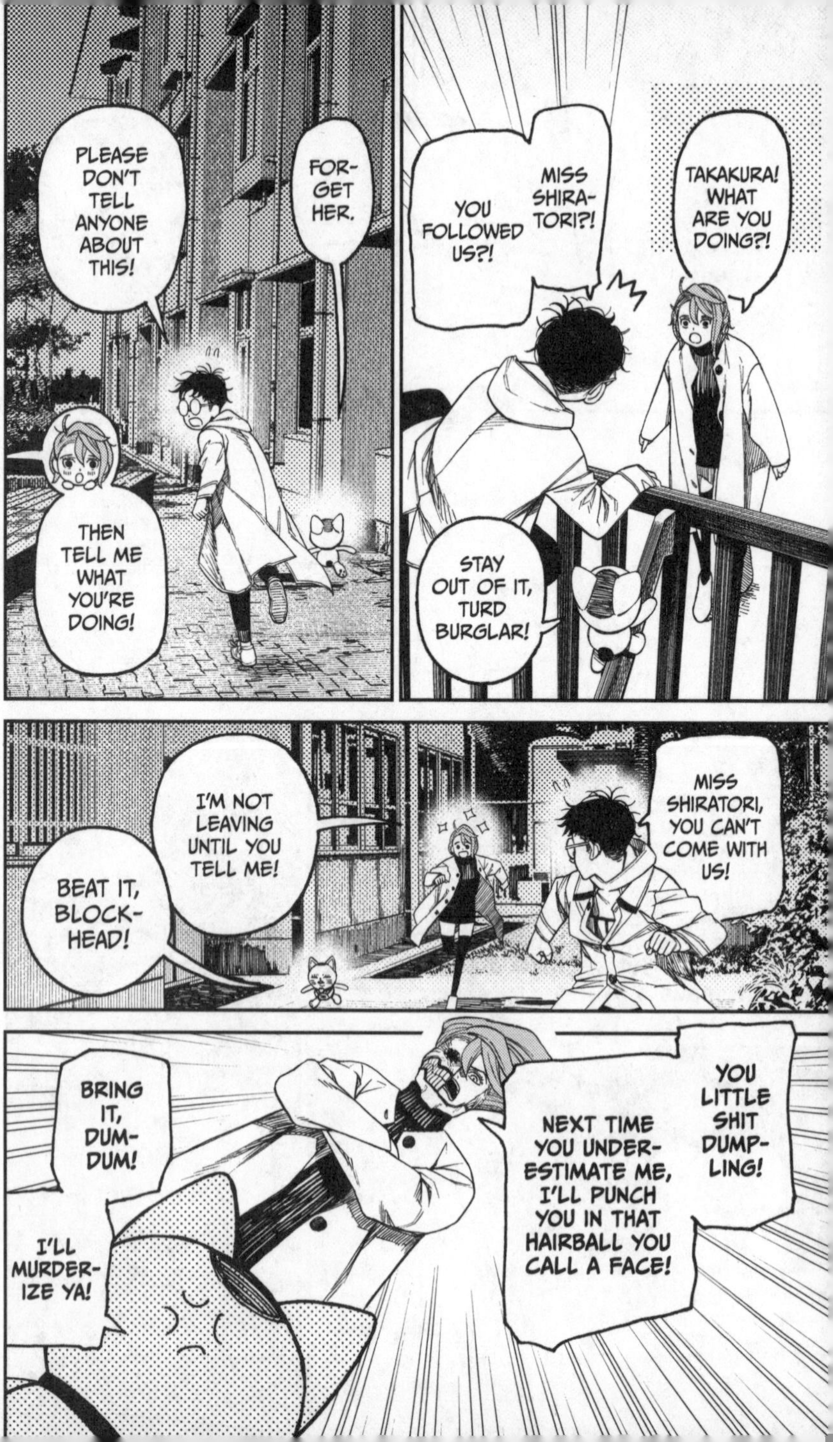
TAKAKURA! WHAT ARE YOU DOING?!
MISS SHIRATORI?! YOU FOLLOWED US?!
STAY OUT OF IT, TURD BURGLAR!
FORGET HER.
PLEASE DON'T TELL ANYONE ABOUT THIS!
THEN TELL ME WHAT YOU'RE DOING!
MISS SHIRATORI, YOU CAN'T COME WITH US!
I'M NOT LEAVING UNTIL YOU TELL ME!
BEAT IT, BLOCKHEAD!
YOU LITTLE SHIT DUMPLING!
NEXT TIME YOU UNDERESTIMATE ME, I'LL PUNCH YOU IN THAT HAIRBALL YOU CALL A FACE!
BRING IT, DUMDUM!
I'LL MURDERIZE YA!

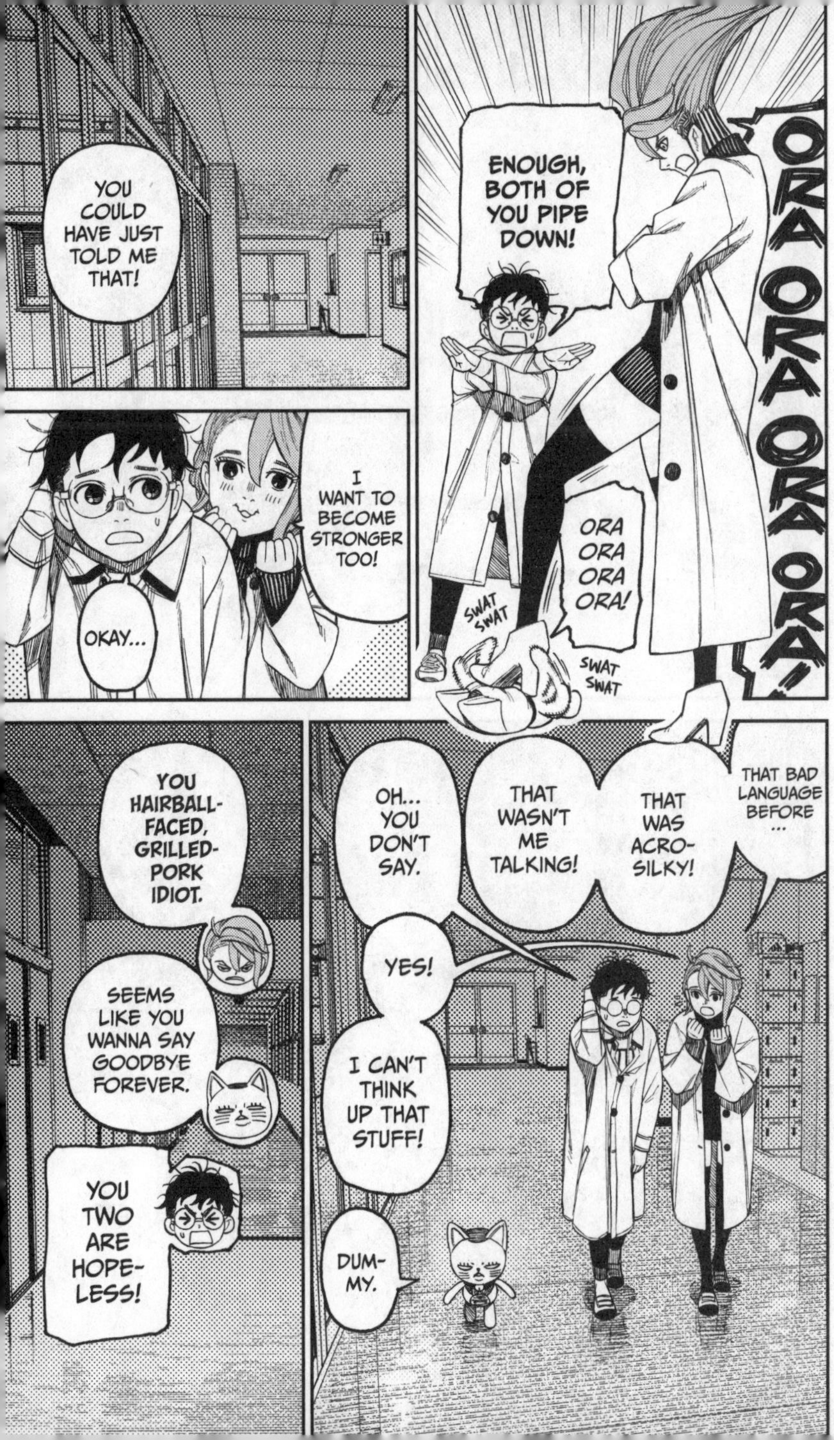
ORA ORA ORA ORA ORA!
ENOUGH, BOTH OF YOU PIPE DOWN!
ORA ORA ORA ORA!
SWAT SWAT
SWAT SWAT
YOU COULD HAVE JUST TOLD ME THAT!
I WANT TO BECOME STRONGER TOO!
OKAY...
THAT BAD LANGUAGE BEFORE ...
THAT WAS ACRO-SILKY!
THAT WASN'T ME TALKING!
OH... YOU DON'T SAY.
YES!
I CAN'T THINK UP THAT STUFF!
DUM-MY.
YOU HAIRBALL-FACED, GRILLED-PORK IDIOT.
SEEMS LIKE YOU WANNA SAY GOODBYE FOREVER.
YOU TWO ARE HOPELESS!

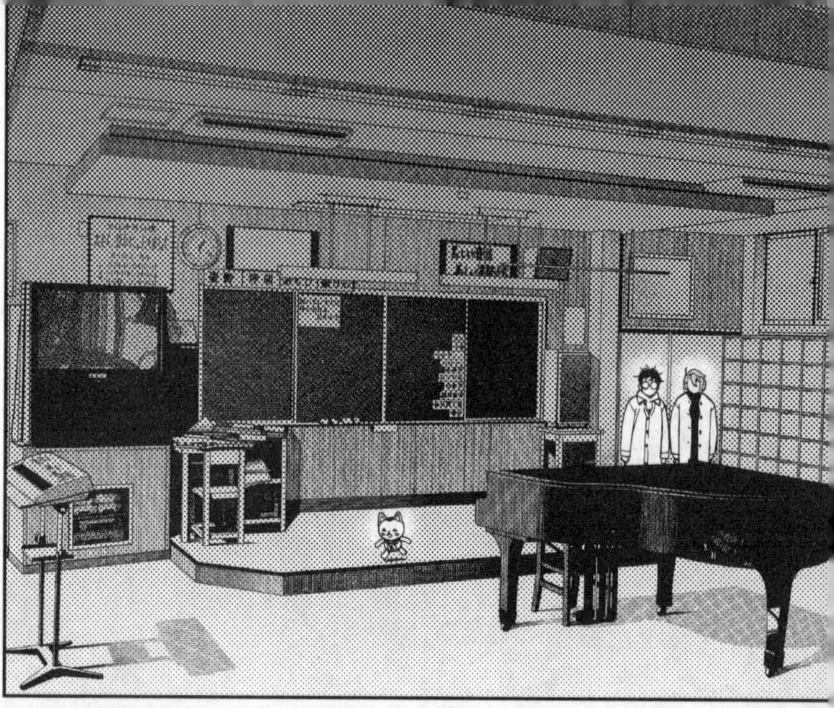
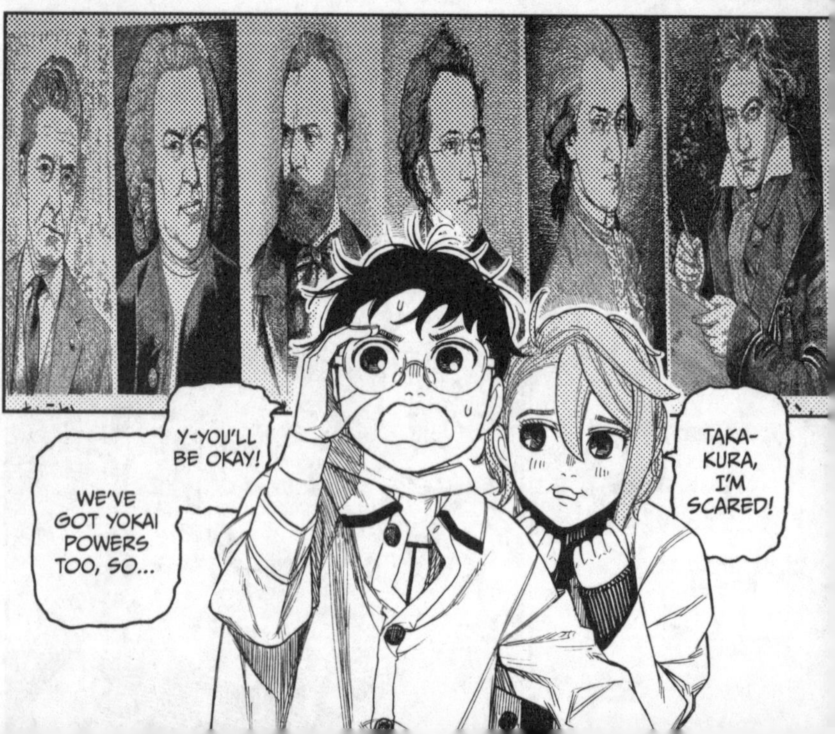
TAKA-KURA, I'M SCARED!
Y-YOU'LL BE OKAY!
WE'VE GOT YOKAI POWERS TOO, SO...

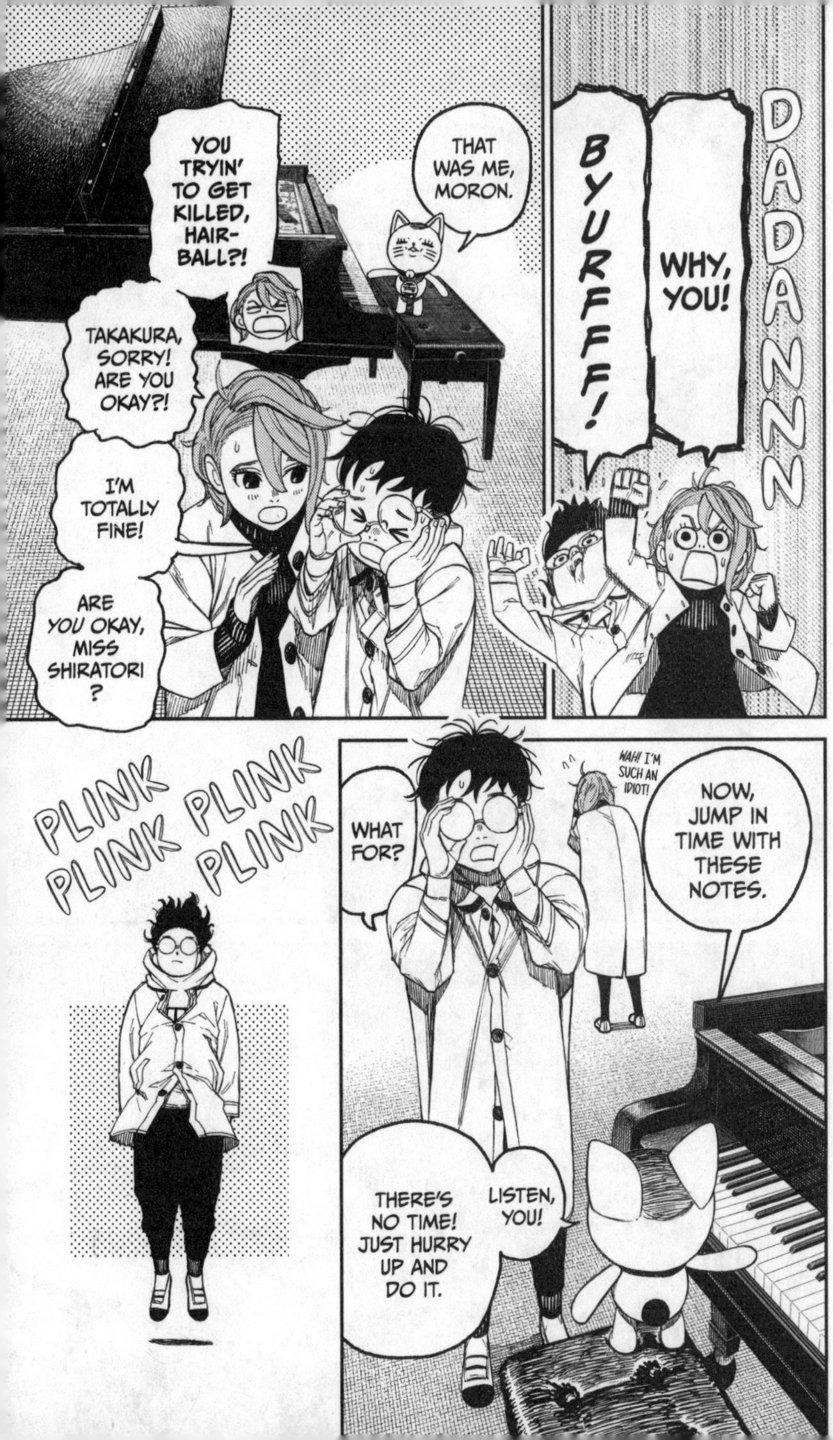
DADANN
WHY, YOU!
BYURFFF!
THAT WAS ME, MORON.
YOU TRYIN' TO GET KILLED, HAIR-BALL?!
TAKAKURA, SORRY! ARE YOU OKAY?!
I'M TOTALLY FINE!
ARE YOU OKAY, MISS SHIRATORI ?
WAH! I'M SUCH AN IDIOT!
NOW, JUMP IN TIME WITH THESE NOTES.
WHAT FOR?
LISTEN, YOU!
THERE'S NO TIME! JUST HURRY UP AND DO IT.
PLINK PLINK PLINK PLINK

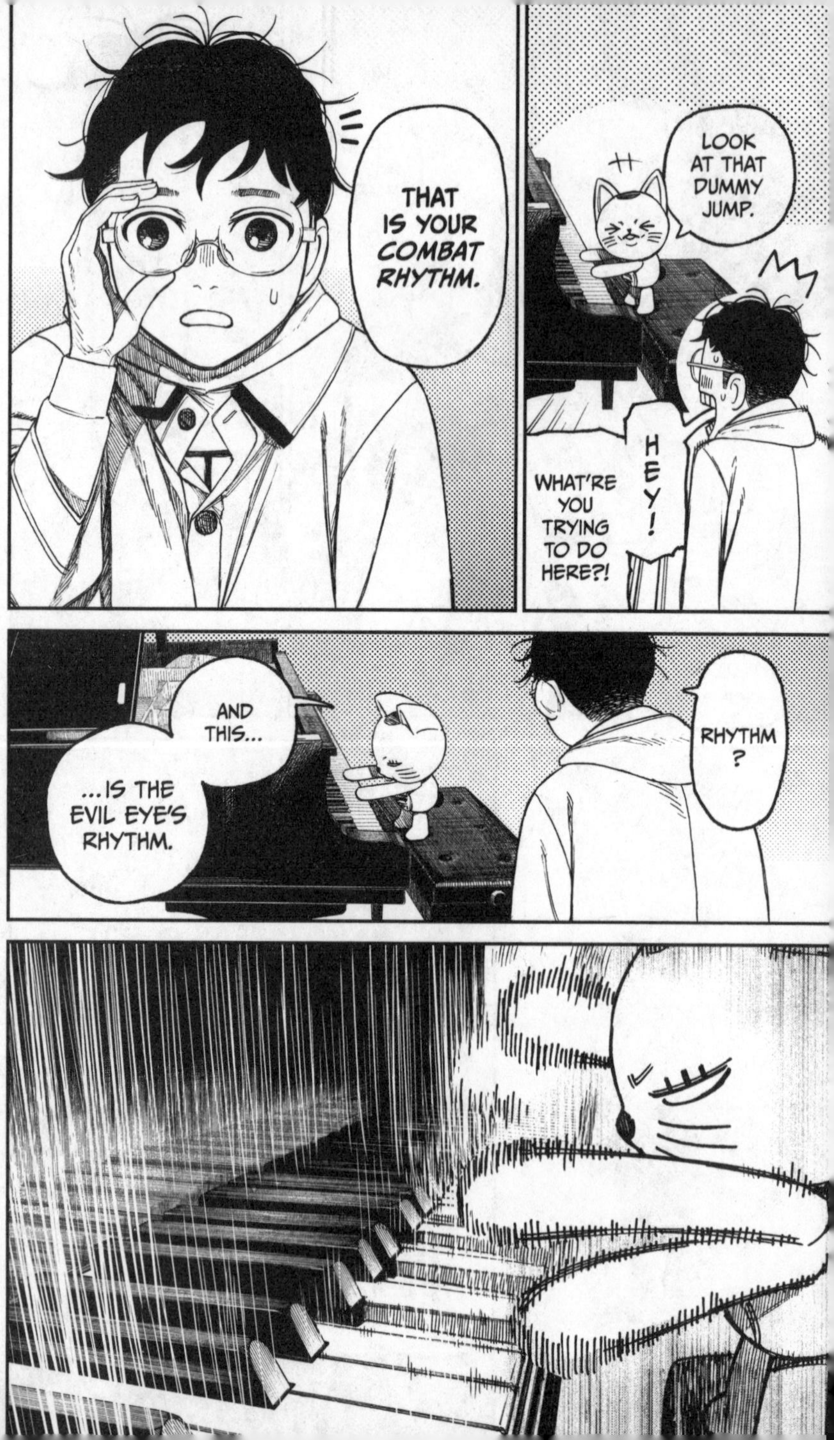
LOOK AT THAT DUMMY JUMP.
HEY!
WHAT'RE YOU TRYING TO DO HERE?!
THAT IS YOUR COMBAT RHYTHM.
RHYTHM?
AND THIS...
...IS THE EVIL EYE'S RHYTHM.

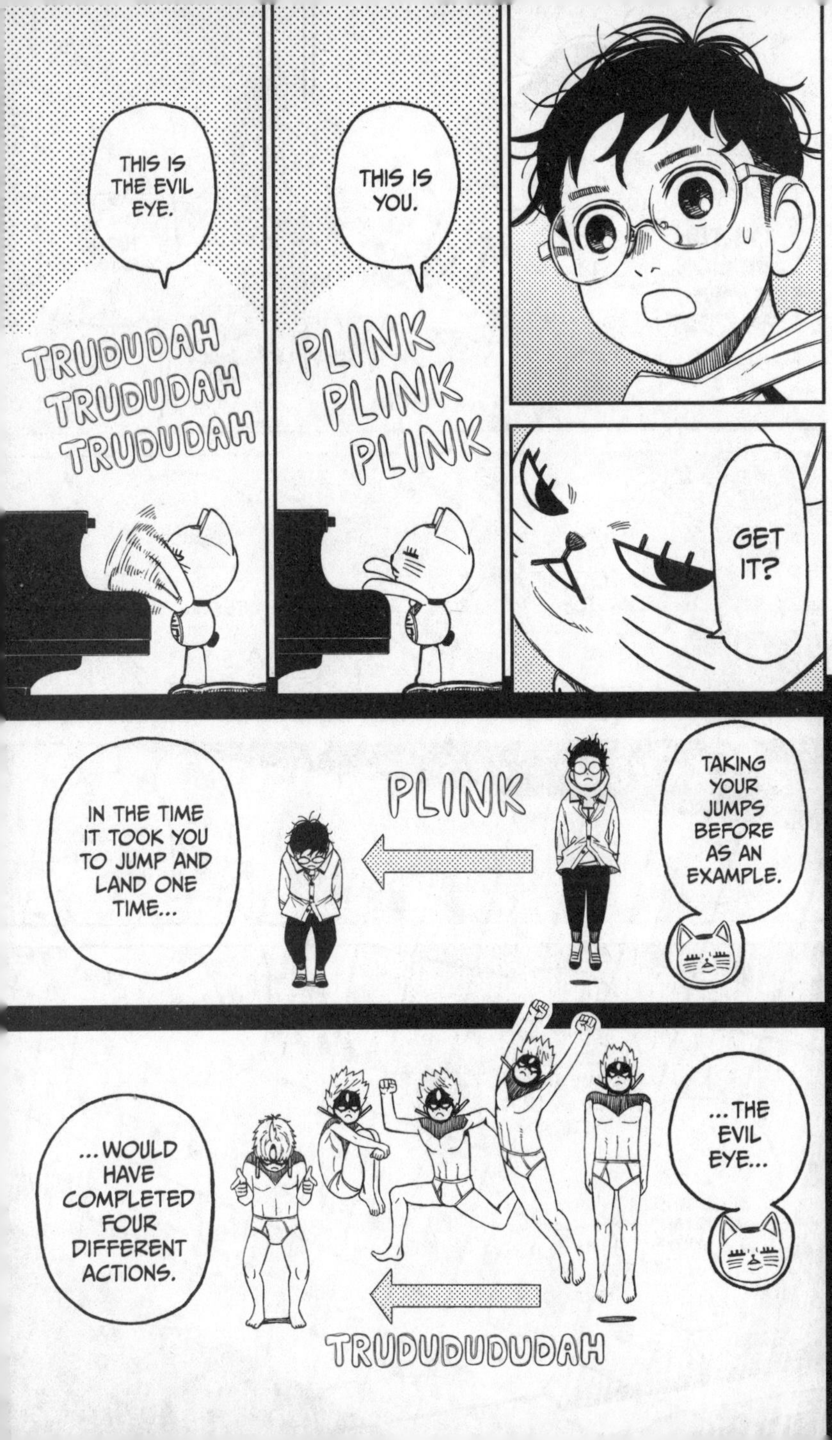
THIS IS THE EVIL EYE.
TRUDUDAH TRUDUDAH TRUDUDAH
THIS IS YOU.
PLINK PLINK PLINK
GET IT?
TAKING YOUR JUMPS BEFORE AS AN EXAMPLE.
PLINK
IN THE TIME IT TOOK YOU TO JUMP AND LAND ONE TIME...
...THE EVIL EYE...
...WOULD HAVE COMPLETED FOUR DIFFERENT ACTIONS.
TRUDUDUDUDAH

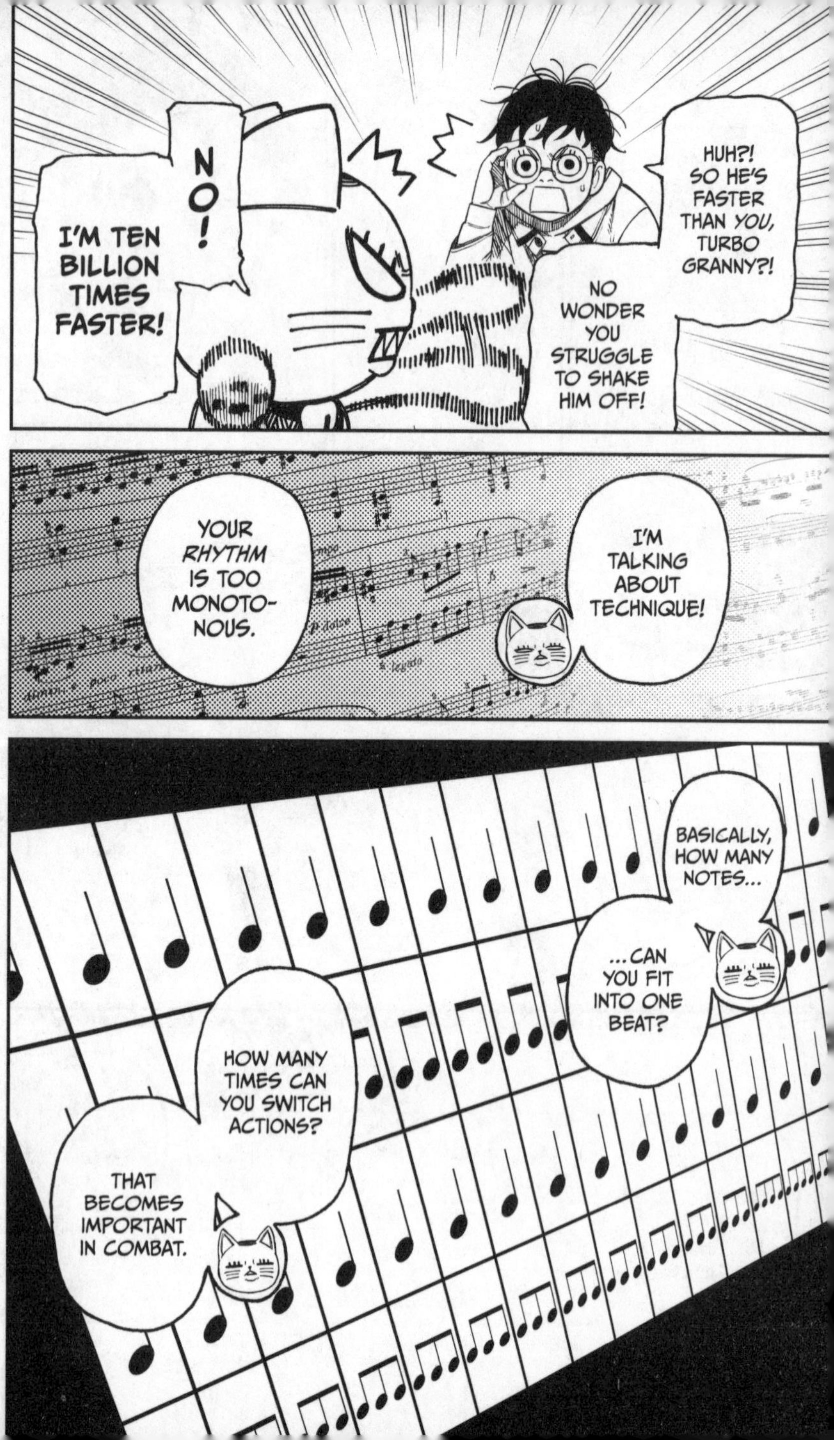
HUH?! SO HE'S FASTER THAN *YOU*, TURBO GRANNY?!
NO WONDER YOU STRUGGLE TO SHAKE HIM OFF!
NO!
I'M TEN BILLION TIMES FASTER!
I'M TALKING ABOUT TECHNIQUE!
YOUR *RHYTHM* IS TOO MONOTO-NOUS.
BASICALLY, HOW MANY NOTES...
...CAN YOU FIT INTO ONE BEAT?
HOW MANY TIMES CAN YOU SWITCH ACTIONS?
THAT BECOMES IMPORTANT IN COMBAT.

WHERE'S IT COMING FROM?!

THAT NOISE!

AN OR-CHES-TRA?!

IT'S SO LOUD, I CAN'T HEAR Y—

HERE?! WHAT'S HERE?!

THEY'RE HERE.

WHOOO'S MAKING THAT NOISE?!

I CAN HEEEAR SOME IMPURE SOUNNNDS.

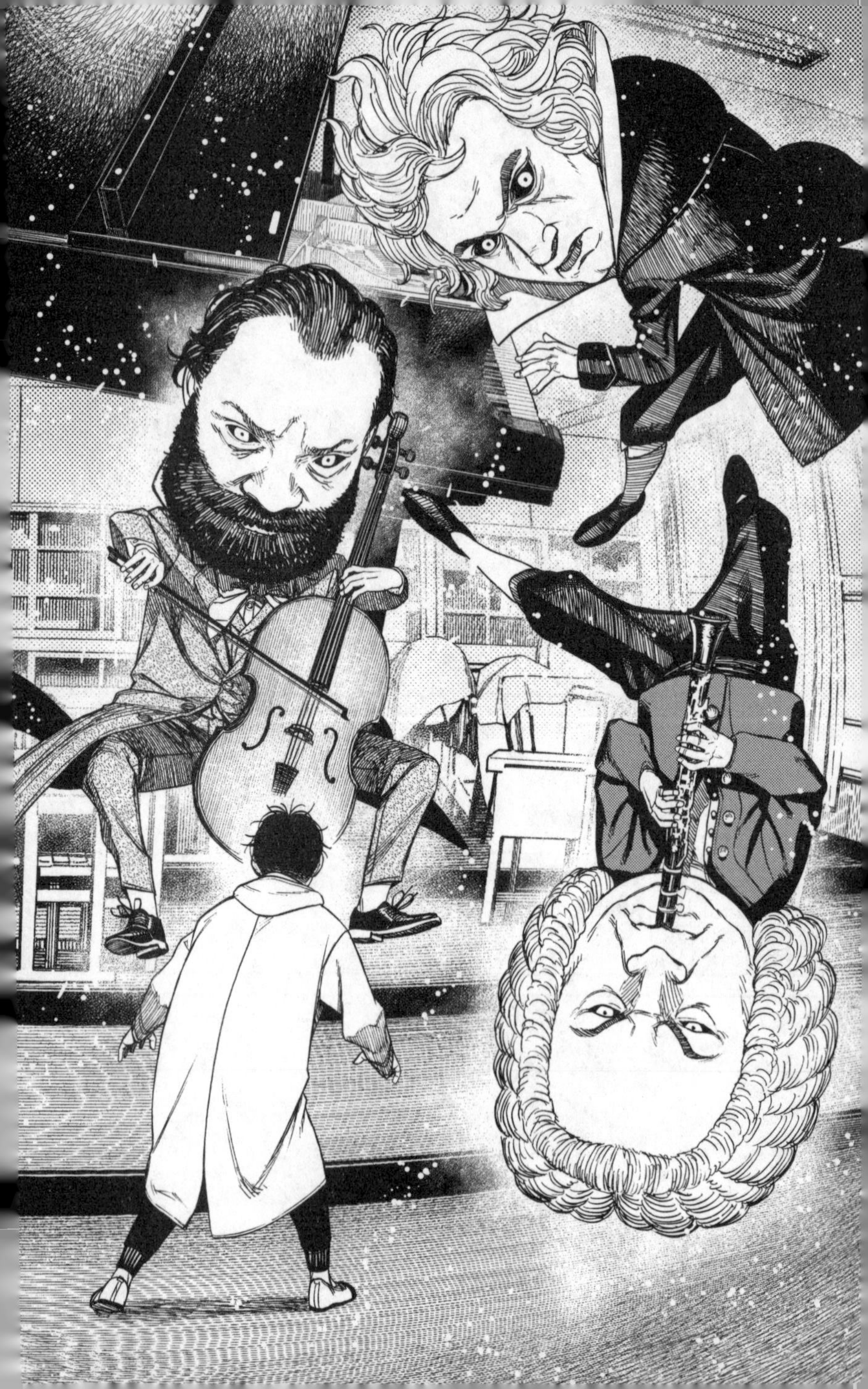

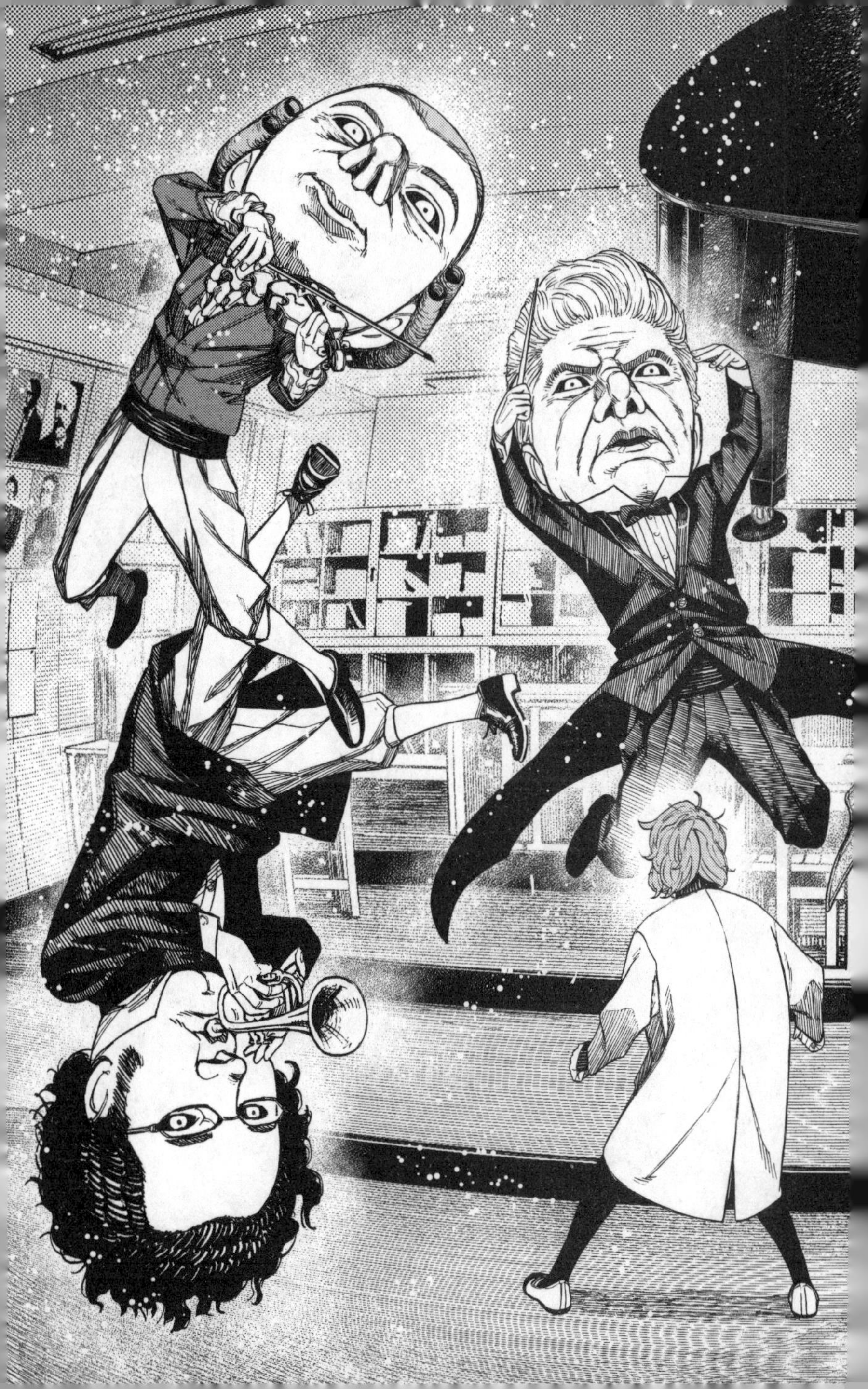

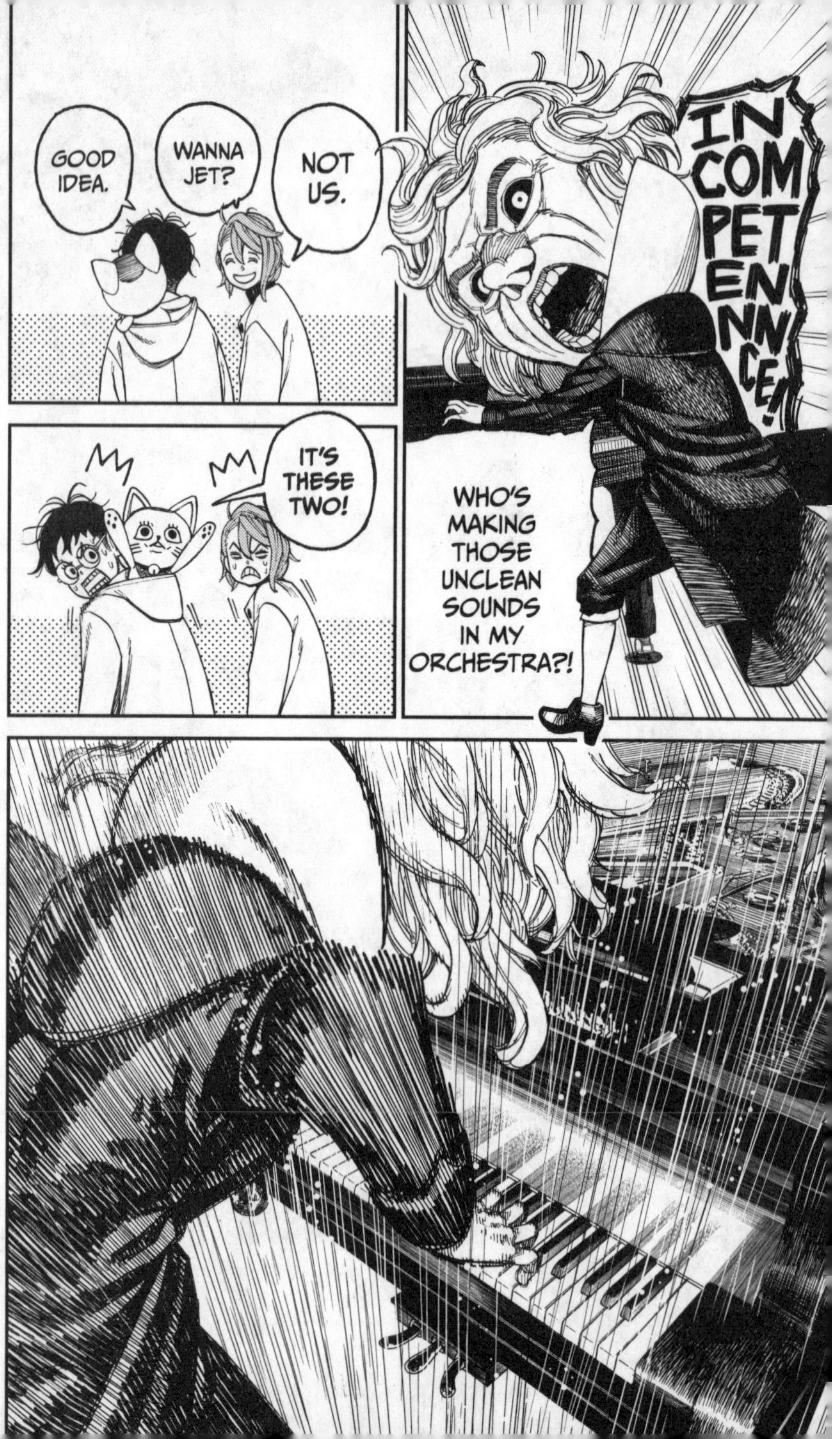
INCOMPETENNCE!
WHO'S MAKING THOSE UNCLEAN SOUNDS IN MY ORCHESTRA?!
NOT US.
WANNA JET?
GOOD IDEA.
IT'S THESE TWO!

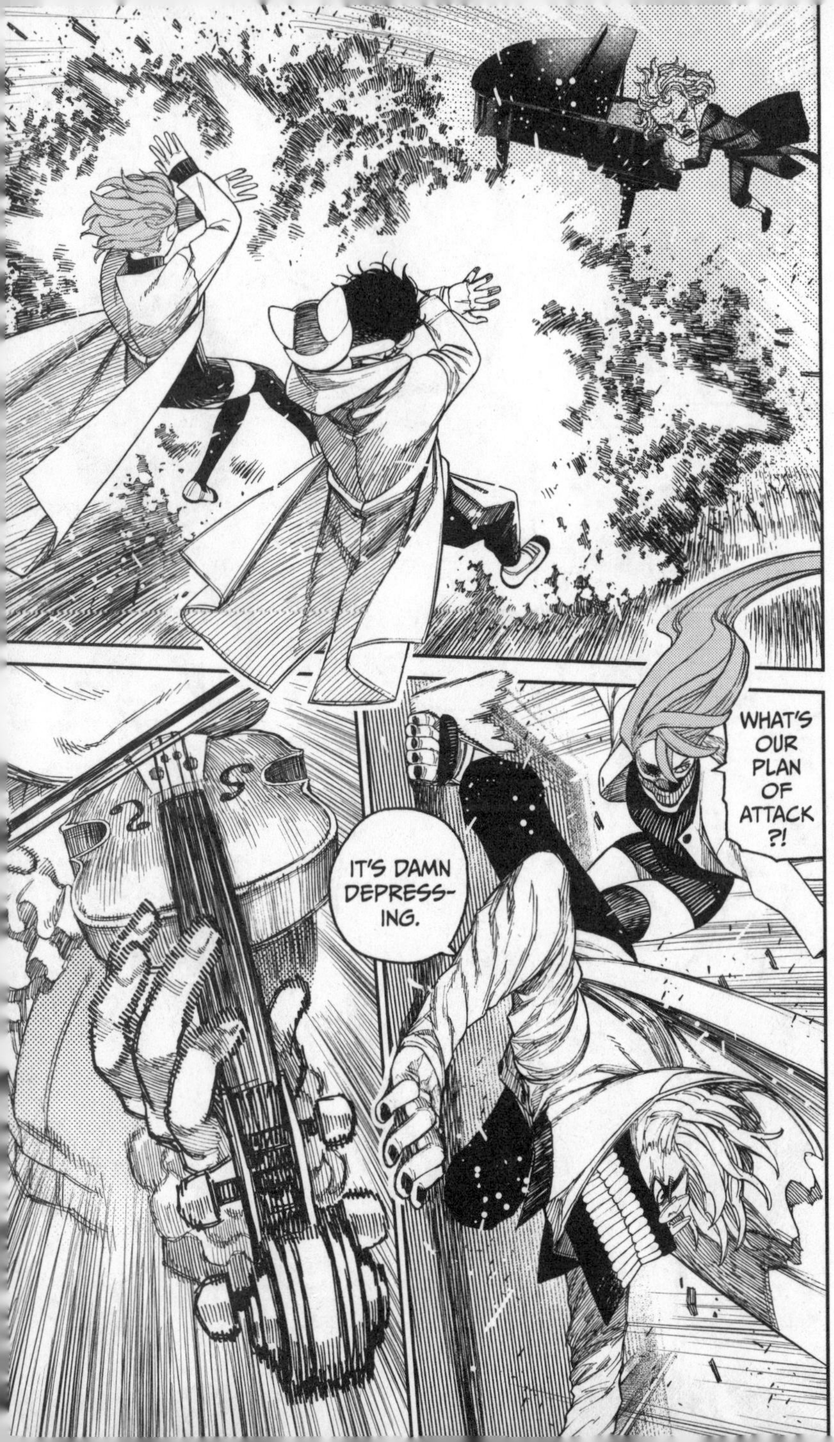
WHAT'S OUR PLAN OF ATTACK ?!
IT'S DAMN DEPRESS-ING.

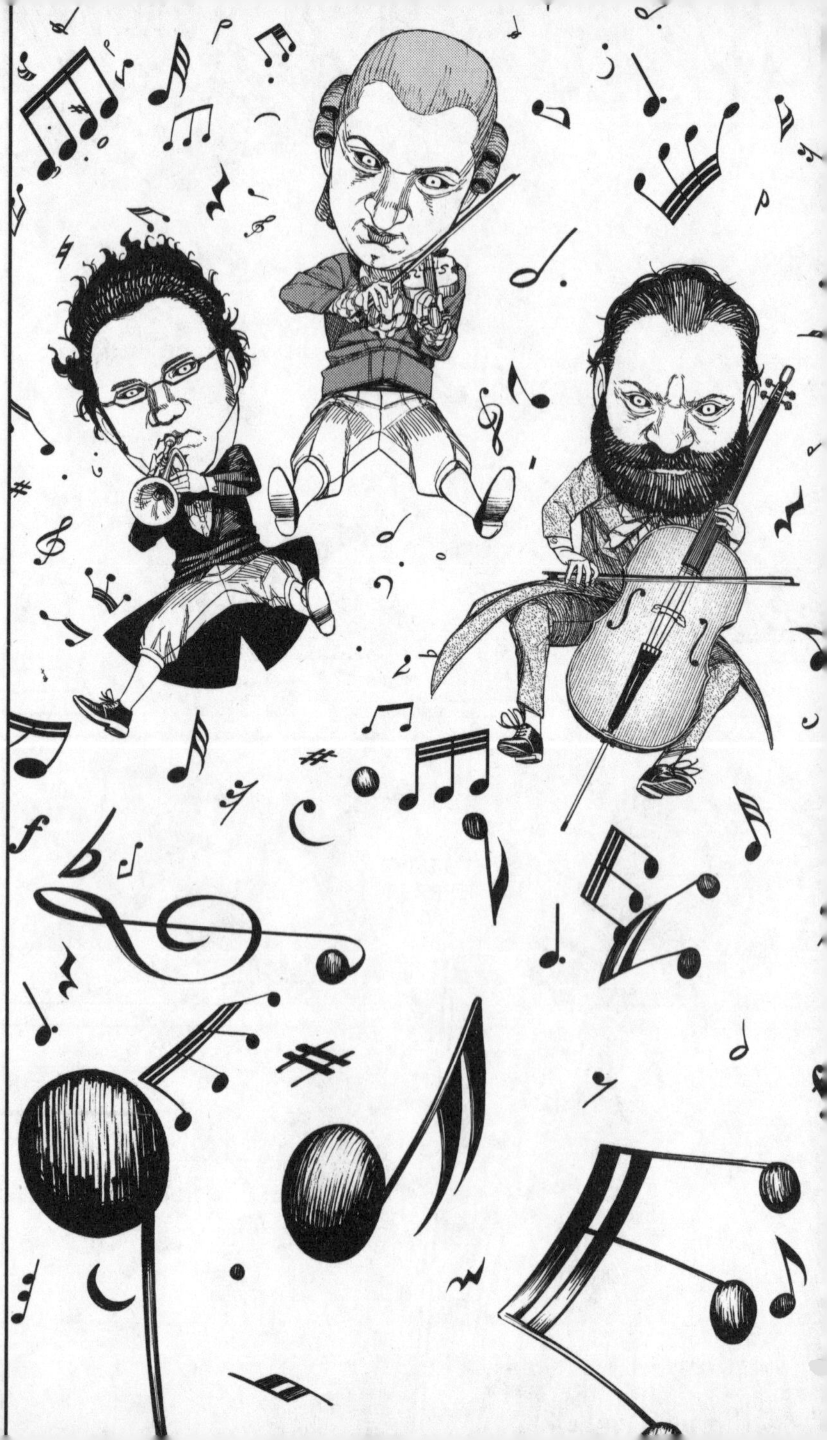

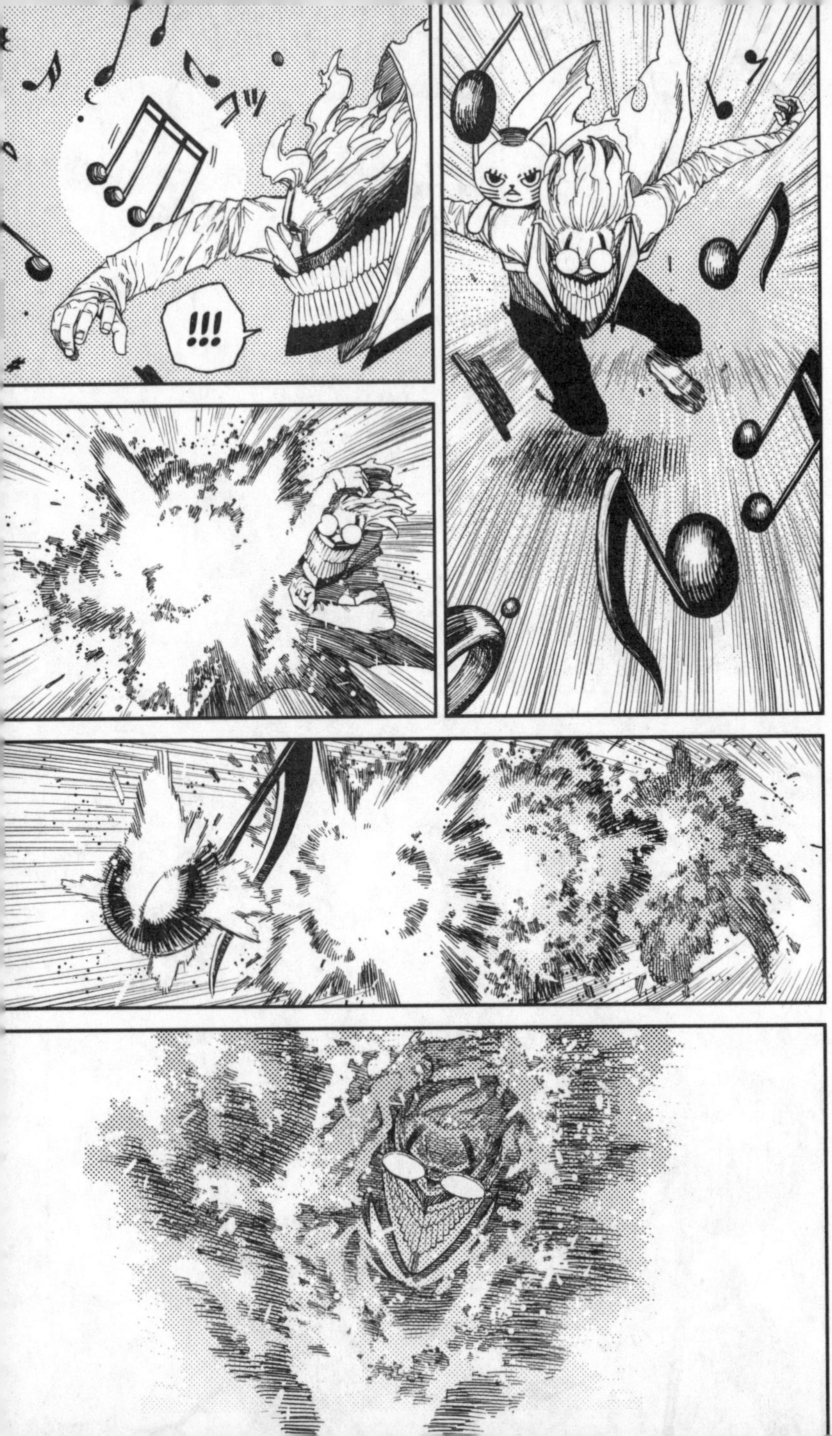
ゴッ
!!!

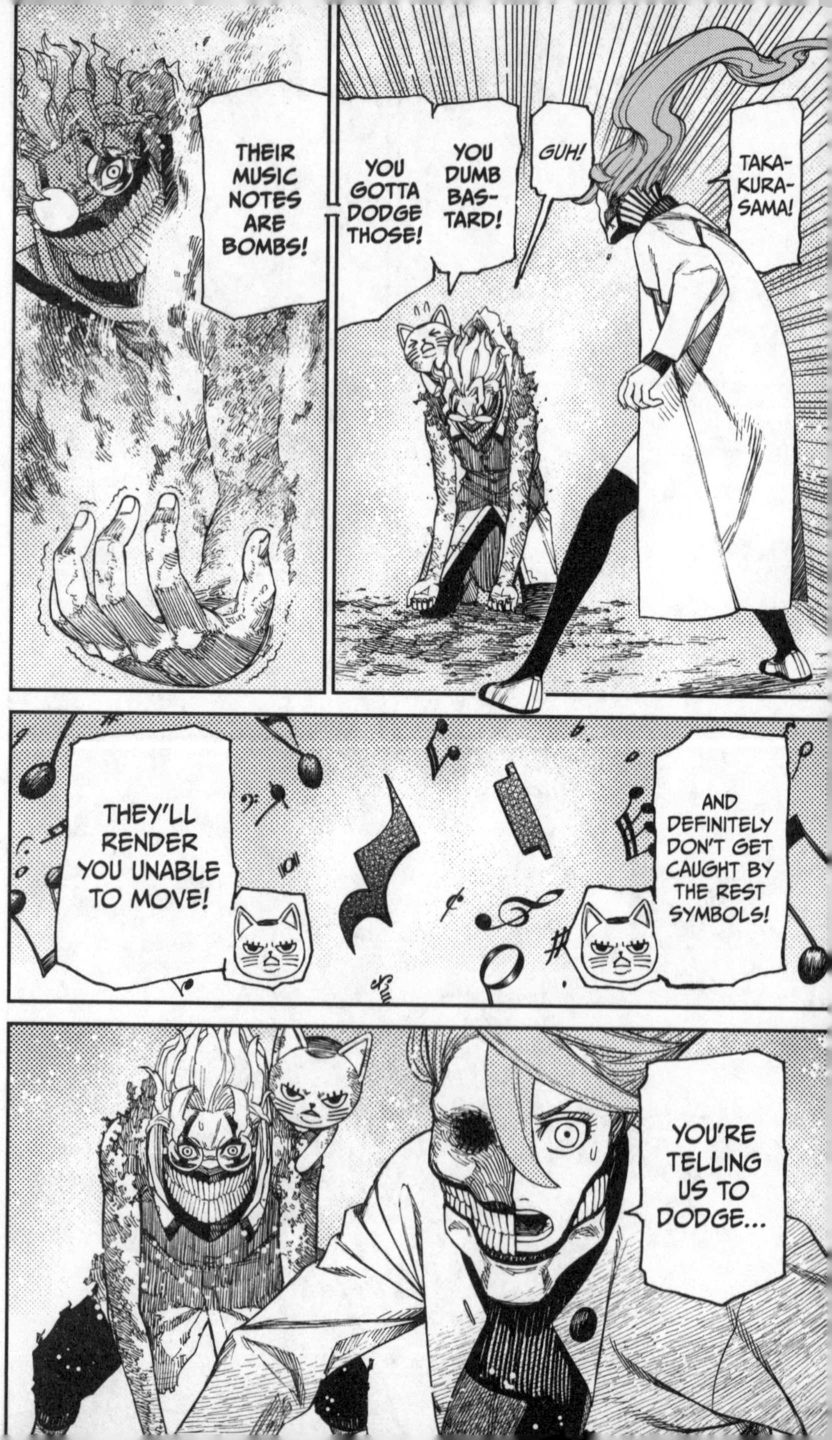
TAKA-KURA-SAMA!
GUH!
YOU DUMB BAS-TARD!
YOU GOTTA DODGE THOSE!
THEIR MUSIC NOTES ARE BOMBS!
AND DEFINITELY DON'T GET CAUGHT BY THE REST SYMBOLS!
THEY'LL RENDER YOU UNABLE TO MOVE!
YOU'RE TELLING US TO DODGE...

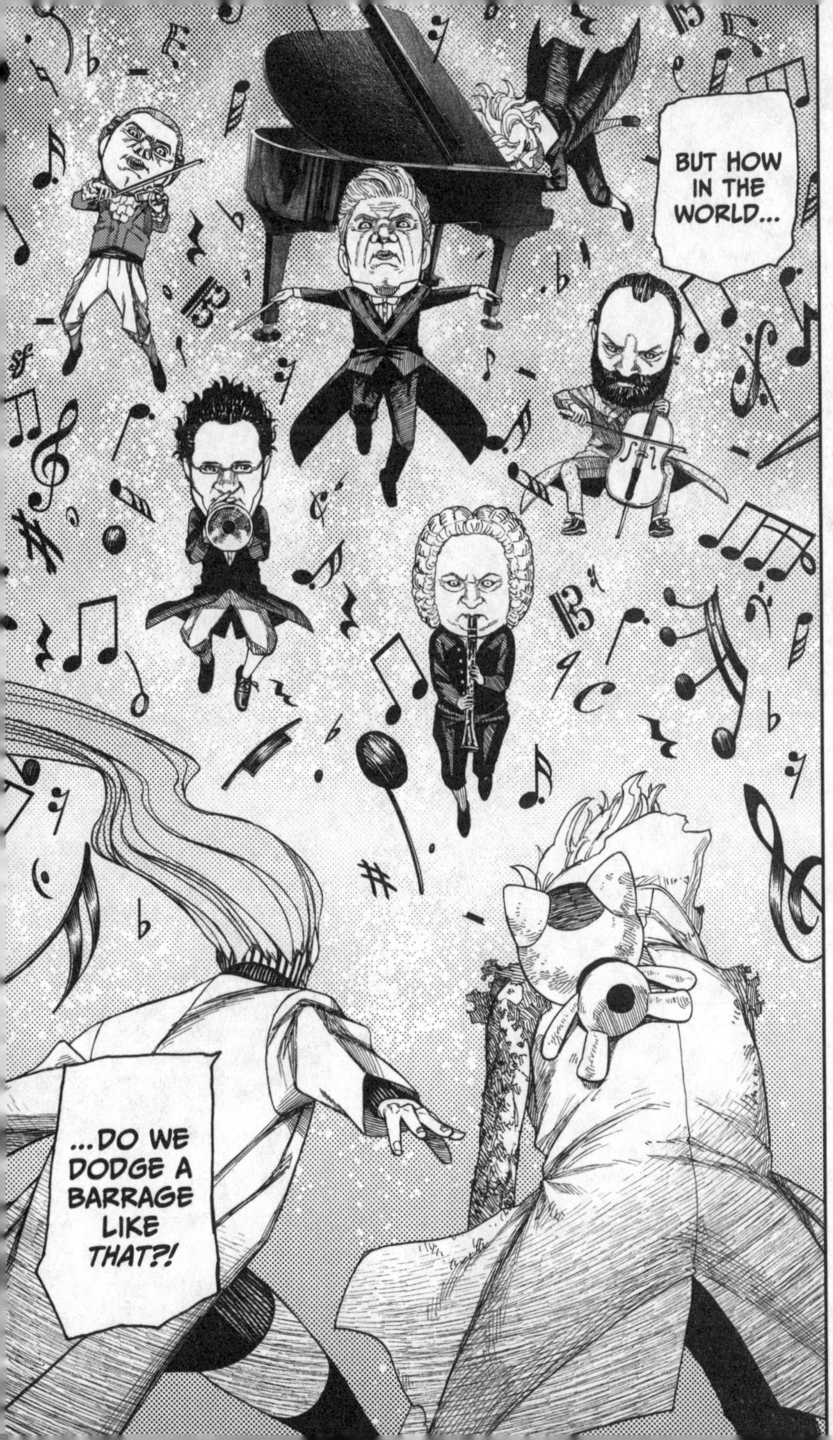
BUT HOW IN THE WORLD...
...DO WE DODGE A BARRAGE LIKE THAT?!

DAN DA DAN

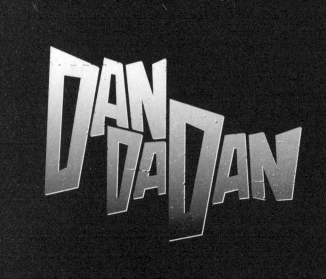

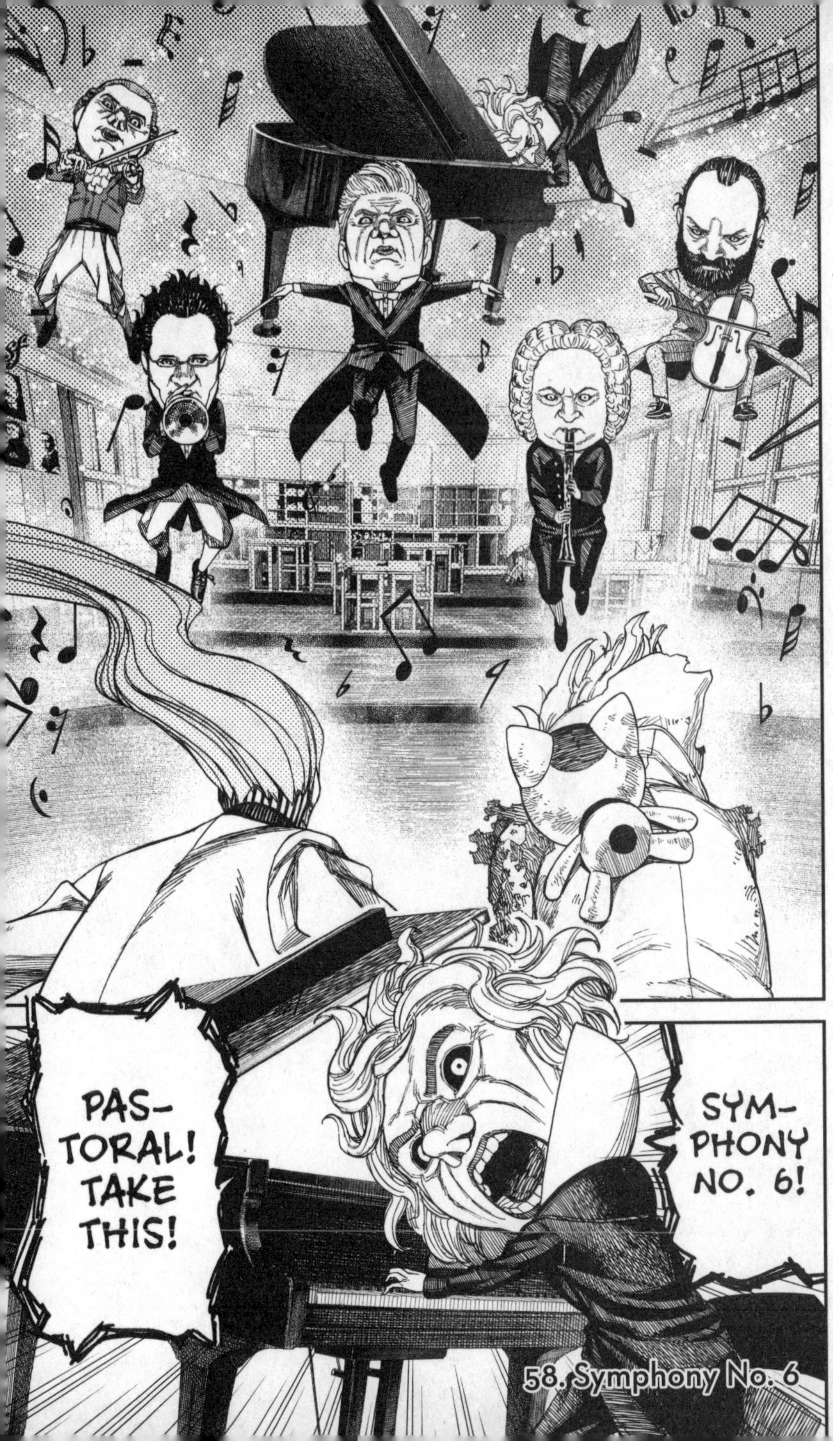
SYM-PHONY NO. 6!
PAS-TORAL! TAKE THIS!
58. Symphony No. 6

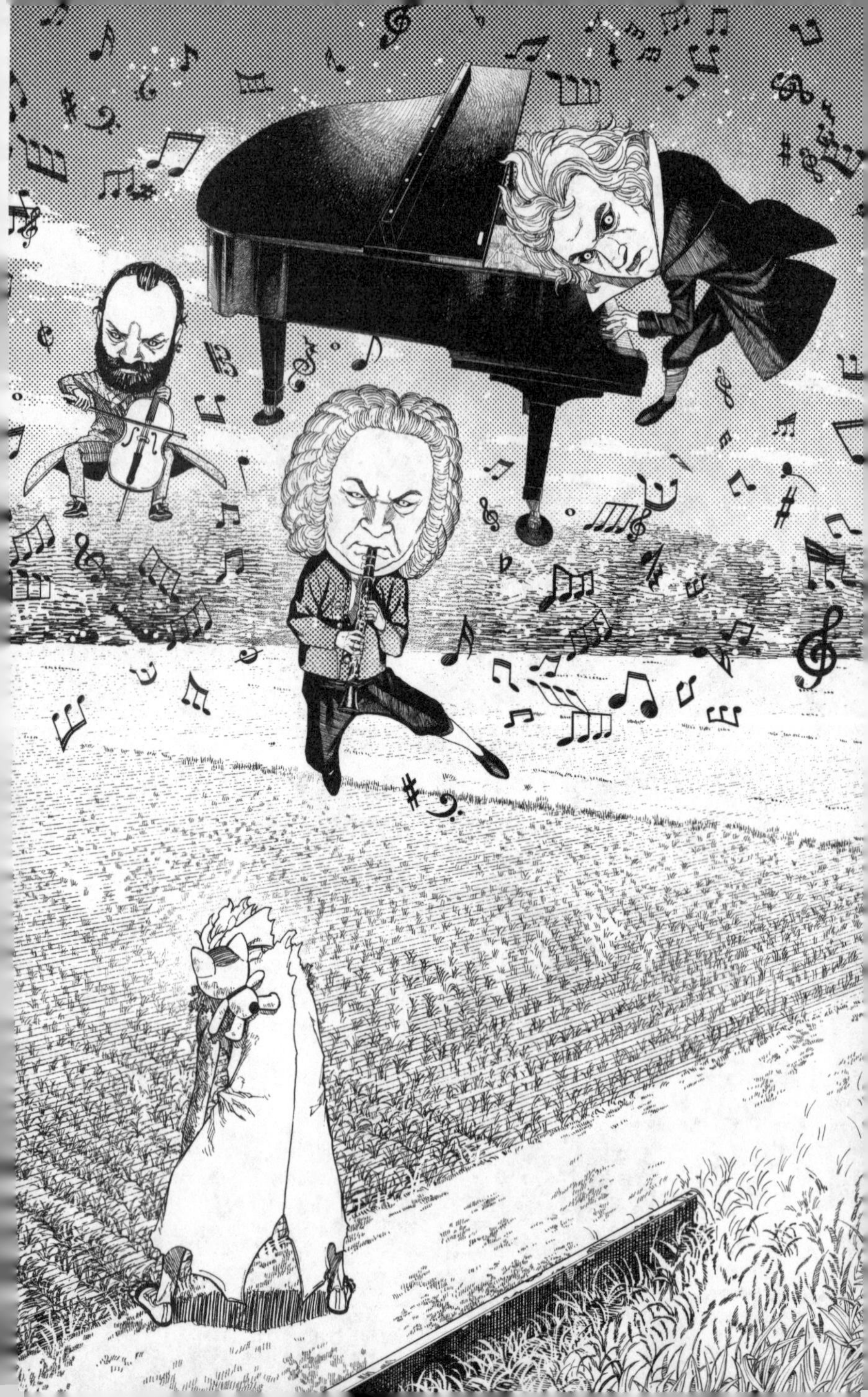

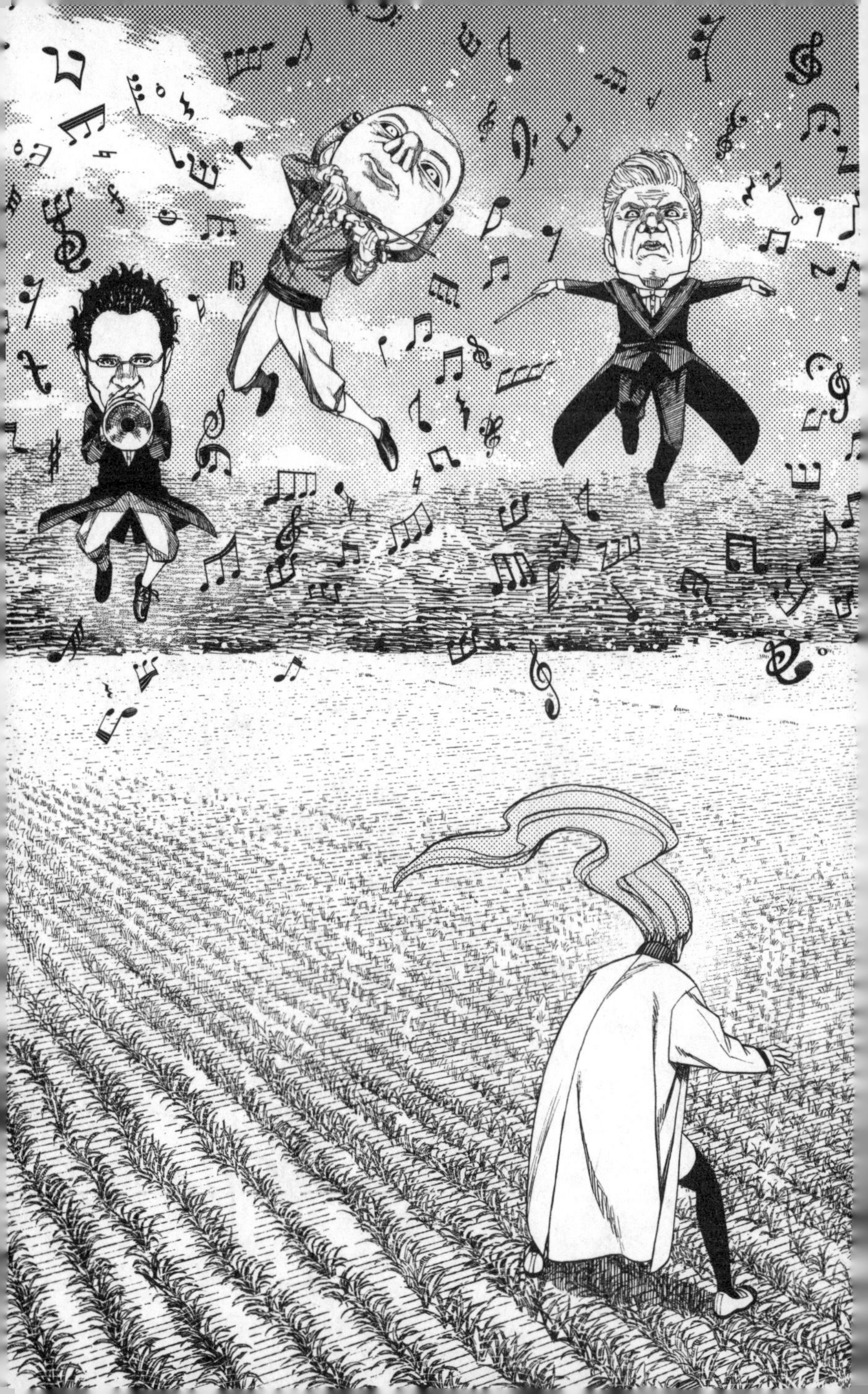

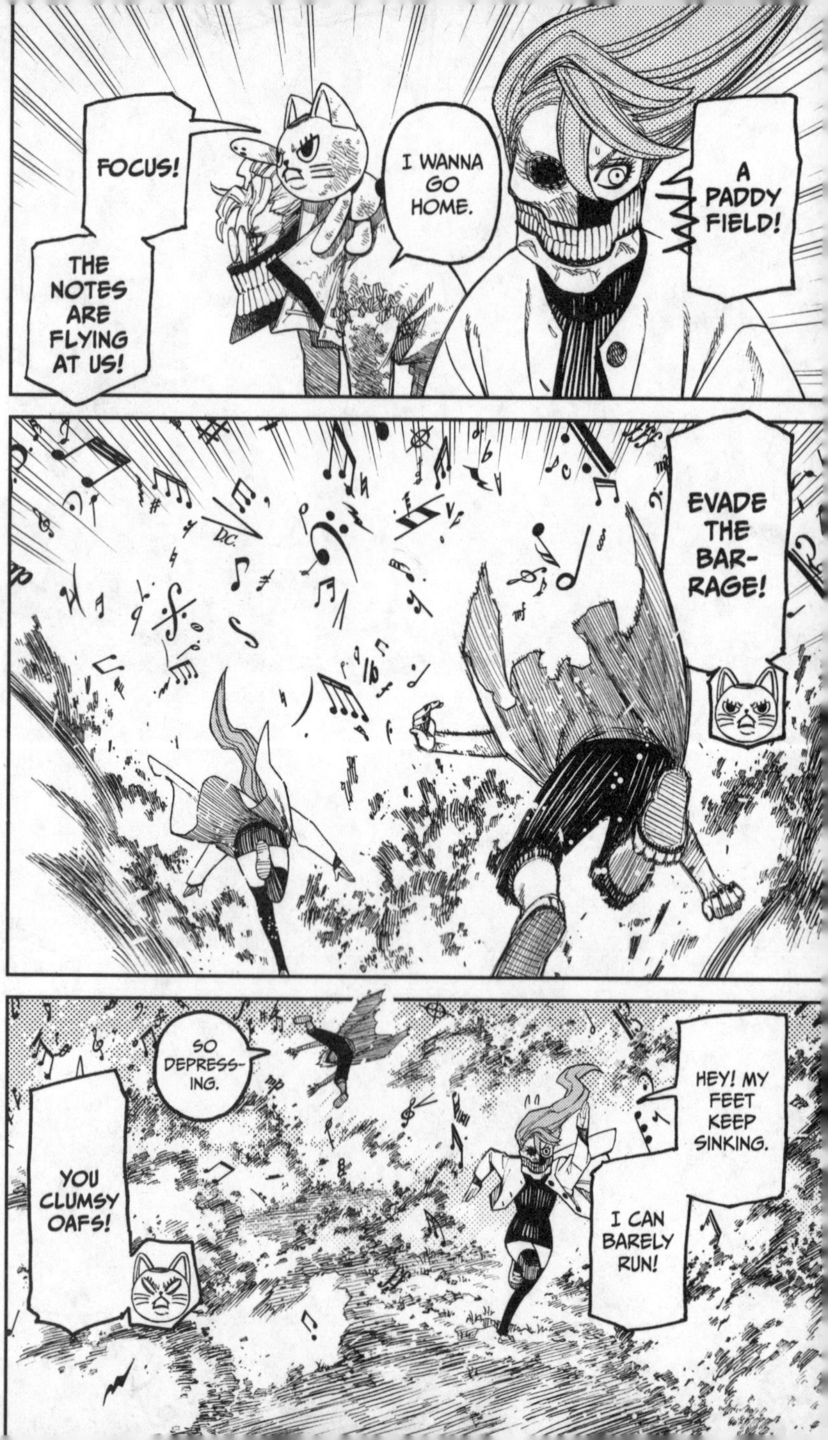
A PADDY FIELD!
I WANNA GO HOME.
FOCUS!
THE NOTES ARE FLYING AT US!
EVADE THE BAR-RAGE!
HEY! MY FEET KEEP SINKING.
I CAN BARELY RUN!
SO DEPRESS-ING.
YOU CLUMSY OAFS!

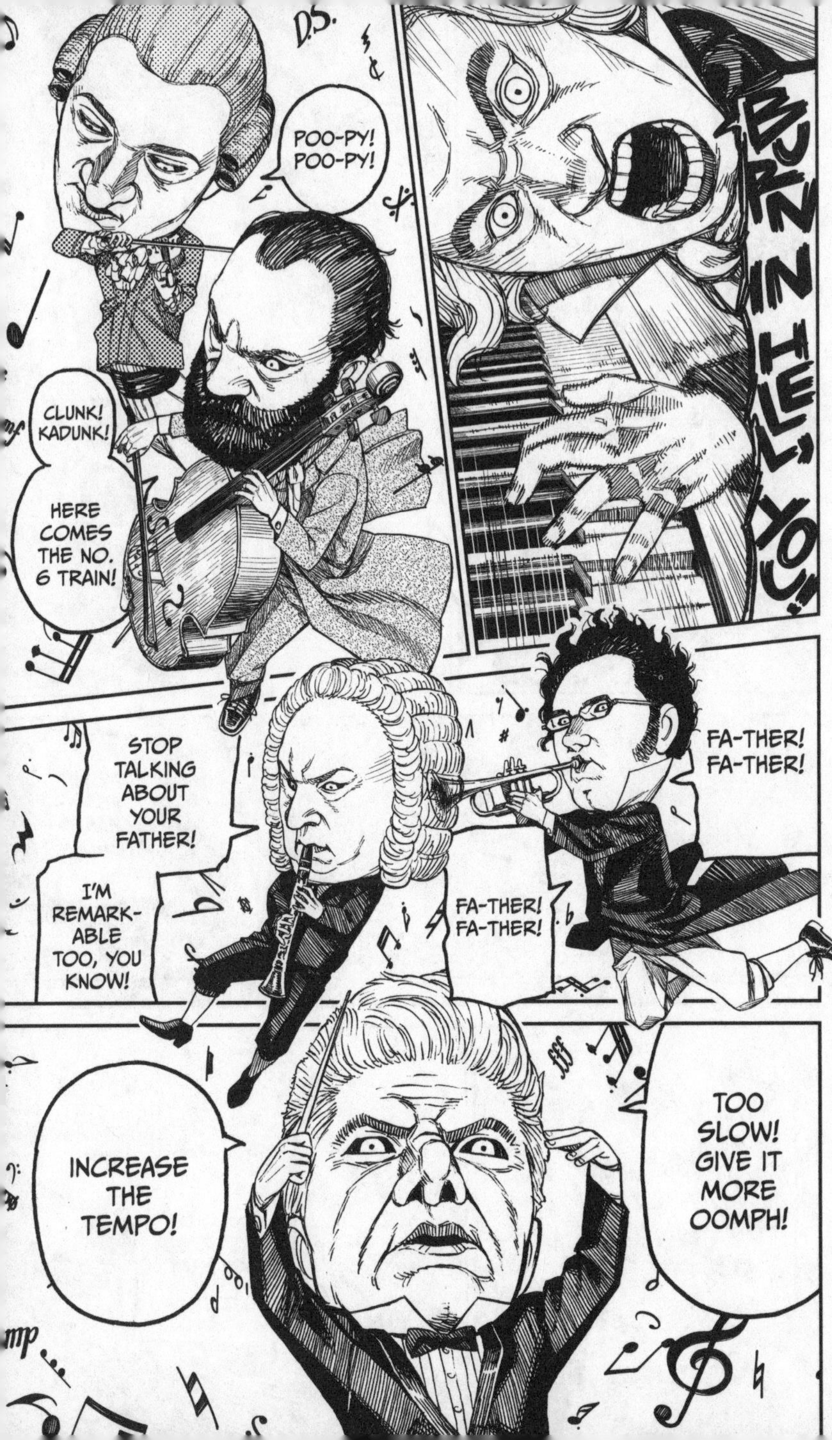
BURN IN HELL, YOU!!
POO-PY! POO-PY!
CLUNK! KADUNK!
HERE COMES THE NO. 6 TRAIN!
FA-THER! FA-THER!
FA-THER! FA-THER!
STOP TALKING ABOUT YOUR FATHER!
I'M REMARK-ABLE TOO, YOU KNOW!
TOO SLOW! GIVE IT MORE OOMPH!
INCREASE THE TEMPO!

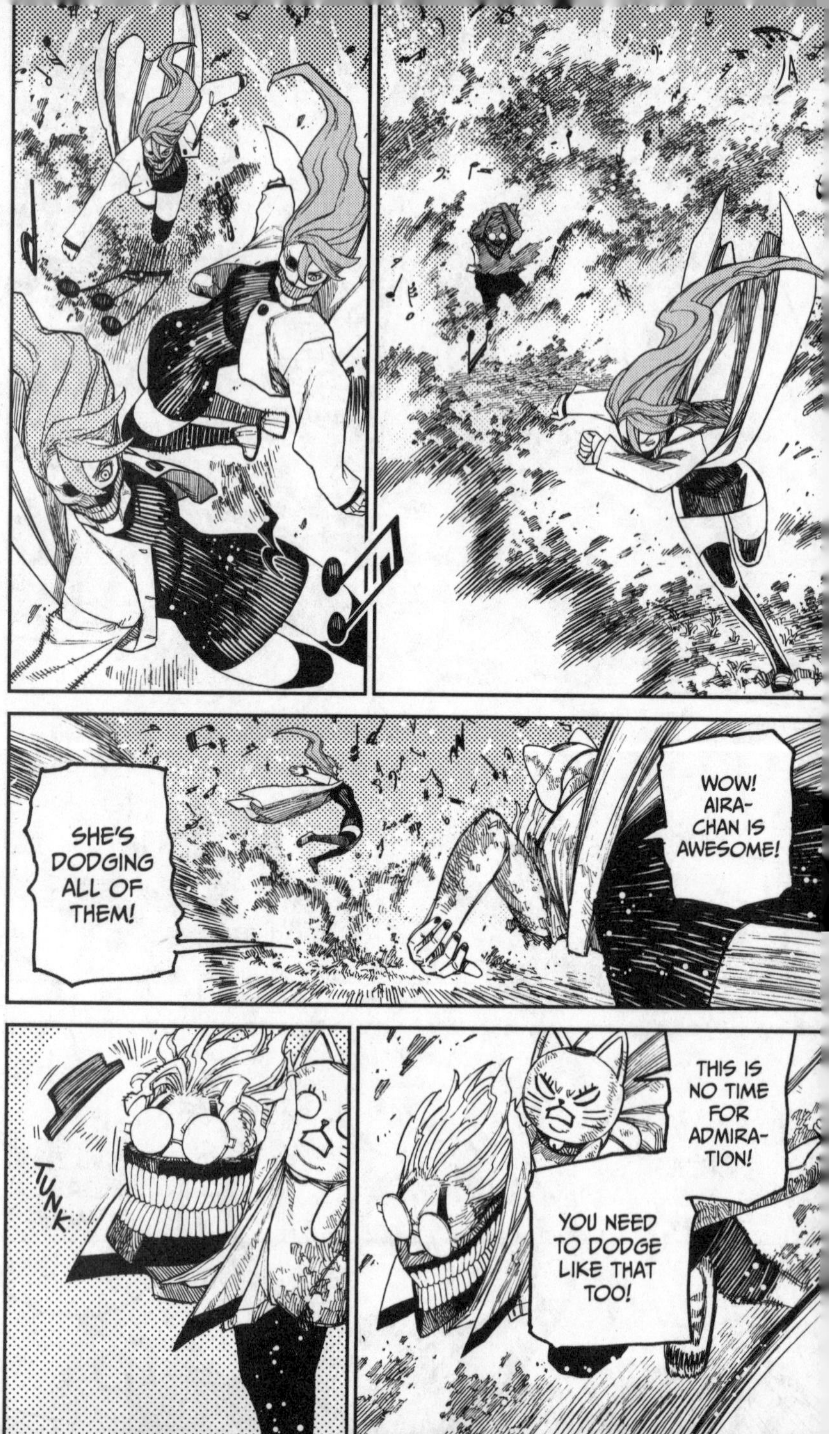
WOW! AIRA-CHAN IS AWESOME!
SHE'S DODGING ALL OF THEM!
THIS IS NO TIME FOR ADMIRA-TION!
YOU NEED TO DODGE LIKE THAT TOO!
TUNK

TAKA-KURA-SAMA!

I CAN'T MOVE!

YOU DUMB-ASS!

I TOLD YOU TO BE CAREFUL OF THE REST SYMBOLS!

SHIT!

YOU COWARDS! GET DOWN HERE!

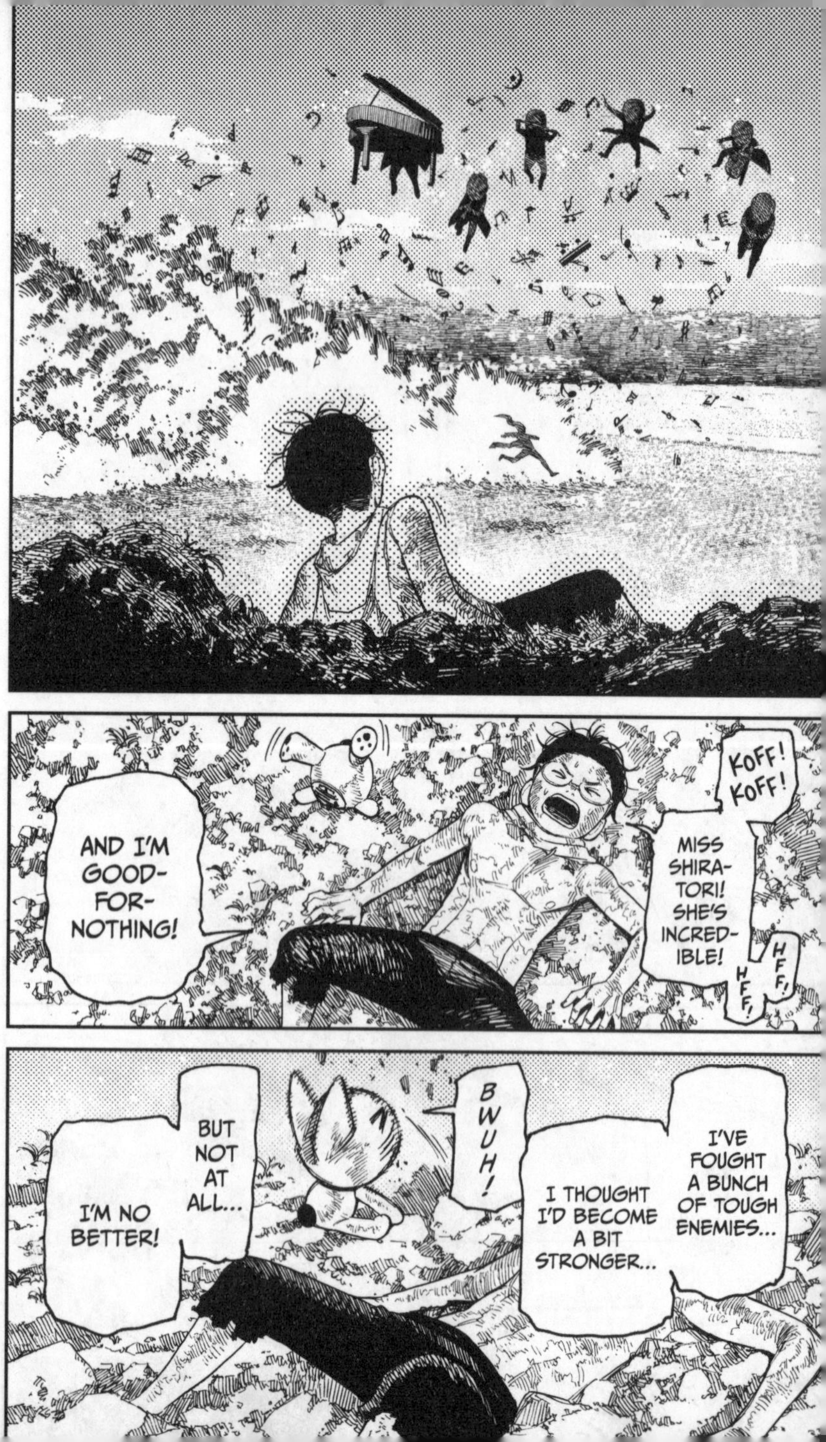
KOFF! KOFF!
MISS SHIRATORI! SHE'S INCREDIBLE!
HFF, HFF,
AND I'M GOOD-FOR-NOTHING!
I'VE FOUGHT A BUNCH OF TOUGH ENEMIES...
I THOUGHT I'D BECOME A BIT STRONGER...
BWUH!
BUT NOT AT ALL...
I'M NO BETTER!

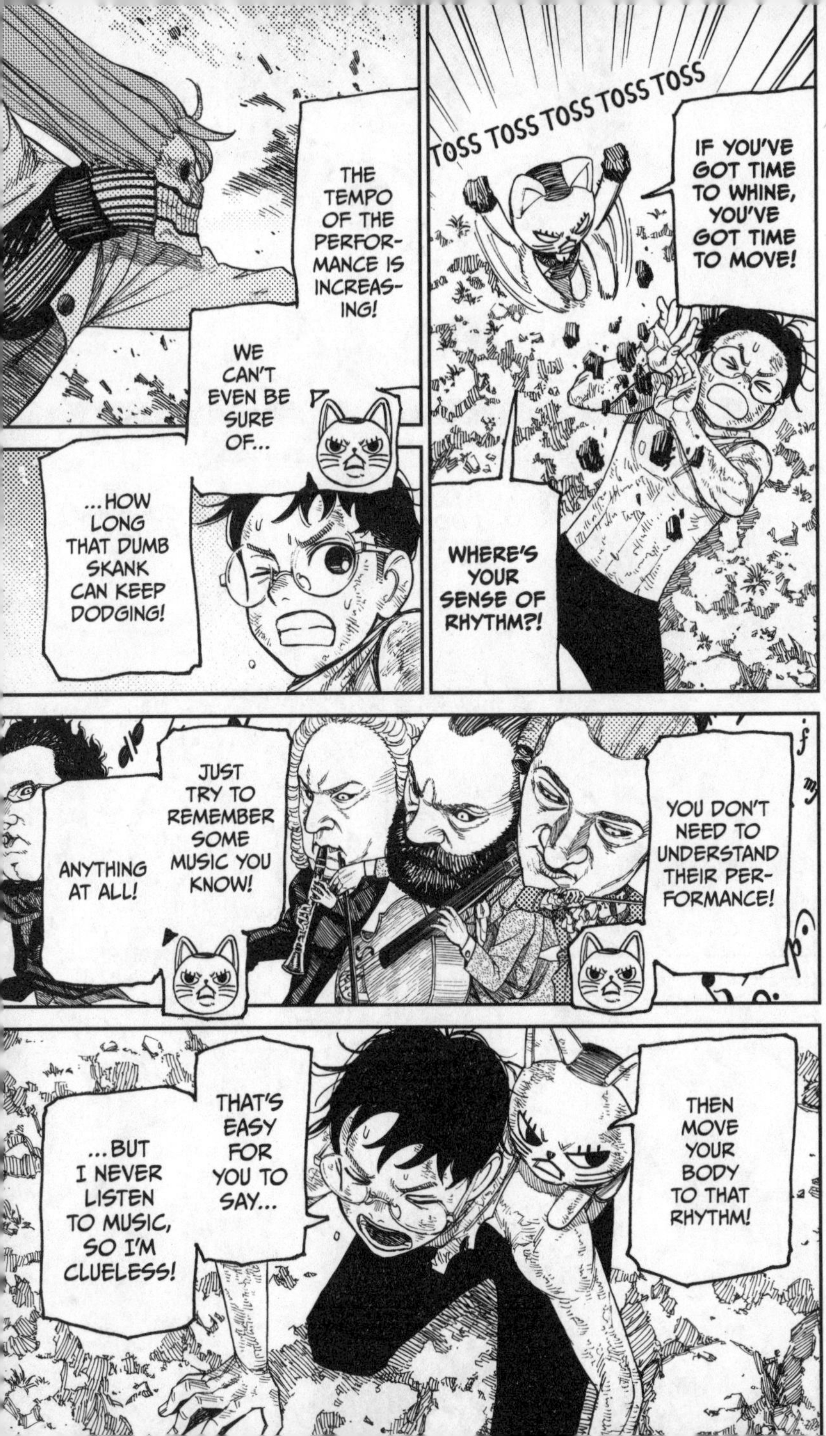
TOSS TOSS TOSS TOSS TOSS
IF YOU'VE GOT TIME TO WHINE, YOU'VE GOT TIME TO MOVE!
WHERE'S YOUR SENSE OF RHYTHM?!
THE TEMPO OF THE PERFORMANCE IS INCREASING!
WE CAN'T EVEN BE SURE OF...
...HOW LONG THAT DUMB SKANK CAN KEEP DODGING!
YOU DON'T NEED TO UNDERSTAND THEIR PERFORMANCE!
JUST TRY TO REMEMBER SOME MUSIC YOU KNOW!
ANYTHING AT ALL!
THEN MOVE YOUR BODY TO THAT RHYTHM!
THAT'S EASY FOR YOU TO SAY...
...BUT I NEVER LISTEN TO MUSIC, SO I'M CLUELESS!

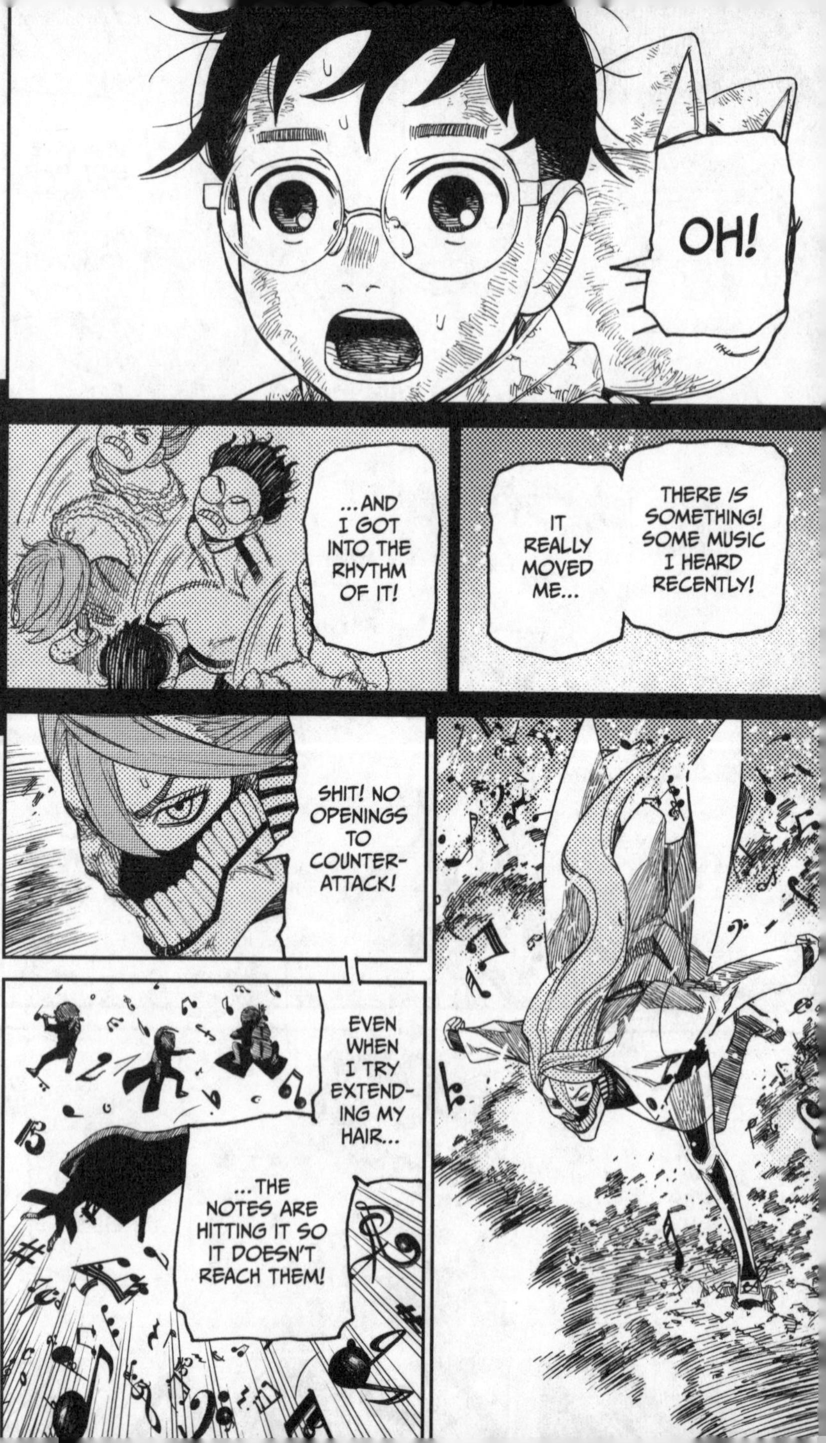
OH!
THERE IS SOMETHING! SOME MUSIC I HEARD RECENTLY!
IT REALLY MOVED ME...
...AND I GOT INTO THE RHYTHM OF IT!
SHIT! NO OPENINGS TO COUNTER-ATTACK!
EVEN WHEN I TRY EXTENDING MY HAIR...
...THE NOTES ARE HITTING IT SO IT DOESN'T REACH THEM!

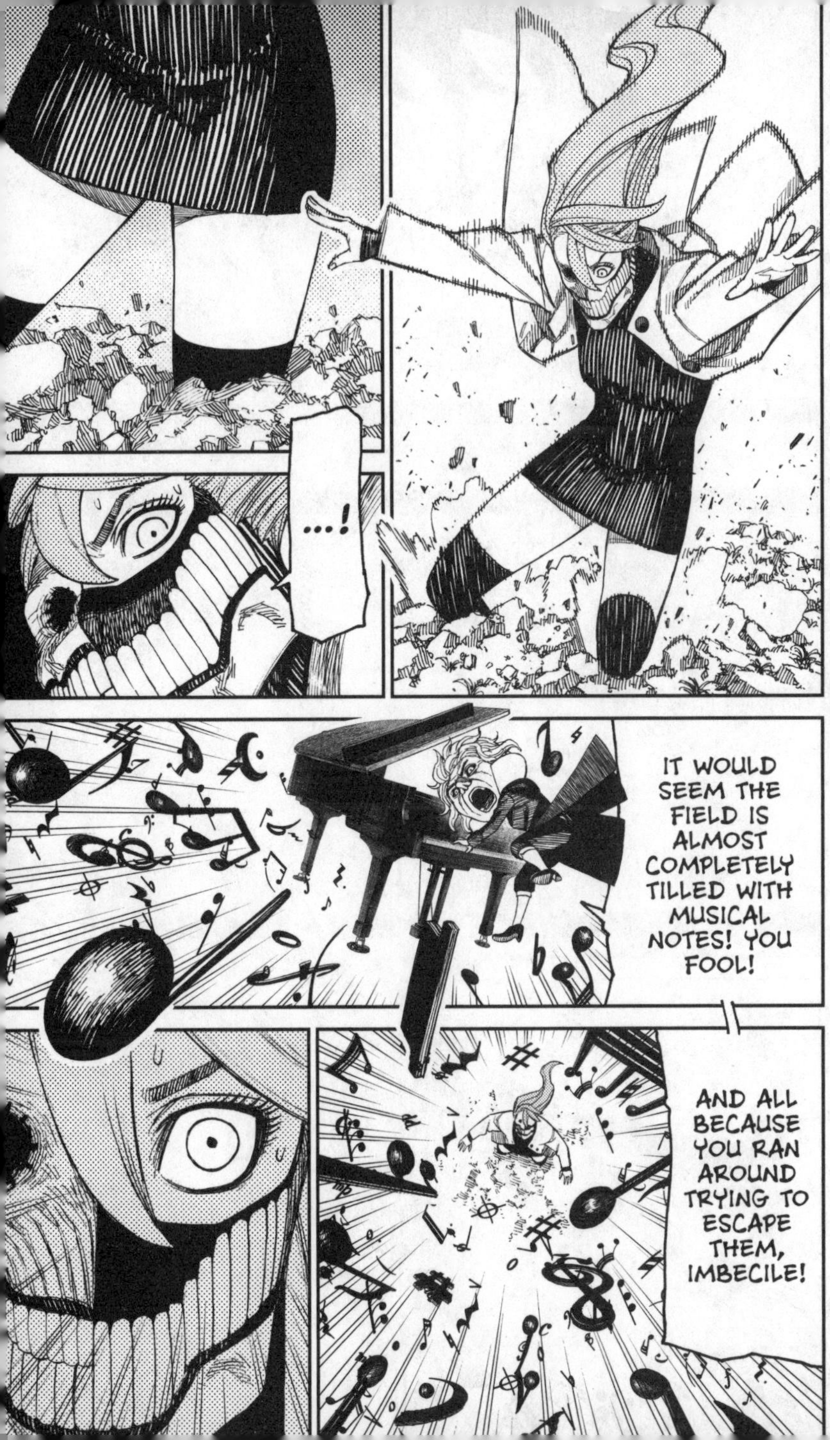
...!
IT WOULD SEEM THE FIELD IS ALMOST COMPLETELY TILLED WITH MUSICAL NOTES! YOU FOOL!
AND ALL BECAUSE YOU RAN AROUND TRYING TO ESCAPE THEM, IMBECILE!

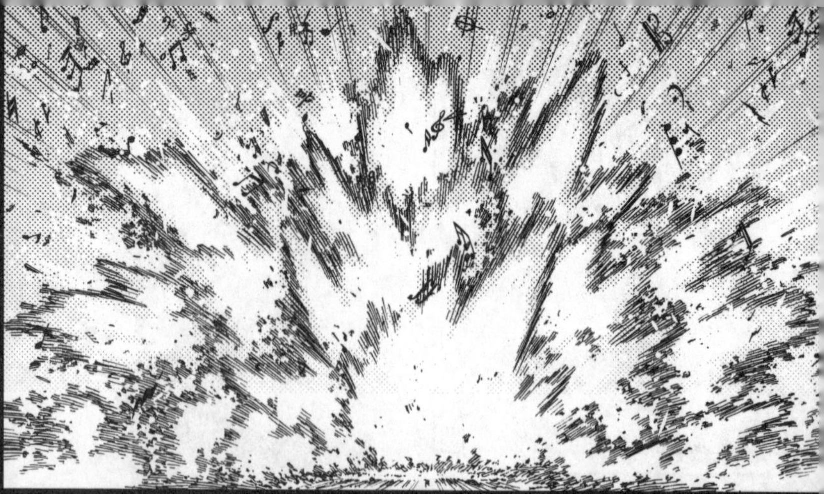
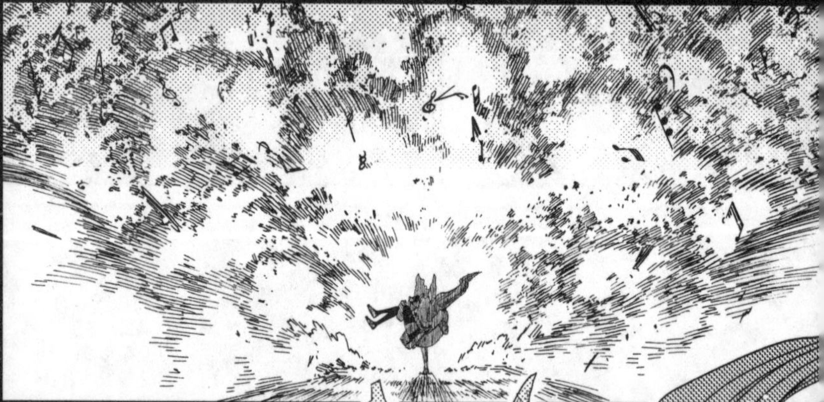
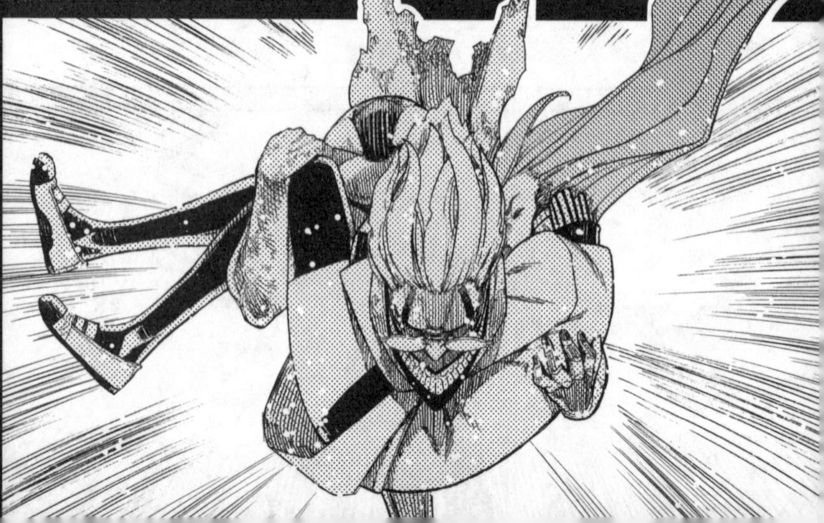

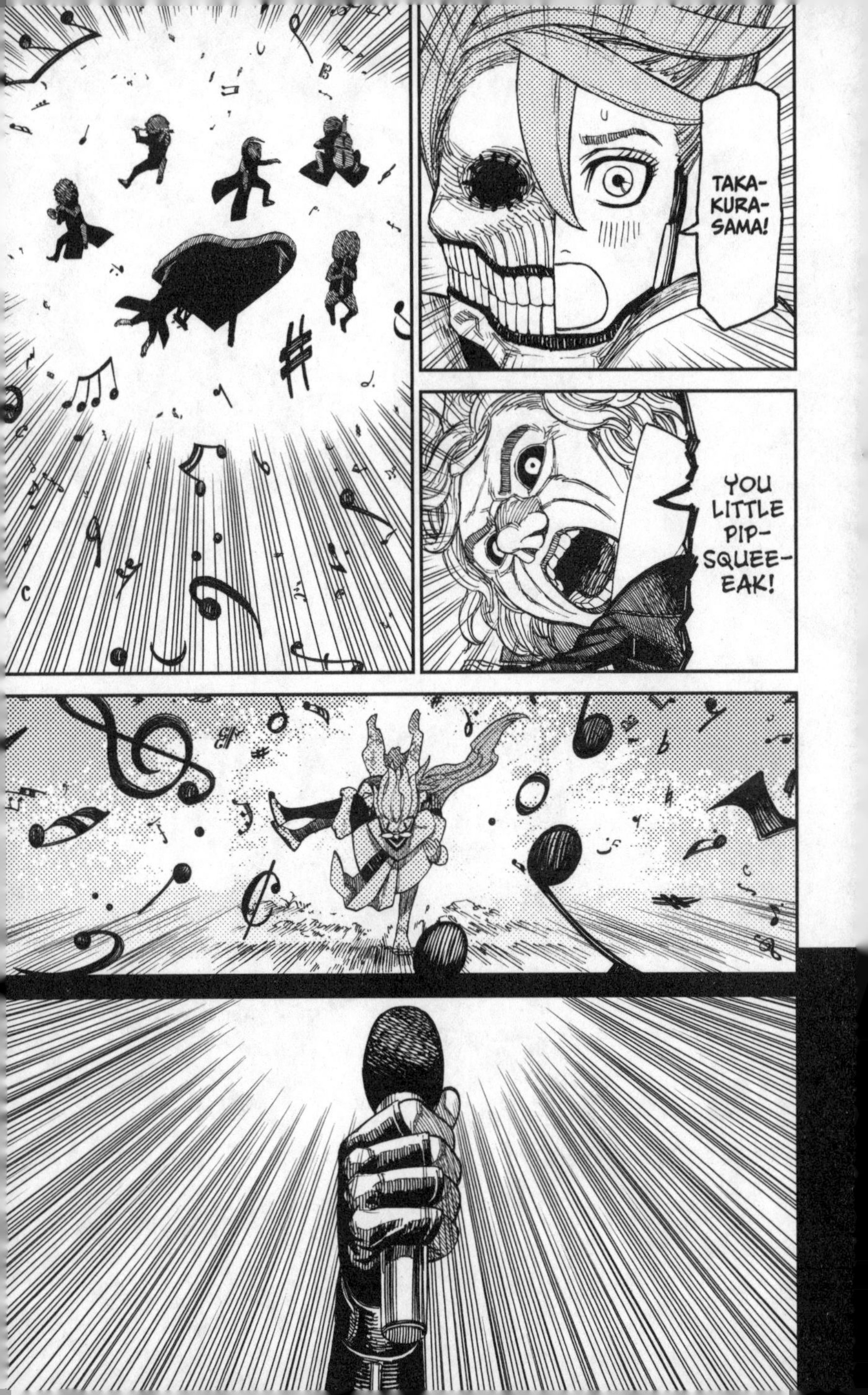
TAKA-KURA-SAMA!
YOU LITTLE PIP-SQUEEE-EAK!

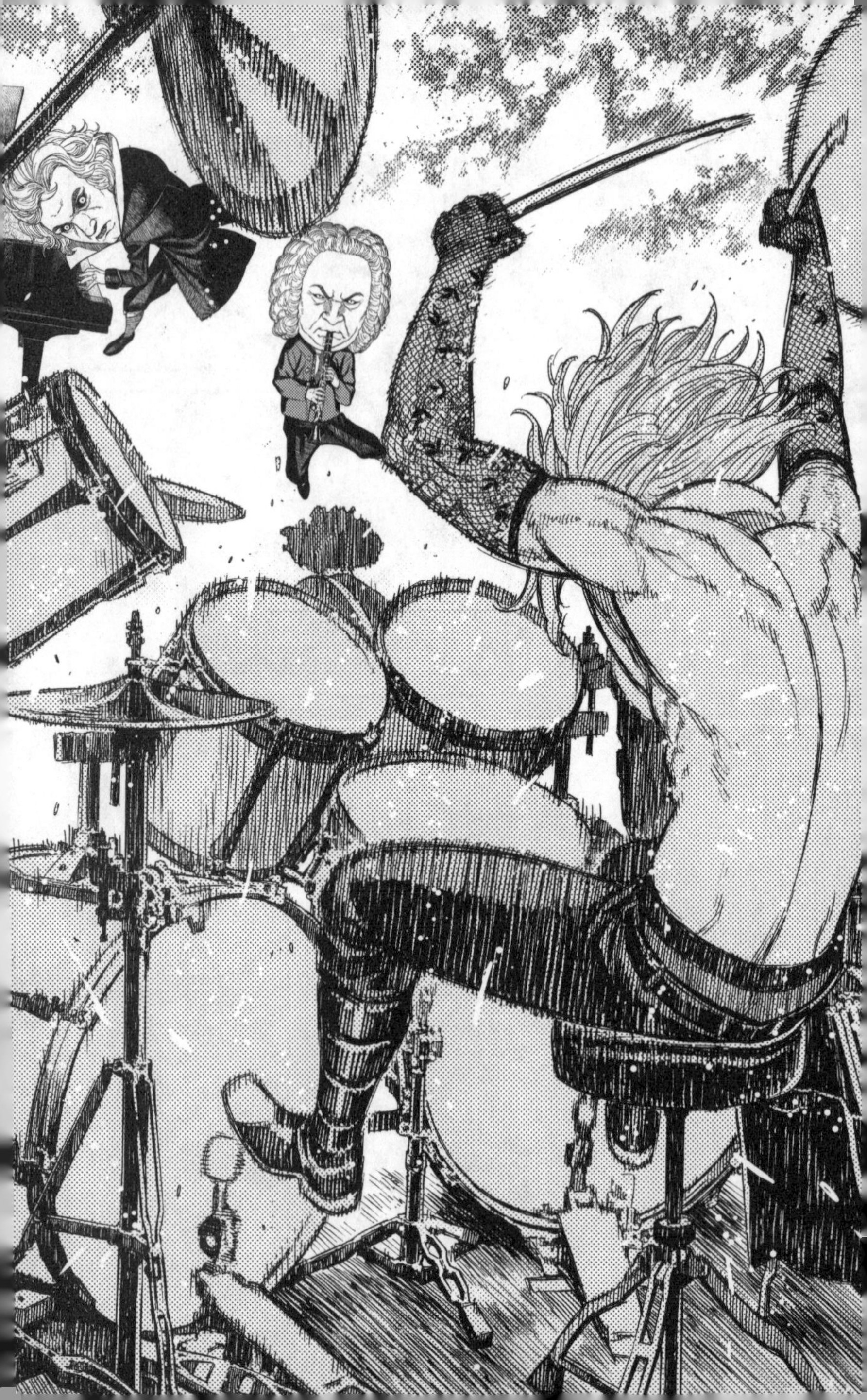

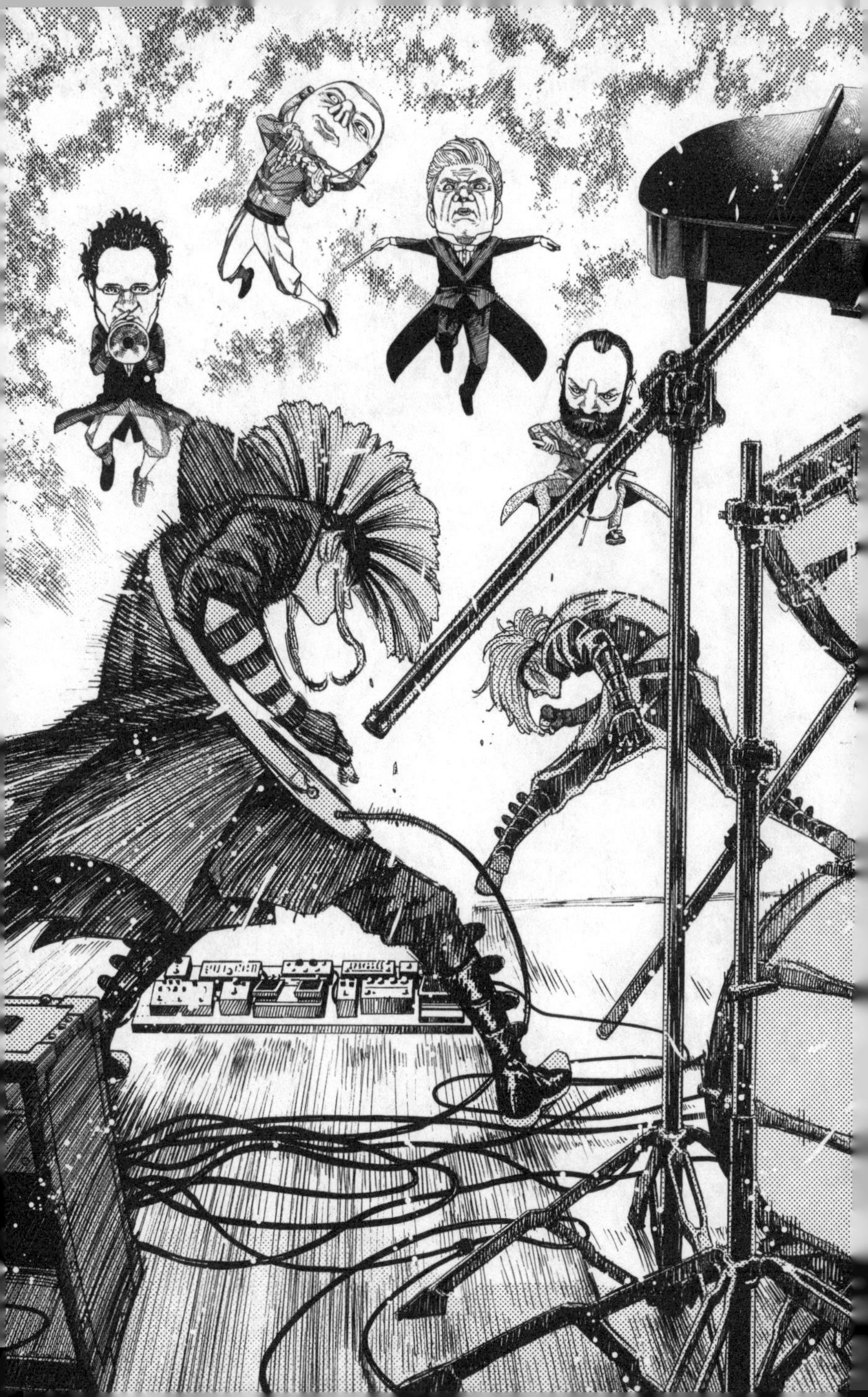

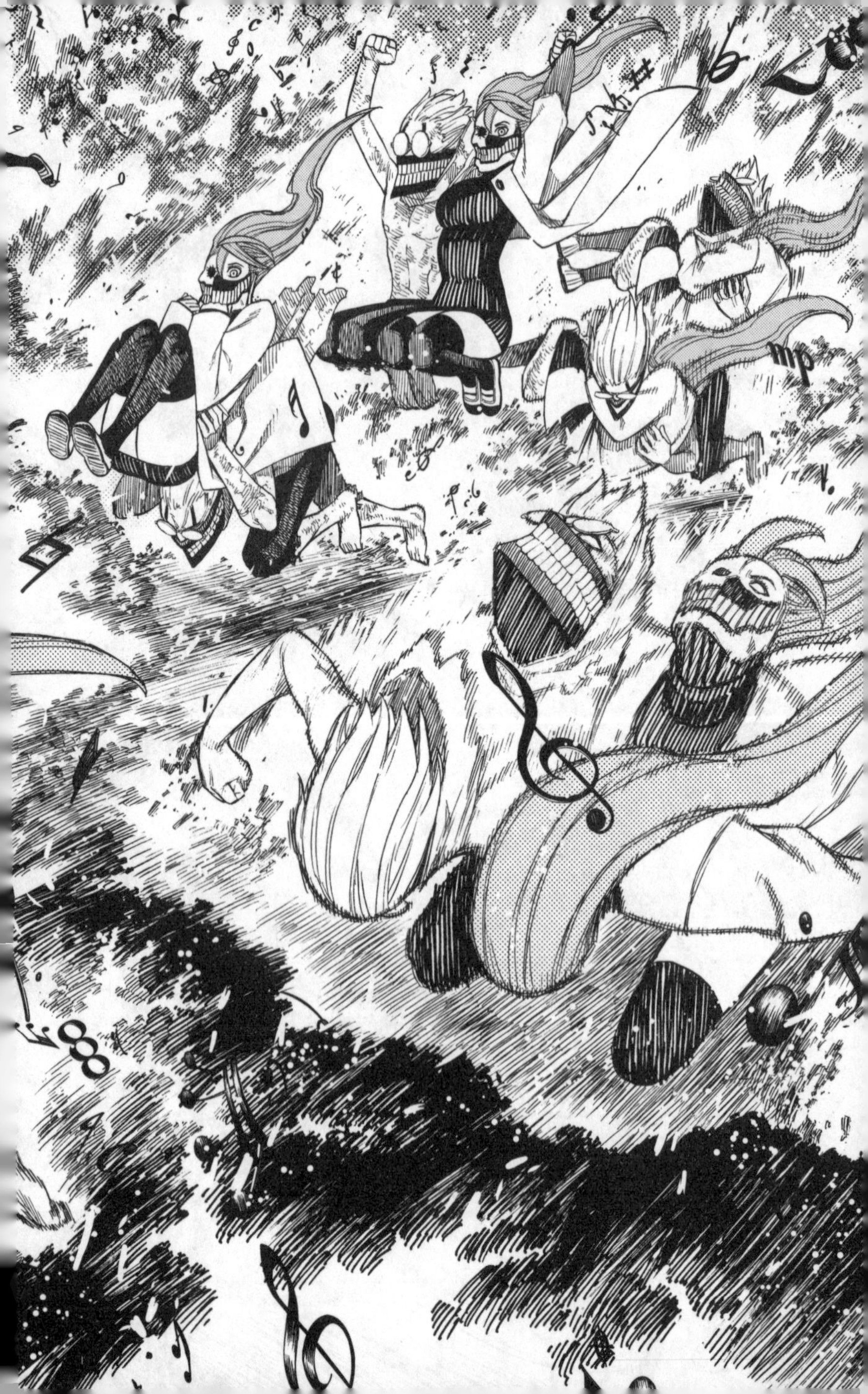

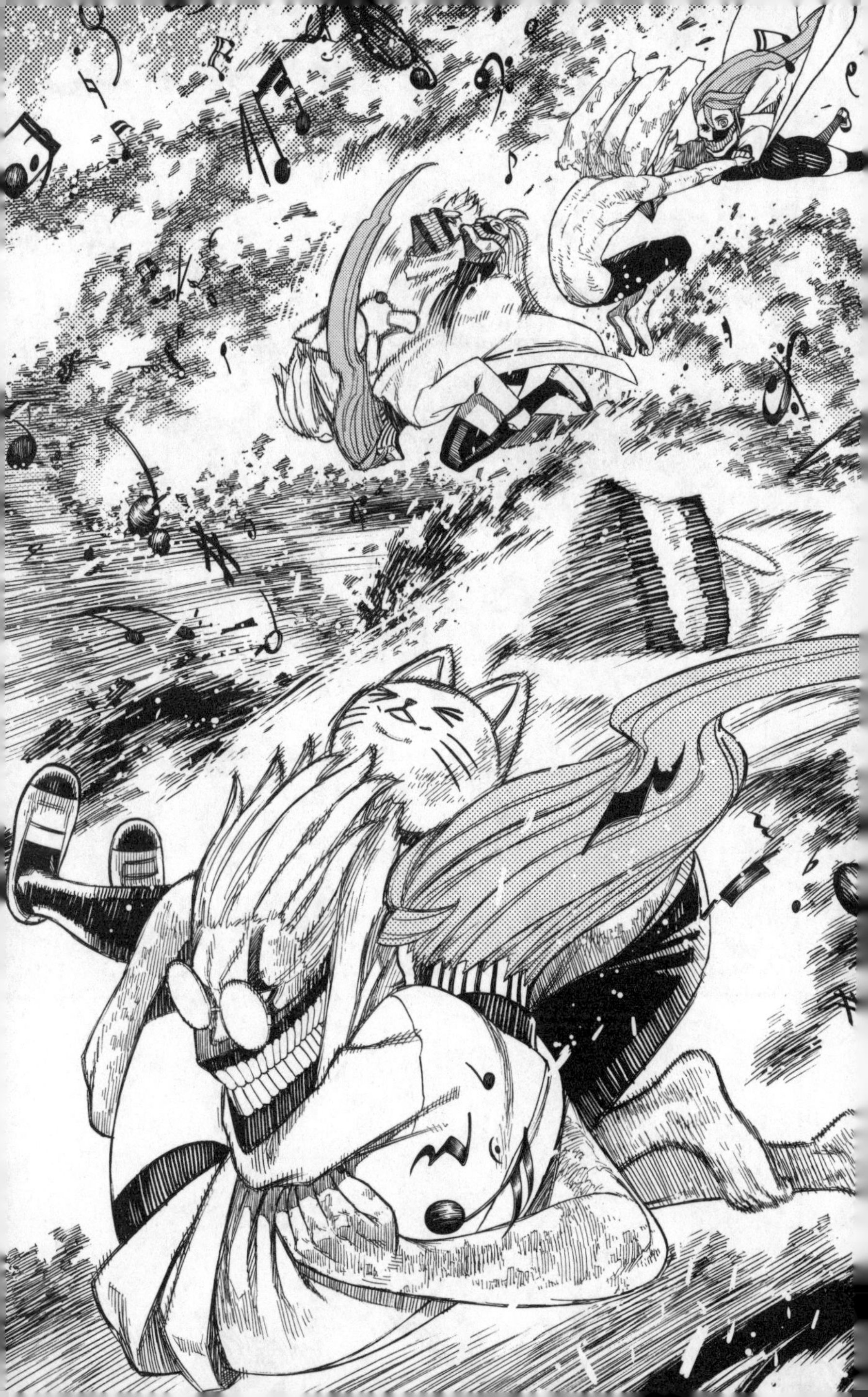

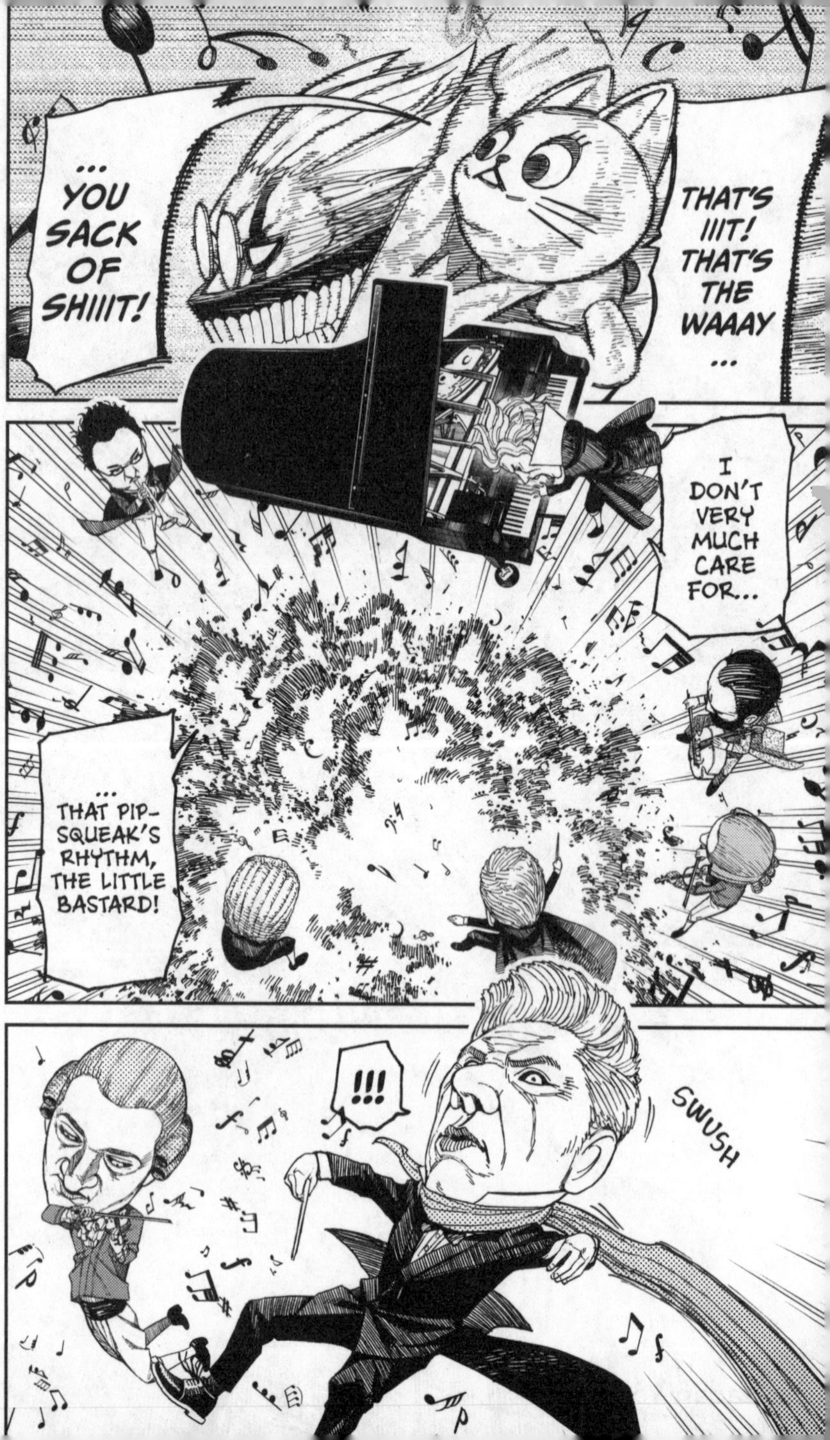
THAT'S IIIT! THAT'S THE WAAAY...
...YOU SACK OF SHIIIT!
I DON'T VERY MUCH CARE FOR...
...THAT PIP-SQUEAK'S RHYTHM, THE LITTLE BASTARD!
!!!
SWUSH

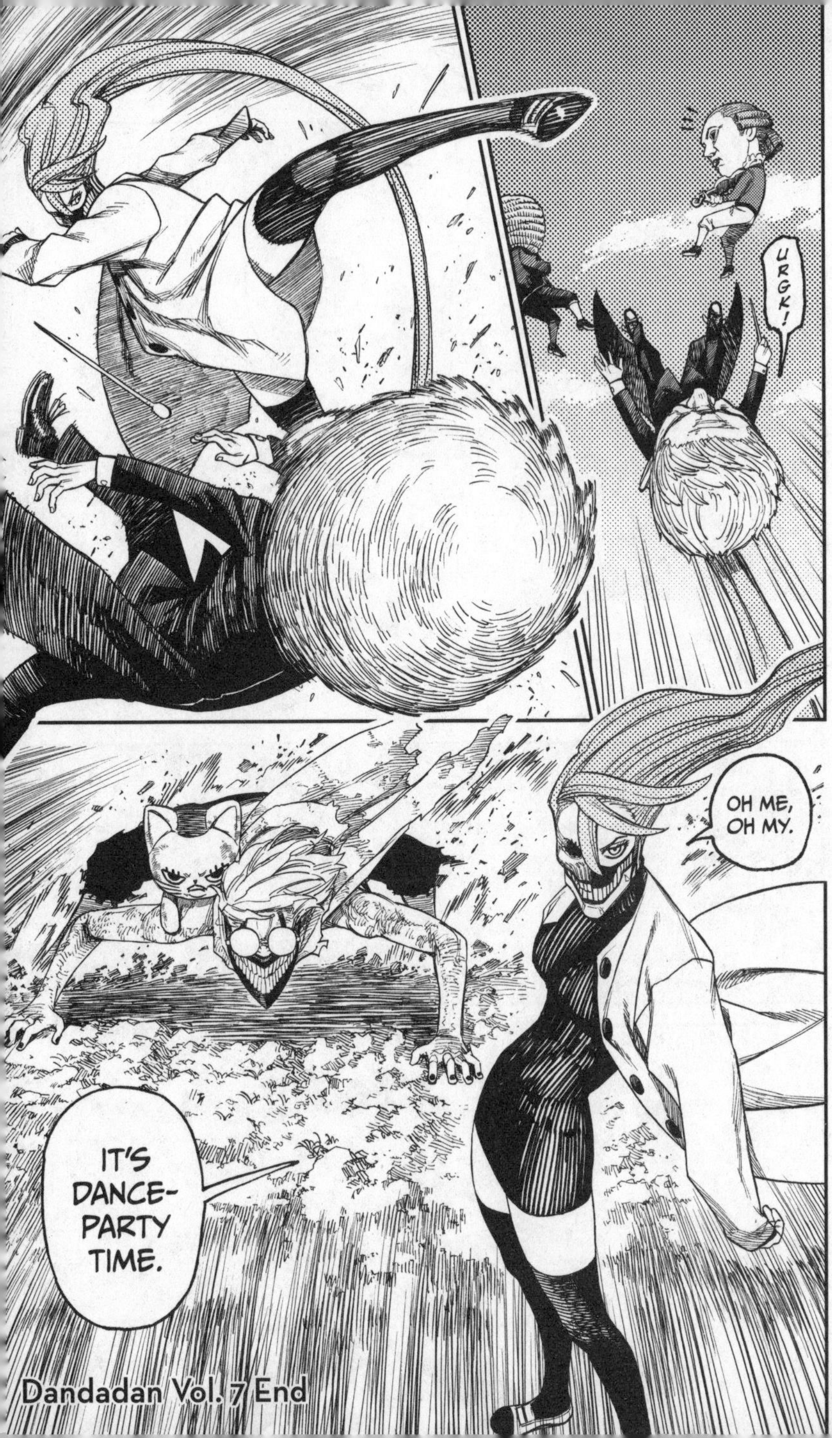
URGK!
OH ME, OH MY.
IT'S DANCE-PARTY TIME.

Dandadan Vol. 7 End

BONUS

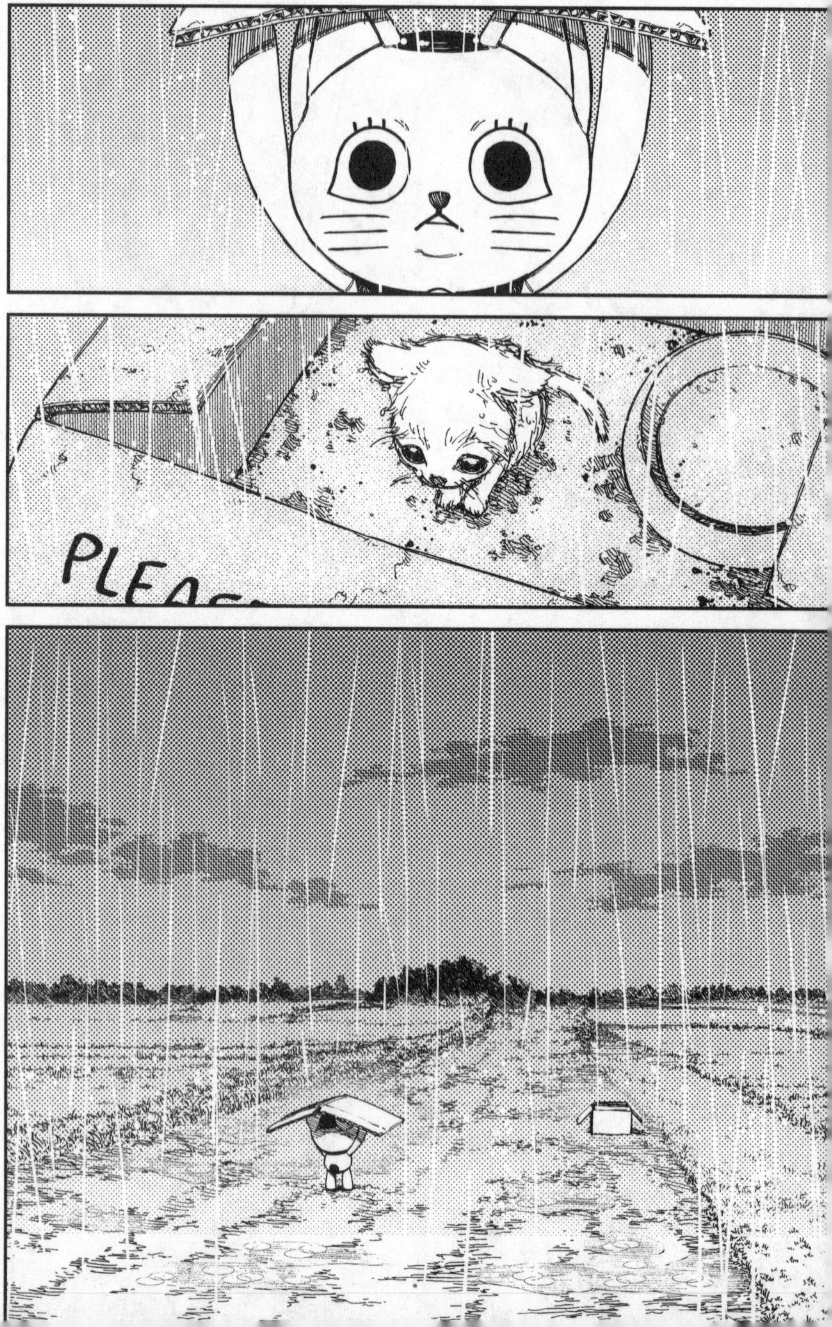
PLEA

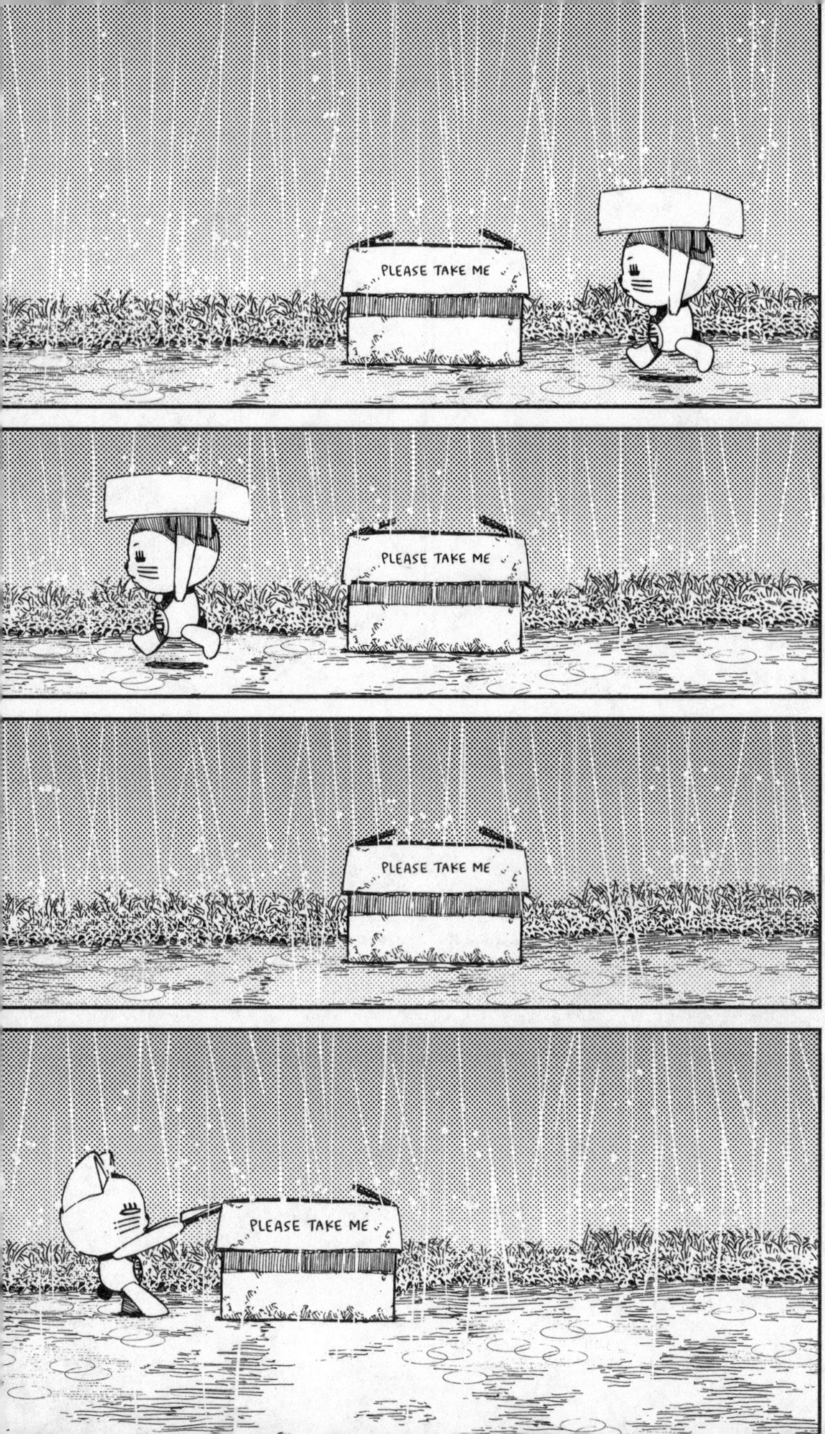
PLEASE TAKE ME
PLEASE TAKE ME
PLEASE TAKE ME
PLEASE TAKE ME

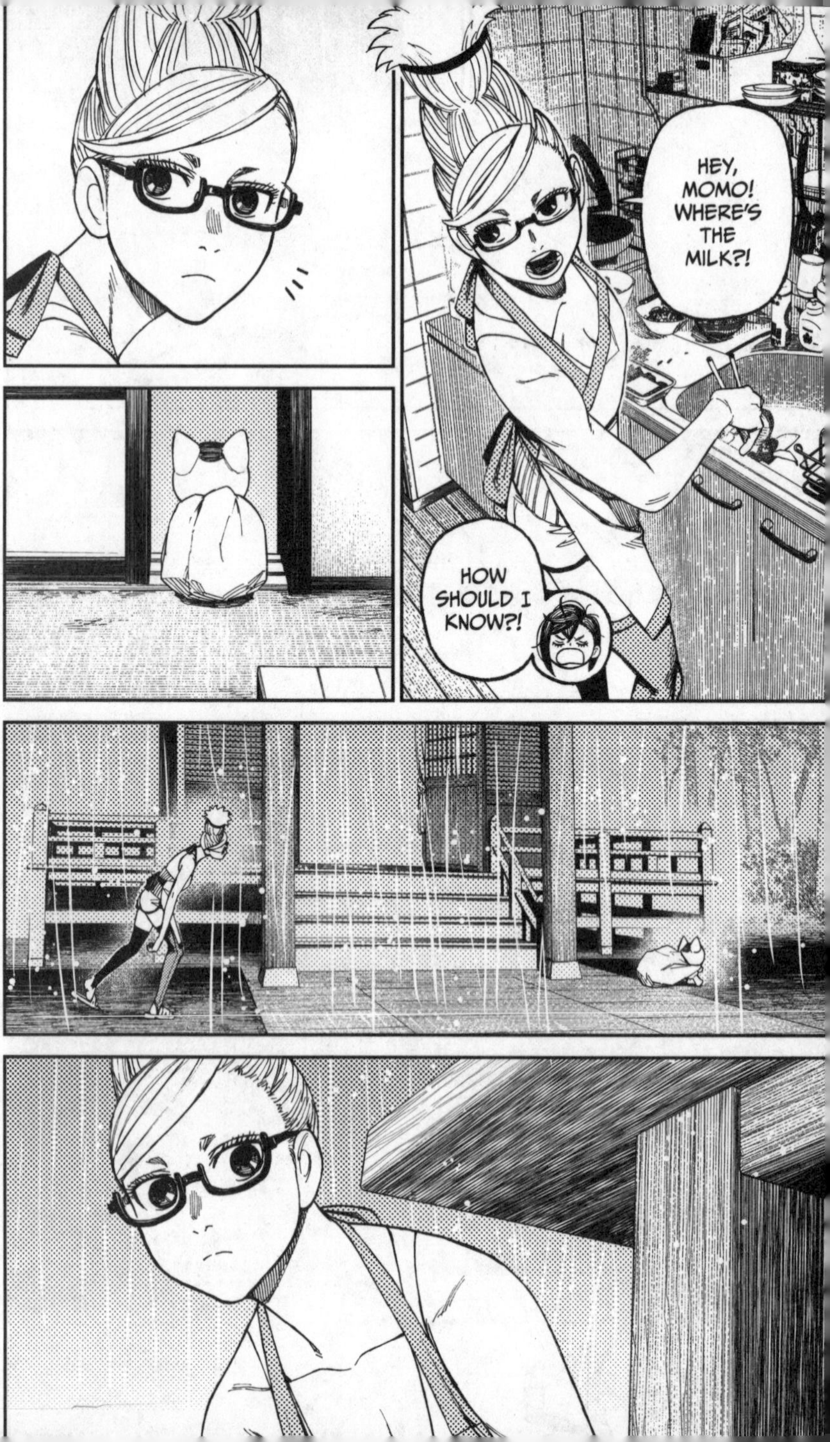
HEY, MOMO! WHERE'S THE MILK?!
HOW SHOULD I KNOW?!

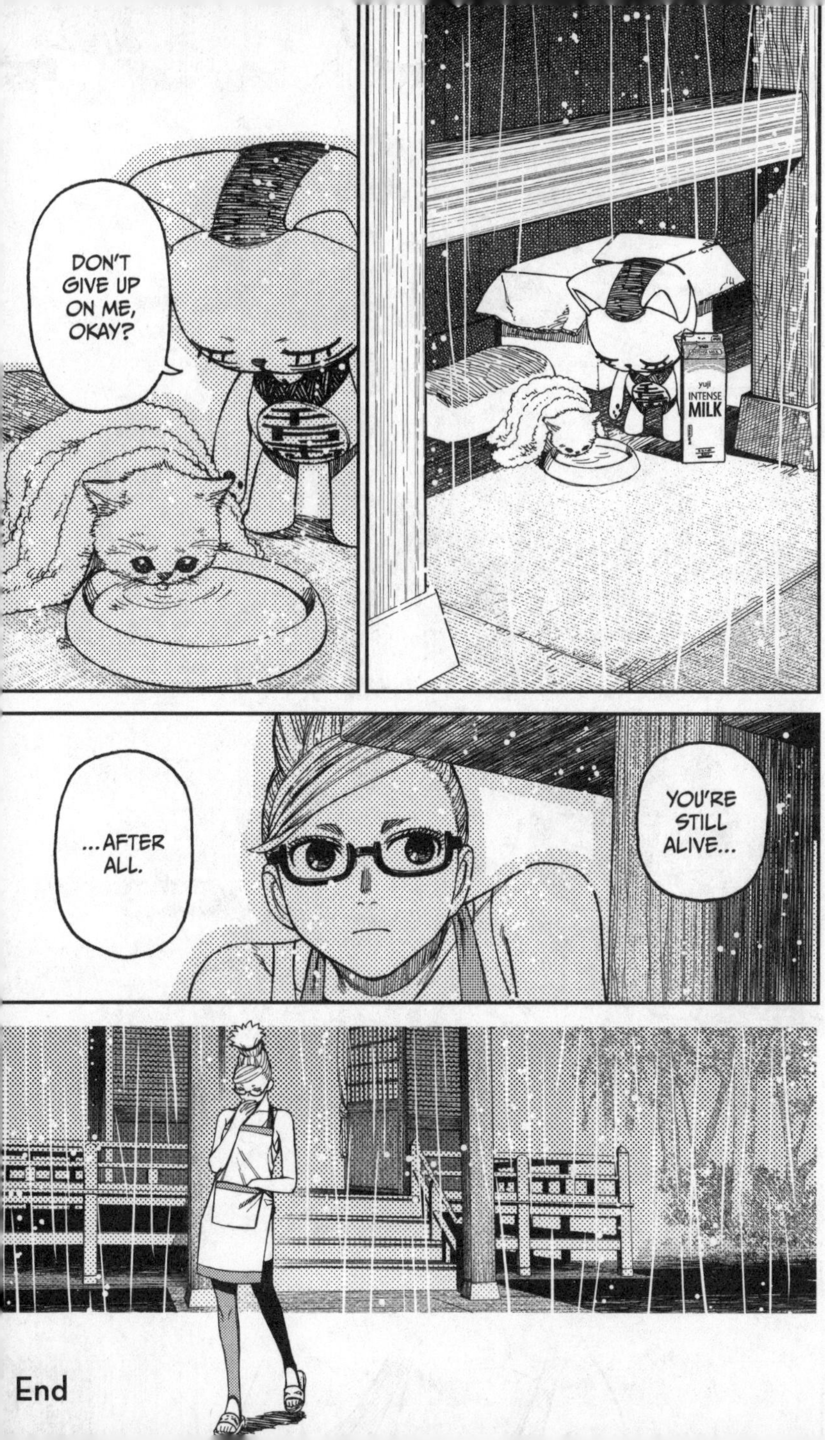
yuji
INTENSE
MILK
DON'T GIVE UP ON ME, OKAY?
YOU'RE STILL ALIVE...
...AFTER ALL.

End

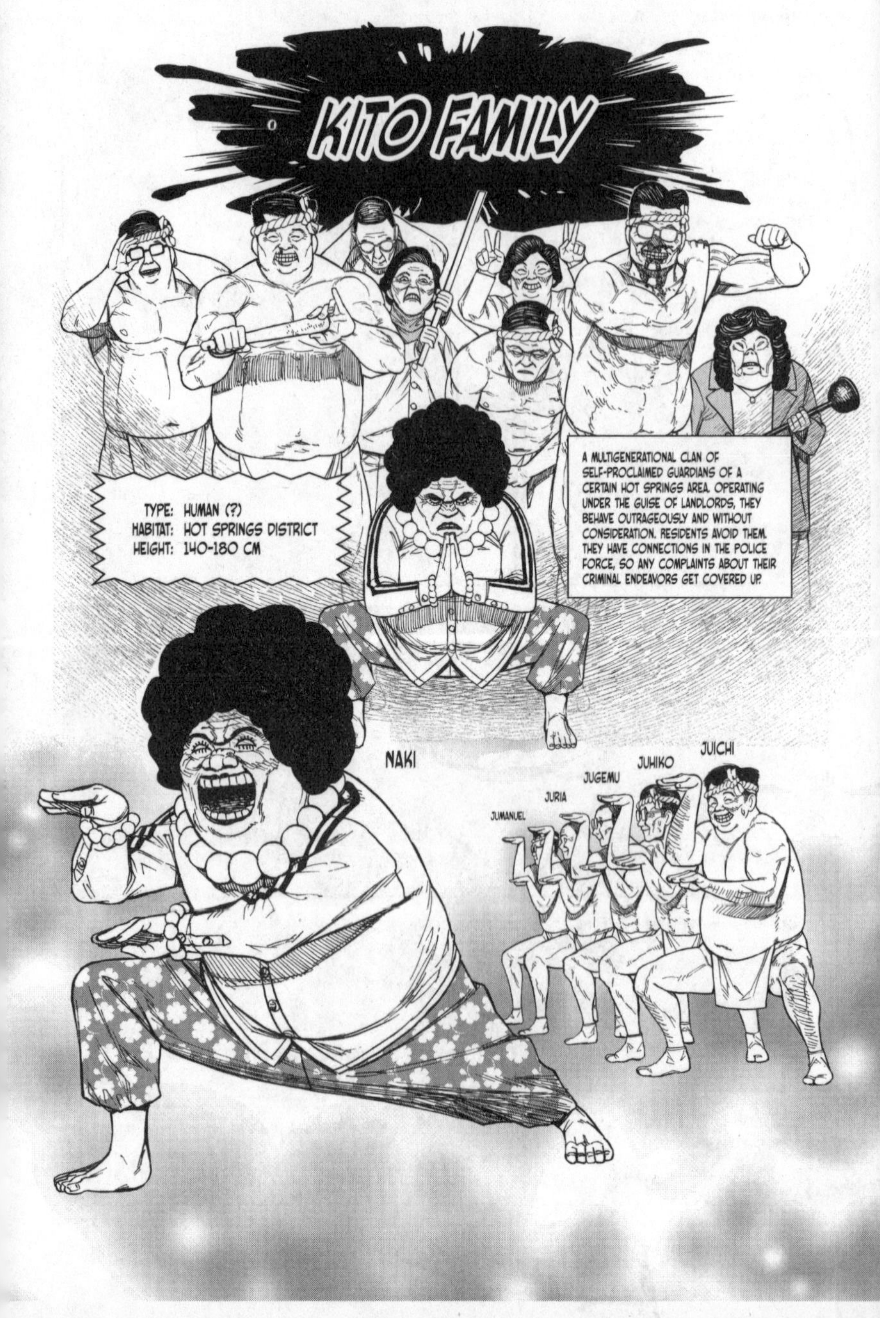
KITO FAMILY
TYPE: HUMAN (?)
HABITAT: HOT SPRINGS DISTRICT
HEIGHT: 140-180 CM
A MULTIGENERATIONAL CLAN OF SELF-PROCLAIMED GUARDIANS OF A CERTAIN HOT SPRINGS AREA. OPERATING UNDER THE GUISE OF LANDLORDS, THEY BEHAVE OUTRAGEOUSLY AND WITHOUT CONSIDERATION. RESIDENTS AVOID THEM. THEY HAVE CONNECTIONS IN THE POLICE FORCE, SO ANY COMPLAINTS ABOUT THEIR CRIMINAL ENDEAVORS GET COVERED UP.
NAKI
JUICHI
JUHIKO
JUGEMU
JURIA
JUMANUEL

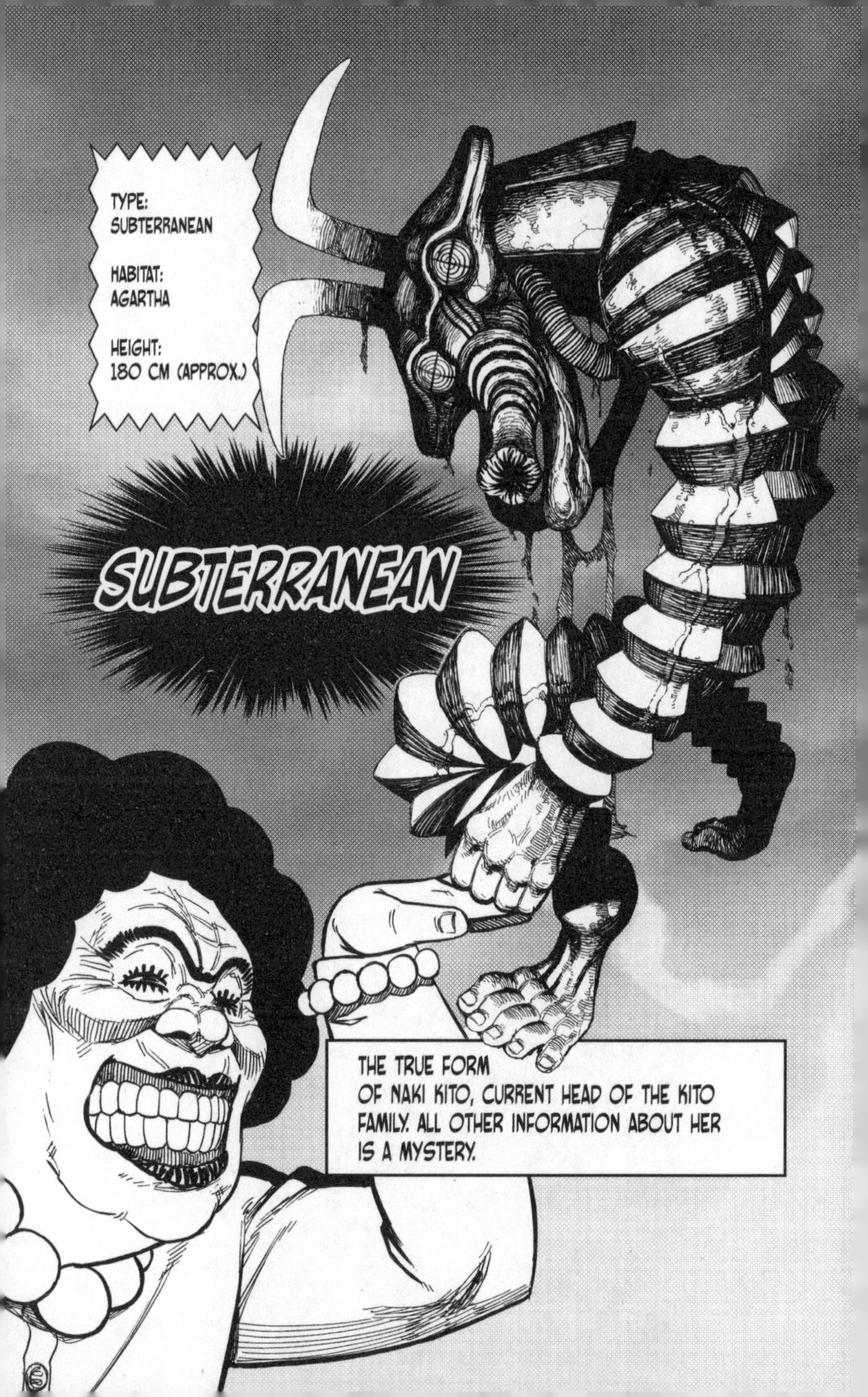
TYPE:
SUBTERRANEAN
HABITAT:
AGARTHA
HEIGHT:
180 CM (APPROX.)
SUBTERRANEAN
THE TRUE FORM OF NAKI KITO, CURRENT HEAD OF THE KITO FAMILY. ALL OTHER INFORMATION ABOUT HER IS A MYSTERY.

YUKINOBU TATSU

I was overexuberant
in my chewing of some
Black Black gum, and
somehow my tolerance
for its spiciness has
now increased.

Yukinobu Tatsu debuted in
Gekkan Shounen Magazine with
Seigi no Rokugou (Rokugou of
Justice). He has also worked as an
assistant for manga artist Tatsuki
Fujimoto on the well-known series
Chainsaw Man and *Fire Punch*.

7

SHONEN JUMP Edition

Story & Art YUKINOBU TATSU

Translation/KUMAR SIVASUBRAMANIAN
English Adaptation/JENNIFER LEBLANC
Touch-Up Art & Lettering/KYLA AIKO
Design/JULIAN [JR] ROBINSON
Original English Logo Concept/SARA LINSLEY
Editor/JENNIFER LEBLANC

DANDADAN © 2021 by Yukinobu Tatsu
All rights reserved.
First published in Japan in 2021 by SHUEISHA Inc., Tokyo.
English translation rights arranged by SHUEISHA Inc.

The stories, characters, and incidents mentioned
in this publication are entirely fictional.

Printed in Canada

Published by VIZ Media, LLC
P.O. Box 77010
San Francisco, CA 94107

10 9 8 7 6 5 4 3 2 1
First printing, April 2024

What happens when an unlucky girl
meets an undead guy? *PURE CHAOS!*

**Story and Art by
Yoshifumi
Tozuka**

Tired of inadvertently killing people with her special ability Unluck, Fuuko Izumo sets out to end it all. But when she meets Andy, a man who longs for death but can't die, she finds a reason to live—and he finds someone capable of giving him the death he's been longing for.

JoJo's

BIZARRE ADVENTURE

PART 5 *Golden Wind*

STORY & ART BY
HIROHIKO ARAKI

A MULTIGENERATIONAL TALE OF THE HEROIC JOESTAR FAMILY AND THEIR NEVER-ENDING BATTLE AGAINST EVIL!

GOLDEN WIND is here! The highly-acclaimed fifth arc of Hirohiko Araki's *JoJo's Bizarre Adventure* shifts the action from Japan to Italy, as Koichi Hirose heads to Europe to find an aspiring gangster named Giorno Giovanna, the secret son of Dio Brando, scourge of the Joestar family. Organized crime meets family drama and unbelievable enemy Stands in *JoJo's Bizarre Adventure: Part 5—Golden Wind*!

VIZ

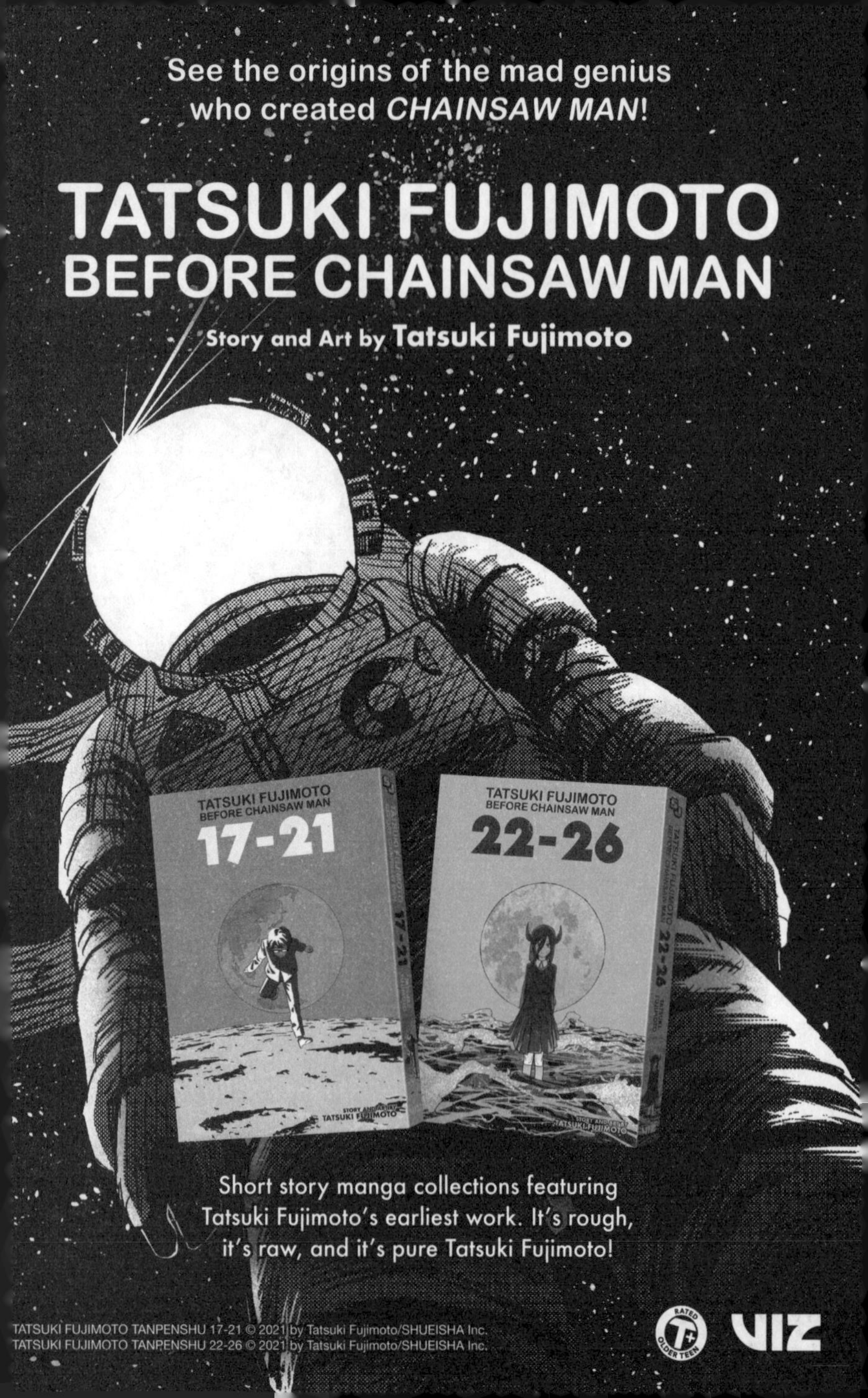
See the origins of the mad genius who created *CHAINSAW MAN*!
TATSUKI FUJIMOTO BEFORE CHAINSAW MAN
Story and Art by Tatsuki Fujimoto
TATSUKI FUJIMOTO BEFORE CHAINSAW MAN
17-21
TATSUKI FUJIMOTO
TATSUKI FUJIMOTO BEFORE CHAINSAW MAN
22-26
TATSUKI FUJIMOTO
Short story manga collections featuring Tatsuki Fujimoto's earliest work. It's rough, it's raw, and it's pure Tatsuki Fujimoto!
TATSUKI FUJIMOTO TANPENSHU 17-21 © 2021 by Tatsuki Fujimoto/SHUEISHA Inc.
TATSUKI FUJIMOTO TANPENSHU 22-26 © 2021 by Tatsuki Fujimoto/SHUEISHA Inc.
RATED T+ OLDER TEEN
VIZ

CAN MUSCLES CRUSH MAGIC?!

MASHLE

MAGIC AND MUSCLES

STORY AND ART BY
HAJIME KOMOTO

In the magic realm, magic is everything—everyone can use it, and one's skill determines their social status. Deep in the forest, oblivious to the ways of the world, lives Mash. Thanks to his daily training, he's become a fitness god. When Mash is discovered, he has no choice but to enroll in magic school where he must beat the competition without revealing his secret—he can't use magic!

Kafka wants to clean up kaiju, but not literally! Will a sudden metamorphosis stand in the way of his dream?

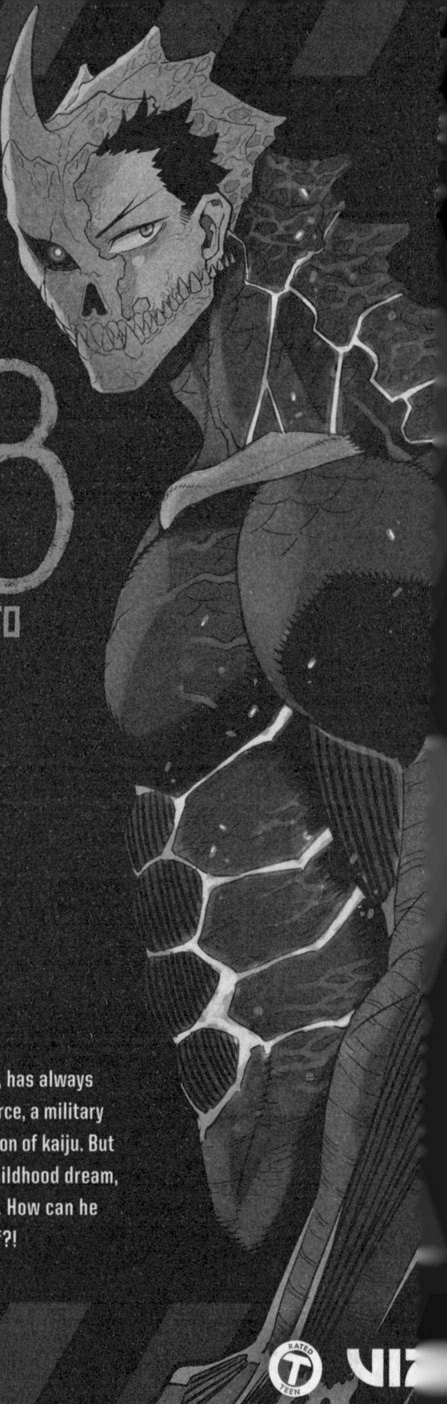

KAIJU NO. 8

STORY AND ART BY **NAOYA MATSUMOTO**

Kafka Hibino, a kaiju-corpse cleanup man, has always dreamed of joining the Japan Defense Force, a military organization tasked with the neutralization of kaiju. But when he gets another shot at achieving his childhood dream, he undergoes an unexpected transformation. How can he fight kaiju now that he's become one himself?!

RATED
T TEEN

VIZ

YOU ARE READING THE WRONG WAY

DAN DA DAN

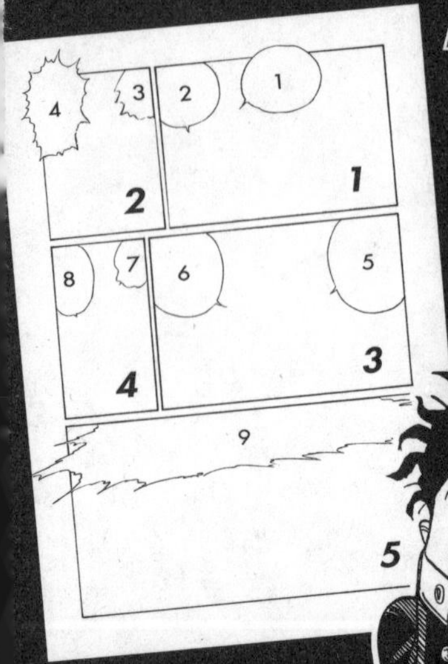

1
1
2
2
3
4
3
5
6
4
7
8
5
9

Dandadan reads from right to left, starting in the upper-right corner. Japanese is read from right to left, meaning that action, sound effects, and word-balloon order are completely reversed from English order.

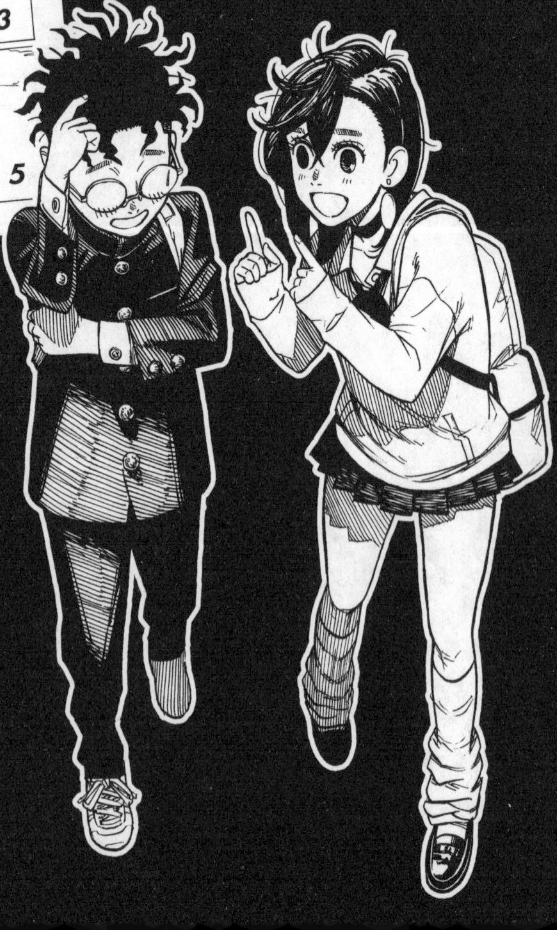